Praise for the first edition

"Tungate's absorbing and thoroughly entertaining book examines the new rules of the global fashion industry… An impressive and authoritative overview of what is arguably the world's original brand name industry."
AdBrands

"Explores the popularization of fashion and explains how marketers and branding have turned clothes and accessories into objects of desire."
Brand Republic

"This is the most fun non-fiction book that I've read in a long time, while simultaneously unique and useful. Written in a witty and readable journalistic style, this book unravels the magic behind an industry that uses more smoke and mirrors than Hollywood."
Anoop Maini, Chartered Management Institute

"Useful nuggets."
Financial Times

"Littered with amusing anecdotes."
Marketing

"Includes brand strategy insights from designers such as Paul Smith and Diesel founder Renzo Rosso, interviews with influential industry figures and behind-the-scenes reports."
Fashion Business International

"*Fashion Brands* includes exclusive quotes and insights into brand strategy from designers such as Paul Smith and Diesel founder Renzo Rosso."
In-Store Magazine

"An interesting read for anyone involved in the fashion or marketing sector."
International Textiles

FASHION BRANDS

Branding Style from Armani to Zara

2nd edition

Mark Tungate

KOGAN
PAGE

London and Philadelphia

Publisher's note

Every possible effort has been made to ensure that the information contained in this book is accurate at the time of going to press, and the publishers and authors cannot accept responsibility for any errors or omissions, however caused. No responsibility for loss or damage occasioned to any person acting, or refraining from action, as a result of the material in this publication can be accepted by the editor, the publisher or the author.

First published in Great Britain and the United States in 2005 by Kogan Page Limited.
Reprinted in 2005, 2006 (twice)
Second edition 2008

120 Pentonville Road
London N1 9JN
United Kingdom
www.koganpage.com

525 South 4th Street, #241
Philadelphia PA 19147
USA

ISBN 978 0 7494 5305 3

British Library Cataloguing-in-Publication Data

A CIP record for this book is available from the British Library.

Library of Congress Cataloging-in-Publication Data

Tungate, Mark, 1967–
    Fashion brands : branding style from Armani to Zara / Mark Tungate.
        p. cm.
    Includes bibliographical references and index.
    ISBN 978-0-7494-5305-3
    1. Fashion merchandising. 2. Branding (Marketing). 3. Advertising—Fashion. I. Title.
    HD9940.A2T86 2008
    746.9'20688—dc22
                                                                    2008011174

Typeset by JS Typesetting Ltd, Porthcawl, Mid Glamorgan
Printed and bound in Great Britain by MPG Books Ltd, Bodmin, Cornwall

For my sister,
whose fashion icons are Audrey Hepburn and the Ramones –
and who somehow manages to combine the two.

Contents

Acknowledgements

Writing a book like this is inevitably a collaborative process – which is just a posh way of saying that I owe a lot of people a drink. Firstly, I'd like to extend my sincere thanks to all those quoted within these pages. I would also like to thank Randy Weddle of the *International Herald Tribune* for inviting me to the paper's conference, Luxury 2004: The Lure of Asia.

I am indebted to Sarah Blackman for suggesting that I get in touch with Virginie Bertrand of Prêt-A-Porter Paris – and to Virginie herself for opening her contacts book. Nick Hurell of M&C Saatchi deserves a special mention for putting me in contact with two of the most famous gentlemen in fashion journalism.

Here, I hope, are the other members of a stylish crew: Alice Playle at Asprey; Antonella Viero and Silvia Rebuli at Diesel; Daria Genoese at Giorgio Armani; Didier Suberbielle at Condé Nast France; Drieke Leenknegt at Nike; Eileen Le Muet at *L'Express*; Iona Peel and Richard Gray at Harvey Nichols; Polly Stevens at MTV; Richard Hill at Beverly Cable PR.

Last, but by no means least, I would like to thank Géraldine Dormoy, without whose knowledge, support and diligent research this book would never have been completed.

Preface to the new edition

This is the first time I've had to revisit a book, and I didn't realize how hard it would be. Once a book is done, it's done. You read the proofs, make a few corrections, and a few months later the thing is sitting on your bookshelf, the object of your proud glances until you get over it and move on to the next project. That was certainly the case with *Fashion Brands*.

And now, unexpectedly, it's back again. Re-reading the manuscript was a slightly painful experience: I suddenly became aware of all its faults; the phrases that jarred, the errors of judgement. And yet there were paragraphs I was surprisingly pleased with. It was as if I'd discovered a neglected T-shirt in a bottom drawer and, holding it up, realized that I still liked it.

The question is, why update the book at all? The answer lies in the final lines of the conclusion: 'This is a book about fashion. Tomorrow, everything will have changed.'

So what has changed since 2005? Most of the predictions I wrangled from fashion luminaries turned out to be – or are turning out to be – on the money. Evidence of the impact of cheap imports from China can be seen all around us. As I write, I am wearing a cashmere sweater that cost absurdly little. Cashmere is everywhere now, and it has become ludicrously affordable. The label always reads, 'Made in China'. Luxury has become accessible, and so the luxury fashion brands have been forced to market harder – to instil those intangible 'values' that justify their profit margins – and to up the ante in terms of quality and innovation.

It seems to me that, if anything, consumers have become even more obsessed with fashion than they were when I started writing the book. The affordability and accessibility mentioned above have undoubtedly contributed to this trend. But we shouldn't underestimate the power of the fashion bloggers, those independent commentators who were barely a blip on the screen just three years ago. Now, it seems, the internet is crammed with consumers expressing their opinions about brands, taking pictures of themselves in their latest purchases, or wandering the streets photographing other style mavens.

Until very recently, the only people who did this kind of work were professional trend trackers working for 'style bureaus': the intelligence services of brands. They were also the only people who had the courage to approach complete strangers and ask them to pose for a photograph. It takes more guts than you'd imagine: try it some time and you'll see what I mean. The interesting thing, though, is that people almost invariably say yes. They're flattered that the photographer admires their dress sense.

Once the bloggers realized this, the barriers came down pretty fast. Now the trendiest districts of the world's cities are full of colourfully-dressed young people taking pictures of one another for their blogs. I believe this phenomenon has changed the comportment of city inhabitants: now, anybody vaguely stylish almost expects to be photographed. In the morning, they dress for a new form of urban theatre.

This need to stand out from the crowd has inevitably influenced purchase patterns. To a certain extent, consumers have begun branding themselves. Individuality has become more desirable than ever – hence the increasing importance of customization. More and more brands are offering services that enable shoppers to adapt existing models to their own tastes, or even to create items from scratch. Men are rediscovering the joys of tailoring. Improved technology is enabling consumers to order customized clothing online. At the time of writing this trend is barely a ripple, but it will gather in size and pace over the months to come.

To reflect these changes, I've added an entirely new section about the rise of bloggers. I've also revisited the chapter about celebrities and fashion, to touch on the phenomenon of stars who try their hand at designing clothes. Partnerships between brands and celebrities for marketing purposes are now so commonplace that they have almost become a cliché, which is only one step away from becoming unfashionable. Nonetheless, the iconic appeal of model-turned-celebrity-turned-designer Kate Moss, as well as the dozens of pop singers and movie stars who've ventured into fashion, has worked its magic on consumers.

I was also compelled to add to the section about 'ethical' fashion. The first edition of the book alighted briefly on this, but at the time it seemed like an underground movement. Now, with the sale of 'fair trade' and 'organic' goods on the rise and climate change firmly on the agenda, many consumers are questioning the ethics behind every item they buy, including clothing.

Other changes are less obvious: I wanted to extend my profile of the designer Matthew Williamson, for example, in the light of his brand's 20th anniversary. And I've made a few nips and tucks here and there to freshen things up, as the fashion industry is wont to do.

In the couple of years since the first edition of the book appeared, I've been surprised and gratified by the number of e-mails I've received from those who took something away from it. Most of them were from people who loved fashion, but weren't afraid to pick at the industry's stitches – to stretch it a bit and see if anything gave way. That was the original intention of this book, and it remains the case.

Introduction

'You don't buy clothes – you buy an identity.'

The model struts towards the battery of cameras, profile held slightly aloft, walking with the curious avian gait that has evolved to flatter the lines of her dress. She does not spare a glance for us mere mortals in the wings; her attention is utterly focused on the arsenal of lenses at the end of the catwalk, which will whirl her image into the global maelstrom of the media barely an instant after she has turned away.

She pauses at the end of her purposeful march, a thigh thrust forward, a hand on a jutting hip, smiling at last as the flashes crackle around her like summer lightning. When she has given her audience what they came for, she swivels imperiously, flinging a contemptuous vestige of inaccessibility in their direction, before marching just as determinedly back to the oxygen-starved planet where only models, fashion designers and billionaires live.

For many consumers, the model's short stroll is the first image that springs to mind at the mention of the word 'fashion'. The runway show – with its combination of creativity, glamour and artifice – is one of the elements that drive us, again and again, to buy clothes we don't really need. It's difficult to think of an industry that does not have recourse to marketing in one form or another, but only fashion has such an overbearing reliance on it. When clothes leave the factories where they are made, they are merely 'garments' or 'apparel'. Only when the marketers get hold of them do they magically become 'fashion'.

There is nothing trivial about fashion. Although there is little consensus on the figure, it is estimated that the amount spent on clothing and footwear around the world tops US$1 trillion a year. According to Verdict Research, the global luxury goods market is likely to be worth US$450 billion by 2012. Fashion and leather goods account for the largest proportion of the sector, followed by perfumes and cosmetics, which are usually sold under the licensed names of fashion designers. Watches and jewellery take care of the rest. This vast industry is driven by a number of highly sophisticated marketing and branding techniques, which are well worth dissecting.

And it would be foolish of us to underestimate the importance of fashion in society. Clothes and accessories are expressions of how we feel, how we see ourselves – and how we wish to be treated by others. During my interview with the fashion photographer Vincent Peters (who has taken pictures of some of the most gorgeous people in the world, wearing some of the most expensive clothes), he said, 'Fashion is too prevalent to be considered trivial. Even when you say you're not interested in fashion, you've been forced to confront it. Fashion is everywhere. What you choose to wear or not to wear has become a political statement. You don't buy clothes – you buy an identity.'

This identity is linked to brand values that have been communicated via marketing. Are you elegant, flighty, debonair, streetwise, intellectual, sexy. . . or all of the above, depending on your mood? Don't worry: we've got the outfit to match.

But it's not only the outfit that is on offer. Over the past decade or so, fashion has stolen into every corner of the urban landscape. Our mobile phones, our cars, our kitchens, our choice of media and the places where we meet our friends – these, too, have become subject to the vagaries of fashion. It's not enough to wear the clothes; you have to don the lifestyle, too. Fashion brands have encouraged this development by adding their names to a wide range of objects, fulfilling every imaginable function, and selling them in stores that resemble theme parks.

People will go to extreme lengths to consume fashion. Not so long ago, there was a clutch of articles about kids being mugged – even killed – for their sports shoes. While I was researching this book, an uncharacteristically sensationalist article in the French newspaper *Le Figaro* suggested that teenage girls were selling their bodies to raise enough cash to satisfy their addiction to fashion. On a less dramatic scale, few teenagers are unaware of the importance of the right brand, in the right colour, worn in the right way. And, as we're all teenagers these days, adults are becoming just as obsessive. The caprices of fashion are both exasperating and alluring. Its alchemy is mysterious. Most people, even if they refuse to be seduced by it, are intrigued by fashion. If I hadn't written this book, I'd certainly want to read it.

THE VIEW FROM OUT HERE

And who am I, anyway – your host for this tour behind the scenes of fashion? A year ago, I could make no claims to being an expert. I was just your average trade hack, writing about complex but faintly geeky subjects such as marketing and the media. Nor was I a fashion victim. Sure, I used to cruise second-hand emporia for those special Levi's with the red stitching on the inseam, but that was eons ago, before 'retro' morphed into 'vintage'.

My non-fashion background proved advantageous. I could ask naïve questions that a fashion journalist might not have dared to pose, for fear of undermining their credibility. I was not in the pay of the industry I was analysing (unlike glossy magazine journalists, who are in thrall to their advertisers), so I could afford to be objective. My distance from the subject enabled me to regard it with a certain irony. I admit to the occasional smirk.

This was not an easy book to research. The fashion industry, as you might expect, can be haughty and insular, and suspicious of outsiders. It was unlikely to open its arms to a journalist who wanted to deconstruct its marketing strategies. The luxury brands, particularly, are built like chateaux – their elegant façades masking impressive battlements. At first I thought the public relations people working at brands such as Chanel and Louis Vuitton were merely dismissive. I was wrong – they were being tactical. Their inaccessibility is part and parcel of their image. The sportswear brands, perhaps more surprisingly, were equally difficult to penetrate. All these brands are constantly on the defensive, as they present large and irresistible targets that the media love to pepper with negative coverage.

In general, the brands that are the most popular with the general public were the easiest to reach. Zara, despite everything I had read about its non-communicative media policy, threw open its doors to me. H&M was equally responsive. Diesel allowed me to wander around its offices. It was amusing to see how the external image of each brand was evident in its internal culture. Diesel was garrulous and faintly surreal. Armani, which runs the gamut from jeans to very expensive suits, managed to be both formal and approachable, as befits a brand with such a wide range of different audiences.

The book owes a lot to the real fashion experts – the consultants and academics who are constantly monitoring the industry. I was aided by the fact that I live in Paris, which still sees itself as the capital of fashion. The French regard fashion in much the same way as the British see soccer – it is a national obsession. There is an unapologetically Francophile thread running through these pages, and I would argue that my location gave me access to books and articles that my Anglo-Saxon readers might not have seen.

I did not stay put, though – far from it. Although Paris and London were my main hunting grounds, my task also took me to Milan, Molvena, Stockholm, Galicia and Hong Kong. That was just the physical sphere of my activity. Via e-mail and telephone, I travelled to New York, Tokyo and Los Angeles, too. Fashion brands, like fashion trends, do not allow borders to get in their way.

GETTING CHANGED

It is a good time to write about the fashion industry. The sector is in the midst of an important phase shift. For one thing, it is still struggling to absorb the impact of changes to textile trade regulations in January 2005. The scrapping of a long-standing quota agreement allowed China – which already dominated the market – to increase its exports, forcing the price of textiles down even further. Many fashion brands are trying to benefit from improved profit margins while resisting downward pressure on their prices. Mid-market chain stores are losing out to cut-price supermarket clothing and cheap and cheerful newcomers like Japan's Uniqlo. The gap (no pun intended) between added-value 'fashion brands' and everyday clothing is becoming more evident. Hence, more marketing imagery is needed to create the necessary aura of exclusivity.

One thing is certain: fashion, even at the top end of the scale, is increasingly about big business. Designers are admirably creative people, but they work for an ever-shrinking number of global conglomerates.

Under-performing brands are sold without a hint of remorse, no matter how talented and artistic the people behind them might be. The clothes a designer sends out on to the runway are worthless unless they increase sales of handbags, sunglasses and perfume. Thus, marketing has taken on a crucial significance, and no designer can afford to neglect it.

The designers are not always at ease with this situation. Lanvin designer Alber Elbaz – a man as softly spoken as he is sharply witty – relates an interesting anecdote. Elbaz learned his craft working for the legendary American designer Geoffrey Beene. One day, Beene asked the young Alber what he thought of a particular dress. 'It's very commercial,' Elbaz opined. Beene took him gently aside and said, 'Alber, you must *never* say a dress is commercial. You must say it is *desirable*.'

Until recently, I considered myself almost immune to brands and their influence. I was certainly suspicious of designer brands that charged a fortune for their labels. I was convinced that their clothes were no better than those of any chain store. I scoffed when a well-known fashion journalist told me during the Paris collections, 'I have two jackets with me, one from Zara and one from Martin Margiela. The Margiela jacket was probably five times the price of the Zara one – but I don't mind, because I like what Margiela stands for. I'm paying for the person, not the article.' *Fine*, I thought, *you do that. But I won't fall into the same trap.* Then, a few months ago, I bought a pair of glasses. 'They're by Yves Saint Laurent,' said my optician. And, instead of yawning, I thought, 'Ah, yes – the pioneer of prêt-à-porter in Europe.'

Working on this book enhanced my respect for fashion designers, past and present. There cannot be many creative professions in which you are expected to prove your talent with a large body of work at least every six months. In addition, many designers are involved not only with their own collections but also with those of other brands. Certainly, they have large design teams working alongside them – to imagine otherwise would be absurd – but they are the ones who take the flack if the press reception is chilly.

For those outside the industry, it's probably easier to be cynical about fashion than it is to be admiring. As my research progressed, I found that I bounced like a pinball from one mindset to the other. I was surprised that many of the people involved in fashion marketing – the photographers, the art directors, the event organizers – retained a sense of humour about it. Yet they enjoyed grappling with an increasingly intellectual challenge. Apart from the stores they are sold in – and the bags we carry them home in – clothes have no packaging. They just sit on shelves, waiting mutely to be judged on their own appearance. All the packaging has to be done externally; otherwise, how would we know that this particular shirt represents a whole range of emotions and messages that we are supposed to be buying into?

Fashion branding may be an ephemeral business, but it is a complex and endlessly fascinating one. How does one turn a mere 'garment' into an object with seemingly mystical transformative powers? Well, let's hear it from the experts.

AUTHOR'S NOTE: The statistics and job titles quoted in this book were correct at the time of writing. All quotes were taken from original interviews or conferences, unless otherwise stated in the text. All translations from French sources are my own, and, although I tried to adhere as closely as possible to the spirit of the originals, I offer my humble apologies to those who feel I have not done their writing or observations justice.

1

A history of seduction

'Fashion is a factory that manufactures desire.'

Everything began in Paris. Later we'll turn to New York and Milan, to London and Tokyo, but most experts agree that fashion, as we know it today, was born in the French capital.

From the days when the couturier Worth designed dresses for Empress Eugénie, the wife of Napoleon III, to the final episode of *Sex and the City* – surely the most fashion-conscious television series of recent times – Paris has been a byword for style. As Bruno Remaury, social anthropologist and lecturer at the Institut Français de la Mode, the leading French fashion school, points out, 'The very word "fashion" comes from the French: *façon* means to work in a certain manner, and *travaux à façon* is the traditional French term for dressmaking.'

Paris still perspires fashion. On the Right Bank, historically the commercial heart of the city, the fashion zone opens like a jewelled fan from the fulcrum of the Musée de la Mode, housed in a wing of the Louvre. It takes in the glittering boutiques along the Rue du Faubourg Saint Honoré (also home to the French edition of *Vogue*), the über-hip designer outlet Colette, the department stores of Printemps and Galeries Lafayette, and several branches of the hyper-successful retail chains H&M and Zara – not to mention acres of billboard space promoting lingerie, perfume, bags or sunglasses, depending on the season. And this is by no means all: outside that better-known fashion zone, there are many other significant style hotspots, including the Avenue Montaigne, Saint Germain and Le Marais.

In all of these places you'll find queues in front of fitting rooms and people drooling over window displays, branded handbags slung over their arms. Those who work in the fashion industry will tell you it's in crisis, but on the streets there is little evidence to back up this claim. The activity during the sales season in Paris is like a cross-breed of rugby and boxing, without the nice manners. At the beginning of the 21st century, it's terribly trendy to be fashionable.

The question is – why?

STYLE ADDICTS

Fashion brands employ many techniques to persuade us to part with our hard-earned cash in return for the transient thrill of wearing something new. In our hearts, we know it's all smoke and mirrors – most of us have plenty to wear, and none of it is going to fall apart for a while yet. So why do we keep buying clothes? Can it really all be about marketing?

As fashion scholar Bruno Remaury points out, 'Traditional marketing is based on need. You take a product that corresponds to an existing demand, and attempt to prove that your product is the best in its category. But fashion is based on creating a need where, in reality, there is none. Fashion is a factory that manufactures desire.'

Many of those who work in the fashion business seem surprised – or at least mildly amused – by consumers' willingness to be seduced. Fashion consultant Jean-Jacques Picart, who has worked with brands such as Christian Lacroix and Louis Vuitton, comments as follows: 'For the people who are genuinely obsessed with fashion, it's a sort of drug. This is a personal theory, but I believe it's because they equate exterior change with interior change. They feel that, if they've changed their "look", they've also evolved emotionally.'

He hints that a preoccupation with fashion reveals a level of insecurity. 'The most extreme fashionistas have a vulnerable quality about them. It's as if they are worried about being judged. They live in a state of perpetual anxiety about their appearance.'

With disarming frankness, Picart describes his job as 'a little cynical, a little perverse'. 'The métier of fashion has a sole objective: to create brand appeal, in the same way that one might try to create sex appeal.

Everything we do is designed to make people fall in love with our brand. All the trimmings of our industry – the shows, the advertising, the celebrities, the media coverage – all of these things work together so that, if we've done our job well, somebody will push open the door of a shop.'

It all sounds fiendishly modern. But of course, although the bait has grown in sophistication, fashion branding has been around almost as long as the Venus flytrap.

THE FIRST FASHION BRAND

For our purposes, fashion originated in Paris at the end of the 19th century. That was when the first designer label was created. Although its main market was France, its founder was English.

Charles Frederick Worth changed the rules of the game. Before he came along, dressmakers did not create styles or dictate fashion; they were mere suppliers, who ran up copies of gowns that their wealthy clients had seen in illustrated journals, or admired at society gatherings. The clients themselves chose the fabrics and colours, and dresses were constructed around them, rather like scaffolding. Worth was the first couturier to impose his own taste on women – in effect, he was the prototype celebrity fashion designer.

Worth was born in the town of Bourne, Lincolnshire on 13 October 1826. Like many of today's most flamboyant designers – Galliano, Gaultier, McQueen – he came from a relatively humble background. (Indeed, the desire to escape a humdrum existence via sumptuous dresses and beautiful women is a thread running through the history of fashion.) He was the son of a local solicitor, William Worth, who appears to have run into financial difficulties when Charles was just a boy. Assuming that it was now up to him to put bread on the family table, Charles headed for London, where he became an apprentice and later a bookkeeper at a drapery firm called Swan and Edgar in Piccadilly. It was here that he developed an eye for sumptuous fabrics, and showed the prodigious flair for salesmanship that was to serve him so well. At the age of 20, and by now burning with ambition, he left for Paris.

Worth got a job at the drapery house of Gagelin and Opigez at 83 Rue Richelieu. When he was not busy attending to the needs of his clients, he designed dresses for his new French bride, Marie Vernet, who also worked in the store. Soon, customers began to notice these elegant creations, which, although adhering to the bottom-heavy style of the day, seemed to have an extra dash of cut and colour. Worth was given a small department at the back of the establishment in which to display his designs. These could be made to measure for customers who admired them.

Gagelin and Opigez were unwilling to let Worth expand his business, so, with the backing of a wealthy young Swedish draper called Otto Bobergh, he branched out on his own. Worth & Bobergh was established at 7 Rue de la Paix in 1858. Although Worth had a number of influential clients, his big break came when he designed a gown for Princess Metternich, wife of the Austrian ambassador to Paris. Empress Eugénie spotted the dress at a ball in the Tuileries Palace, and summoned its designer.

Worth was soon dressing the world's most glamorous women. Unlike his predecessors, he was not a fawning servant, forced to make imitations of gowns his clients had seen elsewhere. As far as he was concerned, he had a better idea of how to enhance their looks than they did. Slowly but surely, he did away with bonnets and crinolines and begun cutting dresses closer to the body. Hoop skirts were replaced by the infinitely more seductive 'sheath' dress – albeit garnished with bustles and trains that required cascades of expensive fabric.

More to the point, Worth was a marketing genius. Previously, dress designs had been displayed on wooden busts. (Scaled-down versions were sewn minutely on to dolls, which were sent out to potential clients as promotional devices.) Worth was the first couturier to sit his clients down and give them a little show – having first dressed a series of attractive young women he called *sosies*, or 'doubles', in his creations – thus inventing the concept of the fashion model. He would also identify fashionable women on whom he could place his dresses, knowing they would create a buzz as they mingled in high society. In private, he contemptuously referred to them as 'jockeys'.

In addition, Worth looked and acted like a proper fashion designer. Dapper and moustachioed, dressed from head to toe in velvet, a beret perched on his head, a cigar between his ostentatiously be-ringed fingers, he would greet clients while reclining on a divan. He had a capricious temper, too – there are reports of him furiously ripping half-finished garments to pieces because they were not exactly as he had envisaged them. Potential clients could be turned down, existing customers banished.

Here, already, we have many of the ingredients of contemporary fashion marketing: runway shows, celebrity models, elitism, and, of course, a charismatic brand spokesman. Dictatorial and flamboyant, this was a man who rose from obscurity to become deified by the fabulously rich – by the time he died, on 10 March 1885, Worth had established a pattern for all other designers to follow. Certainly, he exhibited a high level of artistry, but of all the dressmakers of that period he was the first to wrap his own name in a fairytale, and resell it at a profit.

POIRET RAISES THE STAKES

The one constant of fashion is constant change. Although Worth left his business in the capable hands of his two sons, Gaston and Jean-Philippe, his brand could not remain at the forefront of style for ever. This is not to say that it didn't have a pretty good run. A stand at the Paris Exposition of 1900 did a roaring trade, and the Worth name continued to resonate up to and beyond the 1920s (with a branded Worth perfume being launched as late as 1925). By then, though, the torch had been passed on not once, but twice.

The young designer Paul Poiret, recruited to Maison Worth by Jean-Philippe, soon began to challenge the restrictive styles of his masters. The son of a fabric merchant, Poiret had started out as an apprentice umbrella maker. In his spare time he had begun using umbrella silk to dress dolls in experimental designs. Poiret wanted to free women from the over-complicated structures that encumbered the upper body. Eventually he would banish the corset altogether, revolutionizing the way women dressed. As François Baudot comments in his (1999) book *Mode Du Siècle*, '[Before then] no fashionable woman would, or could, lace herself into or escape from her carapace without the aid of a second person. They had to wait for Poiret before the appearance of clothes they could put on by themselves.'

As is often the case, Poiret's employers weren't ready to embrace his radical ideas, and in 1904 he opened his own shop in the Rue du Faubourg Saint Honoré. In the years that followed, Poiret altered the outline of women's clothing for good. First came his interpretation of the Empire line: long straight dresses falling from a high waist that emphasized the bust. Then there was the 'hobble' skirt, cut so straight and narrow that its wearer could take only tiny steps (somewhat undermining claims that his clothes 'liberated' women). Inspired by fantasies of the Orient and the exotic Ballets Russes, Poiret devised variants of the kimono and baggy harem pants. The latter caused a sensation because, in fashion as in relationships, women were not expected to wear the trousers. Poiret went on to blur the boundaries between art and fashion, recruiting painters such as Georges Lapape and Raoul Dufy to illustrate his catalogues, and decorating his store in a style that prefigured Art Deco.

Like Worth before him, Poiret had a practical yet sophisticated approach to promoting his products. In 1911 he became the first couturier to launch a branded perfume, which he called Rosine after his eldest daughter. Poiret picked out the fragrance and designed the bottle, the packaging and the advertising. That same year, he threw a lavish party called 'The Thousand and Second Night', a fancy-dress extravaganza to which guests came as Persian royalty or cohorts of Scheherazade. The designer himself sported a natty gold turban. The most fashionable names in Europe were there, along with selected members of the press.

Poiret opened branded boutiques in major French cities, and organized travelling fashion shows. He designed dresses for the actress Sarah Bernhardt, his very own celebrity muse. Later, when he refused to sell any more dresses to a certain member of the Rothschild family – who had apparently dared to mutter a criticism at one of his shows – he made sure the decision was widely broadcast.

Not all of his marketing efforts were entirely self-serving, however. In that golden year of 1911, he opened an atelier in which Parisian girls 'from modest backgrounds' were trained to produce fabrics, rugs, lampshades, and other accessories for the home. These were sold in a boutique and several department stores under the Poiret sub-brand 'Martine', this time named after his youngest daughter.

But despite his talent, his marketing prowess and his influence, Poiret could not halt the onward march of fashion. His star was already descending after the First World War, and by the 1920s he was locked in bitter rivalry with the woman who was to become the fashion icon of the era, Gabrielle 'Coco' Chanel. According to Guillaume Erner in the book *Victimes de la Mode?* (2004), Poiret referred to Coco as 'the inventor of misery'. Bumping into Chanel in her black ensemble one evening, Poiret exclaimed, 'You must be in mourning! But for whom?' Chanel is reputed to have replied, 'For you, my dear.'

Poiret wasn't quite ready to slip away. In 1925, during the Art Deco Exposition, he hired three vast Seine barges. The first he turned into a restaurant, the second a hairdressing salon, and the third a boutique selling his perfumes, accessories and furnishings. It was to be his last extravagance. In the words of Erner, 'While the barges stayed afloat, the business sank.'

CHANEL, DIOR AND BEYOND

Gabrielle Chanel considered that Poiret's dresses were costumes rather than clothes, and a growing number of women seemed to agree with her. 'Eccentricity was dying: I hoped, by the way, that I helped to kill it,' she said, as quoted in the book *L'Allure de Chanel* by Paul Morand (1996). Rubbing salt into the wound, she added that it was easy to attract attention dressed as Scheherazade, but a little black dress showed more class. 'Extravagance kills personality,' she pronounced.

Whatever the truth of these claims, there is no arguing with the fact that Chanel took fashion into the 20th century. But the move had actually been precipitated by social change. During the First World War, women worked in factories and fields, and grew accustomed to the simplicity of uniforms. When it was all over, they were underfed but hardy, and unwilling to slip back into the traditional housewife/goddess role. (Many of them had, in any case, lost husbands and fiancés.) This was also the era of the automobile, which led to a more practical approach: short hair, skirts above the knee and tweed car coats. Women became less overtly feminine. Chanel and others – notably Jean Patou – adopted and embellished the androgynous style.

With her quotable wit and her talent for mixing with the right crowd, Coco fits right in to our alternative history of fashion – one that emphasizes the power of marketing. We certainly shouldn't forget her perfume, simply named No.5 because it was the fifth in a series of samples she had to choose from. It was notable for being the first unabashedly synthetic scent, which contributed to its image of modernity. Even today, according to François Baudot, 'a veritable gold mine, [the scent] continues, in the most condensed form, to propagate the style, the allure and the resonance of a personality. . . to equal Picasso, Stravinsky or Cocteau'.

While Chanel was busy twisting the fashion writers around her little finger, other designers were demonstrating that they also knew a promotional trick or two. Although her brand did not prove as resistant as that of Chanel (and, let's face it, few did), Elsa Schiaparelli was a formidable pre-war competitor. Salvador Dali collaborated on her dress designs – notably providing a cheeky lobster print – and the curvaceous bottle containing her perfume, Shocking, was supposed to have been modelled on the bust of the actress Mae West. Unfortunately, such publicity coups could not sustain her business through the dark years of the 1940s.

War, of course, changed everything again. Although a number of fashion houses sprang up in occupied Paris, Jacques Fath and Nina Ricci among them, the focus shifted to the United States. Until that time, fashionable American women bought expensive gowns that had been imported from Paris, or had more affordable copies run up closer to home. Even before the war, manufacturers on Seventh Avenue in New York had begun experimenting with synthetic fabrics, faster production techniques and light, interchangeable garments. This development accelerated in the 1940s, and New York became the birthplace of ready-to-wear. By the time peace broke out, the hegemony of Paris as the world's fashion capital was being challenged. Wartime innovations had shown that 'chic' need not mean personal dressmakers or 'haute couture'. For the first time, fashion was no longer the preserve of the wealthy elite.

Not that Paris had relinquished its importance. The 1950s saw the rise of Christian Dior, a man whose fervour for promotion outstripped even that of his predecessors. As well as being a visionary designer, the inventor of 'The New Look' was a moneymaking machine. He launched his first perfume in 1947 and a ready-to-wear store in New York in 1948. By the end of the decade, he had licensed his brand to a range of ties and stockings. He opened branches all over the world, from London to Havana. By the time he died prematurely, in 1957, he was employing over a thousand people – a situation previously unheard of for a couturier. More than anybody before him, Dior realized that luxury could be repackaged as a mass product. Not only that, he considered it the key to the survival and profitability of a brand. As quoted by Erner, he once commented, 'You know fashion: one day success, the next the descent into hell,' adding, 'I know lots of recipes, and one day. . . they might come in useful. Dior ham? Dior roast beef? Who knows?'

Perhaps it's no surprise that, today, the Dior brand is owned by the LVMH (Louis-Vuitton Moët Hennessy) empire – the ultimate expression of luxury as big business.

Beyond Dior, the dictatorship of the brand took hold. Even in the 1960s, when fashion was democratized and everyone claimed the right to be stylish, the marketers had the upper hand. When asked who invented the mini-skirt, herself or the French designer André Courrèges, Mary Quant replied generously, 'Neither – it was invented by the street.' Nevertheless, Quant was one of several designers who translated Sixties youth culture into profit, with considerable success.

Another such designer, on an entirely different scale, was Pierre Cardin, a man for whom extending the brand was little short of a crusade. A protégé of Christian Dior, naturally, Cardin noted very early on the decline of haute couture and acknowledged the potential of ready-to-wear (prêt-à-porter). He opened one store called Eve and another named Adam. He demanded, and got, a corner of the Parisian department store Printemps reserved exclusively for his brand. A darling of the media, he followed Dior's example by licensing his increasingly marketable identity, and today more than 800 different products around the world bear his name. In her (1999) book *The End of Fashion*, Teri Agins comments, 'There was always a manufacturer somewhere who was ready to slap "Pierre Cardin" on hair dryers, alarm clocks, bidets, and frying pans. "My name is more important than myself," Cardin once said.' Agins goes on to quote Henri Berghauer, who helped to manage Cardin's empire in the 1950s: 'Pierre realized early that he wanted to be more of a label than a designer. He wanted to be Renault.'

Although this strategy generated a vast personal fortune, it also undermined the sense of exclusivity that is the core value of any luxury brand. The Cardin label has languished in the purgatory of the un-hip since the 1990s, and is only now seeing the first glimmer of a resurgence. The future of the brand could depend on whether the designer, aged 82 at the time of writing, succeeds in selling his business – although buyers have apparently balked at the €400 million asking price, according to the French newspaper *Le Monde* (*'L'homme d'affaires chercherait à vendre son empire'*, 2 October 2004). The same article suggests that Cardin's licences continue to rake in around €36 million a year. With that performance, he can afford to dismiss accusations that his brand name is no longer fashionable.

It's impossible to talk about the fashion brands of the 1960s – or indeed the 1970s – without mentioning Yves Saint Laurent. Initially the successor to Dior, Saint Laurent quickly broke away to follow his own path, and it soon transpired that he was able to have his cake and eat it too. He was hailed as a genius of haute couture by the runway-watchers, while at the same time luring shoppers to his 'luxury prêt-à-porter' store, Saint Laurent Rive Gauche, in Paris's Saint Germain district. YSL was keen on licensing, too, but, along with his business partner, Pierre Bergé, he kept a closer eye on quality control than Cardin had done. His biggest hit was a perfume, Opium, which launched in 1978 and remains popular today.

Throughout the 1970s the democratization of fashion continued apace. Art schools pumped out rebellious young designers, rock fell in love with avant-garde clothing, the fashion press exploded and the first generation of 'stylists' – those benign dictators of dress – told consumers what to wear and how to wear it.

In France, the *ancien régime* of haute couture experienced a paroxysm of self-doubt, as prêt-à-porter took the high ground and streetwear usurped aristocratic glamour. The French also faced a new challenge from across the Alps, where the Italian textile and leather merchants began developing their own brands. In *Repères Mode 2003*, a collection of essays published by the Institut Français de la Mode, Ampelio Bucci makes the following note: 'In only 20 years (from 1970 to 1990), [the Italian brands'] notoriety had risen to a global level and they had established a presence in all the principal markets.'

As early as 1965, the Italian leather goods and fur business Fendi was working with a talented young designer called Karl Lagerfeld, who helped to turn the small company into a ravishing brand. And Fendi was not the only Italian player; among the many others were Armani, Gucci, Cerruti, Krizia and Missoni, to name but a few. The London of the 1970s boasted plenty of fresh ideas, associated with names such as Ossie Clark, Anthony Price, Zandra Rhodes and the short-lived concept store Biba, but the real powerhouses of the future were being created in Milan. Until a French tycoon called Bernard Arnault began laying the foundations for LVMH in the 1980s, the Milanese seemed to have the monopoly on luxury as a business. They were traders at heart, and they knew how to marry art with commerce in a way that many French labels hadn't quite grasped.

THE DEATH OF FASHION

When did fashion stop being fashionable? To paraphrase Hemingway, it happened slowly, and then very quickly. Probably the rot set in around the mid- to late 1980s, provoked by a boom-to-bust economy and the emergence of AIDS as a powerful metaphor for the delayed hangover that followed the 1970s. The effect of the disease was terrifyingly real as it tore through the creative economy, robbing it of some of its brightest emerging stars.

Not that this grim decade was entirely devoid of hope. By now the most interesting thing on the catwalk was definitely in prêt-à-porter, with extraordinary creations from Jean-Paul Gaultier, Thierry Mugler and Kenzo. Elsewhere, Karl Lagerfeld was busy revitalizing Chanel – where he was appointed in 1983 – and Christian Lacroix was showing flamboyant dresses inspired by his passion for opera, folklore and the history of costume. This was, after all, the time of the New Romantic. The period also saw the emergence of the Japanese designers, notably Yohji Yamamoto and Rei Kawakubo (of Comme des Garçons), whose ethereal black numbers combined minimalist rigour with futuristic interpretations of traditional garb. More costume than dress, they served as inspiration for the monochrome severity that characterized the tail end of the 1980s.

More than anything, though, this was the era of the yuppie, the young upwardly mobile professional, whose clothing signified success. 'Power dressing' became a buzz phrase. Giorgio Armani's unstructured but easily identifiable suits were worn as a badge of success. In the UK, while providing flashy City boys with eccentrically reworked interpretations of the tailored suit – his trademark 'classics with a twist' – Paul Smith also discovered the Filofax, a leather-bound 'personal organizer' manufactured by a tiny East End company. By popularizing this combination of address book and diary, which implied that its user had people to see and places to go, Smith handed the yuppies their ultimate accessory.

Meanwhile, on the other side of the Atlantic, Ralph Lauren had been steadily building one of the ultimate fashion brands. His rag-trade-to-riches story has been told many times before, but it's worth briefly repeating here.

Born Ralph Lifshitz in 1939, America's most upwardly mobile designer was the son of Russian Jewish immigrants from the Bronx. His father was a house painter, who changed the family name to Lauren when young Ralph was still at school. Ralph was brought up on the Hollywood movies of the 40s and 50s, mentally filing away images of Cary Grant and Fred Astaire so that he could recreate their style. He got his start in the fashion business selling suits at Brooks Brothers, and later became a wholesaler of ties and gloves in New York's garment district. Soon he began designing his own ties, choosing the name 'Polo' for its aristocratic associations. The stylish neckwear proved a big hit at Bloomingdale's, and by 1970 Ralph had taken over a corner of the Manhattan department store with an entire range of upmarket apparel.

According to Teri Agins, 'Lauren will go down in fashion history for introducing the concept of "lifestyle merchandising" in department stores. . . Lauren designed [his] outpost to feel like a gentlemen's club, with mahogany panelling and brass fixtures'. She goes on to say that Lauren's stores 'stirred all kinds of longings in people, the dream that the upwardly mobile shared for prestige, wealth and exotic adventure'. But Ralph Lauren is important for another reason. European luxury brands frequently dwell on their 'heritage' for marketing purposes, using a tradition of craftsmanship as a way of seducing consumers and justifying elevated prices (think of Hermès, Louis Vuitton, Dunhill and Asprey). Almost subconsciously, Lauren realized that, in the USA, history was irrelevant. This was the land of Hollywood, of fantasy for sale.

Lauren created a world of aristocratic good taste, but it was pure invention. In the end, his success rested on the quality of his clothes and his knack for branding. Lauren's shops were film sets, and his advertising campaigns – shot by Bruce Weber – were stills from movies that had never been made. It's no surprise to learn that Lauren designed the costumes for the film *The Great Gatsby*. In many ways, Lauren *was* Jay Gatsby – the man who created himself.

Ralph Lauren was the perfect brand for the 1980s, when fashion became less important than 'lifestyle'. In fact, with the rise of the supermodel, the media seemed more interested in how the models lived than in the clothes they wore.

Fashion clutched its chest and keeled over some time in the 1990s. In *The End of Fashion*, Teri Agins suggests that women lost interest in fashion because they were more concerned about their careers: '[They] began to behave more like men in adopting their own uniform: skirts and blazers and pantsuits that gave them an authoritative, polished, power look.'

In addition, the Paris catwalks had lost their relevance in the face of MTV culture and streetwear. Levi's, Nike and Gap seemed a lot more connected to quotidian reality than some ethereal vision on a runway. Tracksuit-wearing rappers and the chino-clad super-nerds of the dotcom boom were the new icons; 'casual Friday' elided into the rest of the week. Stores selling comfortable but unchallenging garments, mostly run up on the cheap in Asia, made dressing down not only affordable, but acceptable. The elitist stance once taken by fashion brands began to look stuffy and – horror of horrors – old-fashioned. Clothing became a commodity, spare and functional. Even supermodels began to look less 'super'. Kate Moss, in her first incarnation as a grungy teenager, had nothing of the femme fatale about her. Calvin Klein built a phenomenally successful brand around posters featuring Moss and other androgynous youths sporting baggy jeans and nothing else; it was the 'simple chic' ethic taken to the nth degree.

Finally, many fashion houses were acquired by or grew into vast corporations, selling clothing, accessories, make-up and furniture. As Teri Agins explains, 'Such fashion houses just also happen to be publicly traded companies, which must maintain steady, predictable growth for their shareholders. . . Fashion. . . requires a certain degree of risk-taking and creativity that is impossible to explain to Wall Street.' Further, she observes that the utilitarian blandness of Nineties clothing made marketing more important than ever. Branding played a critical role 'in an era when. . . just about every store in the mall [was] peddling the same styles of clothes'.

Today, while branding remains as crucial as ever, its raison d'être has changed. Nine years on from the publication of Agins' book, fashion has – inevitably – transformed itself again. Style has come out of the closet.

THE REBIRTH OF FASHION

The glamour factory had been plotting its resurgence all along, humming away in the background throughout the late 1990s, while industry observers fretted about the rising tide of 'smart casual'. The next wave of upmarket fashion brands would come from Milan and from Paris; clearly, reports of the death of the French capital had been greatly exaggerated.

There is one name you can't escape when you attempt to write a history of fashion branding: Tom Ford. As Carine Roitfeld, the editor of French *Vogue* and a one-time collaborator of the American designer, says, 'In the history of fashion, there's definitely a pre-Tom Ford and a post-Tom Ford period. He was one of the first contemporary designers who really understood the power of marketing. He was not a snob about his work – he wanted to sell.'

The story of Gucci resembles an opera, replete with glamour, envy and murder. More on that later, but for now it's enough to say that Ford realized (like all the smartest designers, from Worth to Lauren) that the key to a successful fashion label lay not just in the garments, but in the 'universe' surrounding them. Or, as Roitfeld puts it, 'He created a dream world.'

It was fine that in winter 1995 Ford showed a collection of sexy, sophisticated clothes that attracted the attention of Madonna and Gwyneth Paltrow. Even better that he reintroduced the bamboo-handled bags that had been the making of Gucci back in the 1950s. But he also redesigned every aspect of the brand, from print advertisements to stores, ensuring that everything gelled to create an 'ideal' of what the Gucci name meant. According to Guillaume Erner, 'The Texan turned the style of the brand upside down: previously everything that bore the Gucci name had been brown, soft, and rounded. With him, it became black, hard, and square.'

So what did the Gucci name mean, exactly? It meant sex. Ford brought lust back into fashion with a series of overtly erotic ads that were quickly tagged 'porno chic'. A famously over-the-top example showed a crouching man gazing at the Gucci logo shaved into a woman's pubic hair – beautifully photographed, of course. While outwardly deploring the trend, the mainstream media had great fun with fashion's filthy new image. Sex, as everyone knows, always sells, and many consumers wanted in. Even those who could only afford to buy their jeans from

Gap found some extra cash for a Gucci belt. As Roitfeld observes, '[Ford] created clothes people wanted to wear, and then he explained to them that if they couldn't afford the dress, they could at least buy the sunglasses.'

Ford was not the only one giving the rarefied world of fashion a much-needed kick up the rear. At the same time, Miuccia Prada – with the aid of her husband and business partner Patrizio Bertelli – was blowing the dust off the old family luggage firm in Milan. Prada, too, understood that the brand message had to be carried right through from advertising to clothing to store. Taking the opposite stance to Gucci's sex-drenched imagery, Miuccia positioned her brand as creative, sensitive and politically engaged. New York intellectuals and London businesswomen loved it. The Prada bag replaced the Filofax as the status symbol of choice, and the shoes and clothing quickly followed.

But what was happening in Paris? By the end of the 1990s the city was a shadow of its former self, its image as the world's fashion capital eroded by the slow decline of haute couture and the rapid ascent of Milan, not to mention the dominance of US pop culture and the influence of American designers. As unlikely as it may seem, the resurrection of Paris as the world's most glamorous city can be credited to one ascetic, understated businessman.

Bernard Arnault was already on the rise in 1984, when he acquired Christian Dior. Two decades later, he is president of both Dior and LVMH, with a glittering portfolio of brands that includes Céline, Kenzo, Thomas Pink, Givenchy, Loewe, Fendi, Pucci, Marc Jacobs and Donna Karan – not to mention Louis Vuitton itself. And although the two men have radically different personalities, Arnault's tactics are not dissimilar to those of Tom Ford.

'I met Bernard Arnault in 1985, and he was already nurturing the idea of a luxury brand that would be at the same time relatively accessible,' recalls the fashion marketing consultant Jean-Jacques Picart, who is also Arnault's personal communications adviser. 'Dior now has 310 boutiques around the world, so it can't be described as a luxury brand in the classic sense of the term, which implies exclusive. [Arnault's] stroke of genius was to bring marketing techniques to a world that had previously claimed to have no use for them.'

As far as Dior was concerned, Arnault's most inspired move was the appointment of a charismatic designer named John Galliano. (Legend has it that Arnault made his choice by arranging a meeting of the world's top fashion journalists, and asking them who they thought was the world's most creative designer.) Galliano didn't arrive at Dior directly: he was first appointed at Givenchy, following the reluctant retirement of the illustrious Hubert de Givenchy. But it seemed as though he was being groomed for Dior all along; when the Italian designer Gianfranco Ferré left the fashion house, Galliano was brought in to replace him. Rebellious Londoner Alexander McQueen then slid into the hot seat at Givenchy, further illustrating Arnault's penchant for shaking up the conservative world of French high fashion, and reaping plenty of media exposure in the process. Arnault would repeat the trick by bringing in hip New York designer Marc Jacobs to revamp Louis Vuitton.

In the opinion of Jean-Jacques Picart, 'One of the things that can enable a fashion brand to stand out is transgression. At the end of the 1990s, when fashion leaned towards the minimalist, John exploded on to the scene with a personal vision inspired by history and costume. It was baroque, excessive, warm, rich, flamboyant, brimming over with decadence and sex. It was also completely at odds with the existing image of Dior. It had the effect of a firework display.'

Gucci, Prada and Dior's formula of young, inventive clothes and affordable accessories, plus aggressive marketing, seemed to reanimate the public's inner fashion victim. Ford and Galliano were personally photogenic and exciting – as entertaining in their own way as rock stars. Fortuitously, their makeover of previously moribund brands coincided with the media's increasing obsession with the cult of celebrity and the rise of magazines like *Heat* and *OK!* When the paparazzi captured Victoria Beckham or Jennifer Lopez swathed in designer brands, millions of young women wanted to imitate them.

Of course, as we've already pointed out, few ordinary folk could afford a Prada suit or a Dior dress. Even if they could stretch to a handbag or a pair of sunglasses, where did they get the clothes to match? Enter Zara, H&M and Topshop – high-street brands employing talented young designers who produced fun, fresh creations that wouldn't look out of place on the Paris runways, and were sometimes directly inspired by them. (See Chapter 3: When haute couture meets high street.) By the end of the millennium, fashion was glamorous again.

SURVIVING THE CRASH

In their latest incarnation as dream merchants, fashion brands seem curiously resilient. In September 2001, a minor war had been pre-occupying industry-watchers for several months. The conflict ranged Bernard Arnault against another French businessman, François Pinault, owner of the retail and mail-order conglomerate Pinault-Printemps-Redoute (PPR). The disputed territory was Gucci.

Arnault had been stealthily buying shares in Gucci with the intention of taking over the company. By 1999 his stake had reached 34 per cent. But neither Tom Ford nor Gucci CEO Domenico De Sole liked the idea of being swallowed up by LVMH, where they suspected they would lose control of the brand. Their white knight arrived in the form of François Pinault, who snapped up 40 per cent of Gucci's shares. He also acquired beauty and cosmetics company Sanofi, which owned Yves Saint Laurent. In a couple of swift moves, Pinault had created Gucci Group, a potential rival to LVMH.

The flurry of acquisitions that followed on both sides looked like a duel between billionaires – Monopoly played for real. As LVMH continued its rapid expansion, the Gucci Group took possession of Boucheron, Bottega Veneta and Balenciaga, and signed partnership deals with Alexander McQueen (who left LVMH's Givenchy amid considerable tongue-wagging) and Stella McCartney. Meanwhile, the bitter dispute over who had the right to take control of Gucci was tied up in court in the Netherlands, where Gucci's shares were listed.

Finally, in the economic dip provoked by the dotcom crash – and almost as if he sensed that he needed to conserve his resources for the difficult period ahead – Arnault gave up the fight. On 10 September 2001, he sold his Gucci shares, allowing his arch-rival François Pinault to take full ownership of the company. The *guerre du luxe*, as the French press had termed the conflict, was over.

We all know what happened the next day. In New York, the fashion carnival was in town for the spring-summer collections. The huge marquees that would be the setting for many of the shows had been erected in Bryant Park, practically within view of the Twin Towers. The industry was therefore witness to the horror that was to cause its latest nervous breakdown.

It seems almost churlish to try to place an event as tragic and far-reaching as 11 September 2001 within the context of fashion. But the interesting fact is that, after a dramatic slump, the industry emerged from the disaster in rather better shape than anyone had a right to expect.

On 19 December 2001, an article in *The Independent* reported, 'Profits fall by half at Gucci and Italian fashion giant predicts no upturn until late 2002'. Fast-forward to 16 October 2003, and a headline in *The Guardian*: 'Fashion back in fashion as Gucci sales surge'. Later (23 January 2004), again in *The Independent*: 'LVMH's luxury defies the downturn'. In *Time* magazine's autumn 2004 Style and Design supplement, an article headlined 'Luxury Fever' commented, 'Despite rising interest rates, staggering energy prices. . . and the general state of unrest in the world, conspicuous consumption is back.'

And it's not just the luxury brands that have weathered the storm. In December 2003, market researcher Mintel pointed out that high-street fashion brands H&M, Zara and Mango had all managed to double their sales between 1998 and the end of 2002, despite slowing growth. At the time of writing, the 'fast fashion' brigade continued to announce healthy sales increases and new store openings.

Such is the magnetism of fashion. We need to take a break from it occasionally, but sooner or later we come back for more. And if they've been smart enough, our favourite brands are waiting for us.

2

Fashioning an identity

'In a lot of ways, branding is simply telling a story.'

Exploring the fashion world occasionally feels like gate-crashing an exclusive club. At least, that's the sensation I experience as I climb a spiral staircase in a building near Place Vendôme – the grand Parisian square that is home to the Ritz. César Ritz opened his celebrated hotel on 1 June 1898, and its rich patrons attracted the attentions of Cartier, Boucheron, Van Cleef & Arpels, and the other jewellery and luxury goods boutiques that crowd the square.

This particular building is the headquarters of a publishing firm, but its location is entirely appropriate. Over the past ten years, Assouline has published a series of glossy books, each minutely dissecting the history of a legendary designer label. With offices in Paris, London and New York, it has become a luxury brand in its own right. I reckon that here, at least, I should get my first insight into what makes a fashion icon.

As so often on these occasions, the claustrophobic staircase and labyrinthine corridors of the old building lead to a large office, with a bright picture window overlooking the potted trees and shrubs in the courtyard. Martine Assouline, an elegant French woman, sits me down at a glossy slab-like table and considers her response to my question.

'At the moment we are in a period where the brand has an exaggerated importance,' she tells me. 'Designers like Tom Ford, John Galliano and

Marc Jacobs injected new life into fashion. They fused it with the music and film industries in a manner that seemed very new, very attractive. This was not always the case – in the era of the supermodel, nobody really cared about brands. Naomi Campbell and Claudia Schiffer were the brands; the clothes were immaterial. But fashion has come down to earth – it appears more accessible, more affordable, even when this is not the case. People identify with Prada, Dior and Louis Vuitton in a way that they never did before.'

But do these brands have anything in common? What's the uniting factor that has enabled them to succeed and survive?

'It's a heritage that makes customers daydream, and the strength to live up to it. The question of succession is important: Chanel was lucky to have appointed Karl Lagerfeld, just as Dior was resuscitated by the arrival of Galliano. The wrong designer can wreck a brand. It is also vital to achieve the correct balance between marketing and creativity. I don't think it is fair to say that fashion is based entirely on marketing. You can do as much marketing as you like, but if the final product does not deliver, the brand loses its power. Pierre Cardin made millions licensing his name, but the products were not always of an acceptable quality. And so. . .' She shrugs.

A few days later, in the rather different setting of a shabby-chic café called Chez Prune near the Canal Saint Martin, I'm sipping coffee with a trend-tracker called Genevieve Flaven, co-founder of Style-Vision, a company that specializes in monitoring and predicting consumer behaviour (see Chapter 6: Anatomy of a trend). Like Martine Assouline, Flaven believes that few consumers are convinced by marketing alone.

'Every consumer can now decrypt advertising messages, so traditional marketing has become less and less significant. Consumers want to know what's behind the brand – what it can give back to them. Sometimes it's just a question of value: the best quality for the price. When people buy a very high-priced garment, they want to see the patience and the craftsmanship that has gone into it. They are paying to possess a beautiful object. And sometimes, when it's a famous brand, they are paying to be part of the story.'

Flaven explains that iconic brands create – and occasionally rewrite – their own narratives.

'It resembles a novel that you, the consumer, can enter. Chanel is a good example. First, through her talent and the power of her personality, Coco created her own myth. And now the legend of Coco is inexhaustible. It's the thread that pulls us into the Chanel universe. Every time Chanel launches a new product, it emphasizes a link with Coco, urging us to own a little piece of the legend. When the jewellery range was launched [in 1993] we were told it was in the spirit of Coco – but in fact she disliked jewellery. In a lot of ways, branding is simply telling a story.'

Few people can create a myth from scratch, which is why many fashion entrepreneurs have chosen to buy in to existing stories. (See Chapter 14: Retro brands retooled.) Take Lambretta, for instance. Like the Italian scooters themselves, the name has plenty of retro buzz: Mods and Rockers battling on Brighton beach, natty suits, sharp haircuts and Cool Britannia all rolled into one youth-friendly package. The scooter launched by Ferdinando Innocenti in Lambrete, Milan in 1947 had long been out of production by the time a UK licensing company acquired the name. In 1997, Lambretta re-launched as a British menswear label with a flagship store in London's Carnaby Street – Swinging Sixties Central. Playing on Lambretta's connection with British Mod culture, the store contained a scooter, a Union Jack-patterned sofa and a range of sleek but street-smart clothing. Womenswear followed in 1999, two more stores opened; by 2003 the brand could claim 'ongoing approval from celebrity wearers in the worlds of film, music and TV, including members of Stereophonics and Groove Armada, Ewan McGregor and Vernon Kay' (*Cool Brand Leaders*, 2003). The clothes, the store design and the advertising skilfully edited the Lambretta story, downplaying the brand's Italian heritage and favouring its role in British popular culture.

Other brands have even more unlikely roots. How to explain the success of CAT, the US-based footwear company that is an offshoot of Caterpillar, maker of lumbering earth-moving vehicles? In fact, the evolution makes perfect sense. CAT boots were originally launched in 1991 as protective footwear for Caterpillar machinery operators. (The Caterpillar brand dates back to 1925, when two tractor makers merged to form Caterpillar Tractor Co, based in California. The name Caterpillar derives, of course, from the 'crawler and track' mechanism that allows the vehicles to traverse rugged terrain.) Licensing companies in the United Kingdom and the United States spotted the potential of the brand's early designs, especially the honey-yellow Colorado work boot, which gelled perfectly with the mid-Nineties 'grunge' aesthetic of plaid shirts and cargo pants. Today, a US-based company, Wolverine

World Wide, holds the global licence for CAT Footwear. Since 1994, it has sold nearly 50 million pairs of CAT shoes.

'The fashion aspect of the brand is more pronounced in Europe,' says Shannon Jaquith, brand communications and international marketing manager. 'In the US we're predominantly a work boot business, which makes sense given our heavy machinery heritage. In Central and South America we provide non-slip footwear for people who work in the shipping industry – and there's a connection because Caterpillar makes marine engines. We didn't set out to become a fashion brand, which ironically helped us develop into one.'

Jaquith says the brand's values remain consistent across all its markets. 'We're gritty, blue-collar and authentic. People like us because we haven't tried to portray ourselves as trendy. Our brand image begins with our work shoes – we're here to protect you. In a world where there are a lot of greedy brands clamouring for a slice of the fashion market, we strike consumers as grass-roots and honest. For instance, when we came out with a vintage collection, it really dated back to the 1920s – it was based on our original designs.'

CAT positions itself as a genuine American icon alongside brands such as Budweiser, Levi's and Harley Davidson. A typical extract from one of its catalogues tells the story thus: 'Whether it's a builder swinging a hammer, a musician strumming a guitar, or a student studying from his local café. . . the toughness, honesty and uncompromising nature of CAT is a badge that represents their preference for cargos over khakis, the warehouse loft over a metro high-rise, and their local garage band over the hottest new dance club.' It is a perfect piece of branding narrative, together with the slogan 'No guff since 1904'. This tinkers slightly with historical fact, as the date refers to one of the two tractor firms that later merged to create Caterpillar. However, the core brand 'promise' is genuine, because CAT continues to provide robust protective footwear across a number of industries.

'We don't have a huge marketing budget, so our main focus right now is in enhancing our retail presence; communicating the lifestyle of the brand at store level,' says Jaquith. Thus, heavy machinery becomes the perfect backdrop for a fashionable brand extension. The message is clear: the more convincing the story, the more attractive the brand.

CONTROLLING THE PLOT

But if consumers are invited to play a part in the story of a brand, what happens when they subvert it? Throughout the history of fashion, consumers have had an irritating habit of sweeping aside carefully constructed marketing strategies and bending brands to their own will. It is doubtful, for example, that Dr. Martens encouraged the skinhead movement to adopt its shiny black boots. To its credit, however, the brand does not try to bury the association. Its website has its own explanation: according to its narrative, the original skinhead was a 'multicultural, politically broad-minded and fashion-conscious individual' with a liking for 'reggae, soul and ska'. It was only later that the look was 'hijacked by right-wing racists'.

Burberry faces a similar problem in the United Kingdom. Some time ago, it joined the pantheon of brands adopted by label-conscious but not particularly upmarket British youth, notably soccer fans. As a direct corollary, and most damagingly of all, Burberry – and particularly its iconic check pattern – has become associated with 'chavs'. The etymology of the term 'chav' is unclear – theories range from the Romany word for 'child' to the straightforward acronym of 'Council Housed and Violent' – but it has been widely adopted by the British media to describe a certain type of downmarket consumer. Chavscum. co.uk, the website that first identified the group, uses the definition 'Britain's peasant underclass'. In the section of the site headed 'How to spot a chav', the first item is a baseball cap in Burberry check. The plaid fabric has become so closely associated with hooliganism that some pubs and clubs have instructed door staff to refuse entry to young people wearing it. An article in *The Guardian* ('The two faces of Burberry', 15 April 2004) cites a picture of a soap opera actress 'clad top to toe in Burberry check: the hat, the skirt, the scarf, her baby dressed up to match' as the moment when Burberry became 'the ultimate symbol of nouveau riche naff'.

The 'chav' association clearly goes against the grain of Burberry's status as a luxury brand. It also threatens to unravel the work Rose Marie Bravo has done to rebuild the label since joining the company as chief executive in 1997. Making the brand younger and more accessible has left it open to re-interpretation.

And yet Burberry has emerged relatively unscathed. For a start, 'chavs' are a purely British tribe, and the UK market accounts for only 15 per cent of the brand's sales. In Europe and Asia, Burberry has successfully maintained its official positioning as English, quirky and fashionable – a 'classic with a twist', *à la* Paul Smith. It has also toned down the trademark plaid, now using it on only five per cent of its clothing, as opposed to 20 per cent a couple of years ago. Bravo told *The Guardian*, 'We had this issue of logoism that was rampant across the industry. But we knew that these things run in cycles, you can have too much of a good thing. We moved on, and we got into a mode of being more discreet with the logo.' The company has also placed more focus on its check-free upmarket label, Burberry Prorsum, which is a step above the largest range, Burberry London, in both positioning and price. The current face of Burberry Prorsum is the aristocratic English model Stella Tennant.

Burberry's non-executive director, Philip Bowman (the chief executive of Allied Domecq), skilfully handled the potentially difficult issue by at first laughing it off – brandishing a copy of a book about chav culture during a press conference – and then suggesting that most of the Burberry items worn by the clan were fakes. He told the world, 'I think the genesis of it is rather sad. In this country there is not an insignificant amount of counterfeit product at the low end' ('Bowman keeps the chavs in check', *Financial Times*, 22 October 2004).

In short, Burberry has trodden a delicate line between nonchalant acceptance and ingenuous denial of the phenomenon. In any case, the chavs have done little to undermine the company's performance. At the time of writing, it had just announced a year-on-year sales rise of 14 per cent.

Lacoste has faced the same challenge in its native France, where the prestigious sportswear with the crocodile logo has been adopted as a uniform by tough teenagers from the *banlieues*, or suburbs.

In 1925 tennis ace René Lacoste was standing in front of a shop window in Boston with Pierre Guillou, captain of the French tennis team, shortly before a vital qualifying match for the Davis Cup. 'If I win,' Lacoste said, indicating a crocodile-skin suitcase, 'you can buy me one of those.' He lost the match, but an American journalist who had heard about the bet reported that 'the young Lacoste [did not win] his crocodile-skin suitcase, but he fought like a real crocodile'. From then on, Lacoste wore a crocodile embroidered on the breast pocket of his shirts. And when he launched a range of sportswear in 1930, it naturally bore the crocodile logo. Today, more than 30 million Lacoste products are sold annually in over 110 countries, generating revenue in excess of €800 million.

With its emphasis on quality and its roots in the exclusive domain of tennis, Lacoste had all the ingredients it needed to seduce upmarket consumers – and it did so, for decades. But when French hip-hop fans began casting around for a home-grown version of the sports brands worn by their American counterparts, they naturally turned to Lacoste. The logo implied performance, taste, and money to burn. Plus, what could be more rebellious than that snappy little croc?

At first, Lacoste observed this turn of events with grave concern, fearing that it would lose its traditional older, wealthier French client base. Soon, though, it recognized an opportunity – one that, after a false start, it utilized with considerable subtlety. While a blatant attempt to target these new consumers might have succeeded in distancing both loyal customers and suburban kids – whose very fascination for the brand lay in the fact that that they had 'hijacked' it – Lacoste adopted an oblique approach. It used the trend as a springboard to rejuvenate the brand. It hired a new designer, Christophe Lemaire (formerly of Thierry Mugler and Christian Lacroix), who introduced a range of 'elegantly functional' clothing: 'Though Lemaire was not allowed to touch the polo shirt – the company still regards it as a perfect classic – he used it as a reference point for his collection of sharp pullovers, hip track jackets, soft pants and sexy pleated skirts.' ('Courtoisie on the court', *Newsweek*, 27 May 2002.) Lacoste showed on the catwalks in New York and Paris, and opened smartly minimalist concept stores in France, the United States, Germany and Japan. Cult film director Wong Kar Wai was brought in to direct a globally-screened commercial in the languorous style of his movie *In the Mood for Love*, raising the brand's profile among culturally savvy consumers while simultaneously catering to the important Asian market. Even the crocodile logo was given a subtle retouching by the design agency Seenk, becoming simpler and more streamlined.

Bernard Lacoste, company chairman and the founder's oldest son, refers to the strategy as 'evolution rather than revolution'. The brand regained control of its identity, while giving a '*merci*' nod to the influential group that had helped perk up its flagging relevance. As one French lifestyle magazine noted, 'In the past regarded as little more than vandals, the "crew" from the high-rise blocks have become sought-after opinion leaders, whose cultural and stylistic codes are scrutinized by trend-trackers. In short, they are the people who define tomorrow's fashions.' ('*Comment Lacoste a rendu accros les ados de banlieue*', *Technikart*, 28 May 2002.)

It's certainly not the last time a luxury brand will be forced to tackle the issue of over-accessibility: at the time of writing, there are reports that Dior intends to drop some of its lower-priced accessories, such as the bracelets sported by teenage girls from the Paris *banlieues*, in order to re-establish its exclusivity. A myth is a fragile entity, easily tarnished.

THE ITALIAN CONNECTION

The connection between Dr. Martens, Burberry, Lacoste and Dior is that they have a lengthy heritage to rely on. They may choose to highlight or mask different aspects of their past depending on prevailing trends, but the elements are readily available – a pick-and-mix bag of anecdotes and attributes. But what if you're starting from zero, without access to a resonant name, a dusty archive, or a famous designer? How do you give your brand a compelling story?

There are two instructive – and very different – examples from Italy. The first is Tod's, the footwear and accessories brand. There is no Signor Tod, and there never has been. When company chairman Diego Della Valle created the brand in 1979, he invented the name JP Tod's to give his ultra-comfortable loafers an air of Anglo-Saxon classicism. But his real stroke of genius was an advertising campaign featuring black and white photographs of Cary Grant, Jackie and John F. Kennedy, Audrey Hepburn and David Niven, with a single Tod's loafer superimposed at the bottom of the image. Della Valle was not claiming that these people had actually worn his shoes – let's be clear – he was simply linking the brand with a certain insouciant style. Add a high price point to underscore a suggestion of luxury, and the legend falls smoothly into place.

The second example is perhaps even more impressive. It concerns a young man from rural Italy who ran up a pair of jeans on his mother's sewing machine, and went on to build a global brand.

On the day I went to meet that young man, we were barrelling down the *autostrada* in a functional four-by-four, when my driver pointed out a gleaming flame-red car. 'Look at that – a Ferrari,' he said. 'Now that's what I call a car. *Che bella!*' He looked on with envy as the Ferrari roared to a pinpoint in the distance.

Diesel founder Renzo Rosso wouldn't be quite so impressed. He's more of a Harley Davidson, rock and roll sort of guy. He likes things beaten-up, frayed and oil-stained, preferably mixed in with a bit of retro kitsch. The Diesel universe frequently resembles a 1950s sci-fi movie, sometimes the attic of a junk shop, occasionally an *Easy Rider* psychedelic road trip, and very often a blend of all three. Mostly, it looks like the contents of Rosso's own head.

'I bought a sports car once, when I was younger,' confesses Rosso later, over lunch in the small town of Molvena, where Diesel is based. 'It was a Dodge Viper. I drove it maybe twice. The second time I was sitting at the traffic lights and I became aware of the fact that everyone was looking at me. I didn't like that feeling. I sold the car not long after that.'

Rosso has come a long way from his parents' farm – but, in a sense, he is still in the same place. Diesel's surprisingly small light industrial unit is tucked within the folds of the hilly Bassano del Grappa region in northern Italy, not far from where he grew up. He remains close to his native soil, with the major difference that he now has his own farm, as well as a vineyard producing the red wine that we are currently sipping.

'I have some luxuries,' he says, 'a beautiful home; but I'm still the same person. Basically, I'm a meddler. When I was a kid, I used to take my moped apart and put it back together again, to see if I could get it to go faster. I've always been like that. I look at things and try to work out how they could be better, more fun, more amusing. I'm allergic to the ordinary.'

Rosso ran up his first pair of jeans at the age of 15, on his mother's Singer sewing machine, because he couldn't afford a pair of the flares that were fashionable at the time. 'A couple of my friends liked them, and asked me to make some for them too. Every night I sat at home stitching jeans for my friends. But it was okay, because I charged them 3,400 lire – about two euros. I said to myself, "You know; there might be a future in this business."'

This insight led him to the local technical college in Padua, where he studied textiles and manufacturing. Afterwards, he got a job as a production manager at a company called Moltex, which made trousers for various Italian labels. The enterprise was run by Adriano Goldschmied, who became Rosso's mentor. Rosso is quick to acknowledge, 'He taught me how to survive in the fashion industry.'

A couple of years later, in 1978, Rosso approached Goldschmied with the idea of starting his own jeans label. 'So we went into business together, producing jeans for ourselves instead of other people.' It was Goldschmied who came up with the brand name Diesel. 'We wanted something that didn't sound Italian; that had an international feel. Did you know the word is pronounced the same all over the world?'

The business developed slowly. By his own admission, Rosso was young, inexperienced, and unwilling to risk the future of the joint-owned enterprise by trying some of the wilder ideas that lurked in the back of his mind. Then, in 1985, he bought Goldschmied's half of Diesel: 'That was when I started producing things that were a little more personal, a little more crazy. Everything I did was inspired by vintage. Now everyone uses that word, "vintage", but we were the first to do that. When I began producing stonewashed jeans and jeans with holes in them, retailers would send them back, saying the quality was not good enough. I was obliged to travel – to New York, to Stockholm, to Los Angeles – to explain the concept. It's hard to imagine today, but 25 years ago department stores weren't stocking a great deal of casual-wear, particularly in the States. It was rows and rows of suits. Imagine trying to convince them to stock jeans that already looked old.'

In addition, Rosso had set his prices high. 'Because of the production process that had gone into ageing the jeans, I was selling them for 80 or 90 dollars, when the average at the time was about 50 dollars. I remember going into a vintage store called Antique Boutique in New York, which I thought our jeans suited very well. The guy said no, but I told him, "Don't say no! I believe in this thing! Give me one metre of space, and if you don't sell them all, I'll buy the rest back."'

Needless to say, he didn't end up empty-handed. 'The reason this company has succeeded is because we're always trying to be different. We stand out from the crowd. For instance, in 1995 we started doing accessories. We produced a really strange pair of sunglasses [the cult 'Sister Yes' model] when there was absolutely no innovation in that market. Then we turned to wrist-watches, and gave them the Diesel treatment too. We've changed many aspects of fashion, although few people would give us credit for it.'

It's impossible to talk about Diesel's idiosyncratic style without turning to Wilbert Das, the brand's creative director and head of design.

The Dutchman joined the firm in 1988, straight out of art school, having hassled Rosso for a job. 'I'd seen his clothes in small boutiques in Holland, and I could tell right away that what he was doing fit in with my ideas. Everyone had big catwalk dreams, but I wanted to design clothes that I would see on the streets. That's where the really innovative stuff in fashion was happening – and it still is.'

Das joined the company as assistant designer on the men's line, gradually working his way up the ranks to the top slot. These days he's as essential to the Diesel image as Rosso himself, enjoying an almost symbiotic relationship with the founder of the brand. So how does he define the Diesel identity?

'We've always been fascinated by things that are kitsch, colourful, decorative. Sometimes we refer to it as "retro-futuristic", but that doesn't quite capture it. We like to clash styles, piling references on top of one another. We go out of our way to challenge definitions of good taste. We're not interested in fashion – we prefer to create things that are entirely our own. Diesel is anti-fashion fashion.'

Rather than attending catwalk shows, disembowelling glossy magazines or hooking themselves up to the internet, Diesel's designers travel to urban hotspots around the world. They return with posters, postcards, CDs, club flyers – and, of course, second-hand clothes. Diesel's design studios are cluttered with racks of unlikely vintage items in lurid colours, migraine-inducing patterns and crackly fabrics; all of which might resurface in a mutated form as part of a Diesel collection.

'We have a lot of freedom because we design our clothes on an item-by-item basis, rather than by co-ordinated "looks". We've always considered our consumers to be intelligent, not brand junkies who go to a single store for an entire outfit. We expect them to mix us with other brands, with vintage clothes, with anything they like. These are people who expect a lot of choice. For that same reason, we offer them a huge range of jeans: something like 45 styles and 67 different washes in each collection. Multiply that by lengths and waist sizes and you can see that it gets quite insane.'

Insanity, or at least eccentricity, doesn't seem to be a disadvantage at Diesel. The company traffics in irony, a rare commodity in the fashion world. This is evident in its widely acclaimed advertising, which has played a crucial role in establishing the brand's notoriety. Although Diesel employs an advertising agency, which is unusual for a fashion brand (see Chapter 7: The image-makers), Das oversees the creation of all marketing materials: 'This is vital, because we look upon communications as one of our products. The same standards that we apply to our clothes, we apply to our external communications.'

Diesel's decision to embark on an international advertising campaign in 1991 was a turning point in its history. Its first agency was a small Stockholm-based outfit called Paradiset. The relationship lasted until 2001, by which time Paradiset had racked up shelf-loads of advertising-industry awards and Diesel had exploded into a global brand.

'Our distributor in Sweden recommended the agency to us. It was tiny, maybe four or five people,' Das recalls. 'As soon as we met them, we loved what they were doing. In our sector there are not many people who are brave enough to try different things. And in the advertising industry as well, people are not very courageous. But Paradiset really had balls.'

Paradiset came up with the slogan 'Diesel: For Successful Living', which referred to the improbable advertising promises of the past, while utilizing the company's trademark irony. Print ads resembled the centrefolds of ancient porn magazines, Bollywood movie posters, army recruitment campaigns, ads for superannuated domestic appliances – anything but fashion spreads, in fact.

Renzo Rosso says, 'Once again, we broke through by doing something completely different. If you think back to 1991, fashion advertising was all black and white: Donna Karan, Calvin Klein. . . Tasteful, beautifully shot, black and white. And then we came out with these ads that were colourful, brash and surreal – it's not surprising people noticed us.'

The company has switched advertising agencies a few times since then, but the strategy remains the same. Diesel's ads delight in causing offence, combining the garish and the beautiful, the twisted and the sublime. One ad, showing an improbably leggy model perched on a giant cigarette, was emblazoned with the words 'How to smoke 145 a day'. But the skull at the foot of the image indicated that this was an off-the-wall anti-smoking message. Rosso has often used Diesel's advertising to make acerbic observations about Western society. A poster showing a pistol-toting male model, a comment on gun culture in the United States, caused uproar in that country. A more recent campaign portrayed consumers as ageless, wrinkle-free drones. The images were accompanied by instructions offering the keys to eternal life.

Whether Diesel's advertising carries a genuine message, or whether it is merely designed to provoke, entertain and draw attention to the brand, it has certainly been effective. Diesel began as a small Italian jeans maker with 18 staff and a clutch of sewing machines. Now it is present in more than 80 countries, with almost 6,000 points of sale and 255 branded stores. Alongside the main product line, the company embraces Diesel Kids and the younger, sportier 55DSL line. Through the Italian manufacturing company Staff International, which it acquired in 2000, it obtained licensing agreements to make clothes for designer brands Vivienne Westwood, DSquared and Martin Margiela. (Rosso has since become the majority shareholder of NEUF Group, the owner and operating company of Maison Martin Margiela.) It even owns a hotel, the Pelican in Miami's South Beach, which, with its Art Deco façade and eyeball-frazzling interior, perfectly captures the Diesel vibe. In fact, when studied carefully, all these elements remain true to the brand's skewed, avant-garde outlook.

The rise of Diesel proves that building a fashion brand is as much about communication as it is about clothes. It's about creating a playground, a diverting fiction. Renzo Rosso is often quoted as saying, 'Diesel is not my company, it's my life.' But his real genius has been to sell the world the product of his imagination.

3

When haute couture meets high street

'It's not enough to be fashionable – one wishes to appear intelligent as well.'

In the end, the *New York Daily News* summed it up best of all. 'Fashion king Karl Lagerfeld is a mega-hit for the masses from Manhattan to Milan,' the newspaper gulped, the day after the pillage (13 November 2004). 'Throngs of style-seekers stormed H&M stores around the world to scoop up the first moderately priced collection from the world-famous Chanel designer. By the end of the day, the Karl Lagerfeld for H&M line had sold out at the chain's seven Manhattan stores and across the Atlantic in cities from London to Milan, Munich to Stockholm.'

It was the same story in Paris, where Lagerfeld lives and works. The great man may have even cast a bemused eye upon proceedings from the shadows as shoppers ransacked a store in Les Halles. 'I reckon I've got a collector's item now,' 34-year-old Fabrice told *Le Journal du Dimanche* ('*Razzia chez H&M*', 14 November 2004), after snapping up a €150 Lagerfeld suit, clearly unaware that six-Euro pairs of sunglasses from the collection were already being hawked on eBay. Fabrice confessed that, rather than selecting his size and waiting for a changing room, he'd wrenched armfuls of jackets and trousers from their hangers and tried them on in the corner of the store. The newspaper opined that we could expect to see a lot more of these 'new adepts of low-priced luxury'.

The Scandinavian brand has since tried to repeat this coup – with, it seems, ever-diminishing returns. Designers who have followed in Lagerfeld's footsteps include Stella McCartney, Viktor & Rolf and Roberto Cavalli. By now, though, consumers have grown blasé about the idea. When it was announced, the launch of Lagerfeld's 'capsule' collection for H&M was the consummation of a long-time hot and heavy flirtation between haute couture and high street; the two disparate worlds had been moving inexorably towards each other for some time.

STRATEGIC ALLIANCES

There may have been a time when fashion was constructed like a pyramid, with haute couture at the apex, designer ready-to-wear just below, challenger brands in the middle, and a big slab of mass retail at the base. This is no longer the case today – if, indeed, it was ever that simple. Hovering around the structure are streetwear, sportswear and semi-couture, among others. Consumers, too, rather than being content to stay in their allotted sectors, scurry promiscuously from one to the other, picking up a Louis Vuitton bag here and slinging it over a Zara jacket there; wearing a Topshop T-shirt and Gap jeans under a coat from Chanel.

'It's not enough to look fashionable – one wishes to appear intelligent as well,' remarks fashion guru Jean-Jacques Picart. 'There are two different shifts happening at once. First of all, Chanel, Dior, Gucci and the others will continue to develop luxury as a business. At the same time we are seeing a complementary reaction, which is that a consumer may accept paying for the latest Dior bag, very trendy, that she's seen in all the magazines and advertisements; but she'll see no shame in going to Zara and buying a T-shirt for 10 euros, because it's pretty and it's a fair quality for the price. Then she may go to another store, a bit more expensive but not as well known, perhaps run by a young designer, where she'll buy a skirt. And these items, when brought together, reassure her and send a message to others that she's an intelligent consumer, not dazzled by marketing, in charge of her own image.'

In other words, the era of slavish brand worship is over. Just as everyone today is to some extent a marketing expert, we are also our own stylists. The designer Alber Elbaz, of Lanvin, recently commented, 'We've reached a turning point. Nobody wears logos any more. People aren't hesitating to mix Lanvin with Topshop. Everything is becoming more democratic.' ('Mr Nice Guy', *Numéro*, August 2004.)

The thinking behind the partnership between Lagerfeld and H&M was simple: if the mass market was attracted to the rejuvenated luxury sector, even to the extent of saving up for the occasional pricey item, and if upmarket customers were getting their kicks from unearthing fashionable fripperies at inexpensive stores, then why not formalize the relationship? Luxury brands could show they knew how to talk street, the chain stores would benefit from the glitter, and there would be lots of free publicity for everyone.

The trend can be compared to a parallel evolution among sportswear brands. Rappers have long enjoyed mixing solitaires and sneakers, and multi-brand lifestyle stores such as the pioneering Colette in Paris have been selling sports shoes alongside designer dresses for years. So it's not surprising that names previously associated with the rarefied world of the catwalk have started hooking up with sportswear brands.

Perhaps the most successful of these chimeras is Y-3, the partnership between Yohji Yamamoto and Adidas. The collaboration began when Yamamoto contacted Adidas to ask if he could produce a customized version of the brand's classic Stan Smith sports shoe. Talks led to a co-branding exercise that now has its own identity, complete with stand-alone outlets. The collection runs not only to trainers, but also to clothing, accessories and swimwear. Many of the items utilize the three-stripe Adidas logo. As a whole, the collection resembles a futuristic take on vintage sportswear, as if somebody has strapped a bundle of 1970s Adidas gear to a time machine and hurled it into 2020.

Michael Michalsky, global creative director of Adidas, describes it as a 'win-win situation'. ('Teaming up from arena to runway', *International Herald Tribune*, 10 October 2003.) He has good reason to do so. A sportswear brand that forms this kind of partnership gets the kudos of working with a major design talent, while the designer gains an extra layer of gritty credibility. Adidas is clearly pleased with the outcome, because it has since teamed up with a second top-name designer, Stella McCartney, to create a 'functional sport performance range' for women. Other designer/sports collaborations include a Fred Perry shirt by Comme des Garçons and a Reebok dress designed by Diane Von Furstenberg.

Taking a slightly different (and arguably more imaginative) tack, Puma has embarked on a partnership with French designer Philippe Starck. Starck is best known for architecture and interiors, although he is increasingly branching out into other areas, from eyewear to beer bottles. In a press release announcing the alliance, Puma's director of global brand management, Antonio Bertone, explained the thinking behind the collaboration: 'The objective of Puma's co-op projects is for an outside designer to share a different perspective so that we can learn from one another.' He added that the project was all about 'pushing the boundaries of design'. But the venture also adds sheen to the brand's image, pushing it further from the locker room and closer to the loft conversion.

CHIC BATTLES CHEAP

Upmarket brands may have begun stalking mass consumers, but the trend labelled 'massluxe' (or 'masstige', take your pick) is more about chain stores smartening up. Gap, for instance, recruited the likes of Roland Mouret and shoe designer Pierre Hardy to try and inject some pizzazz into its outmoded image after a long period of declining interest from consumers. In a variation on the theme, cut-price UK brand New Look launched a range by witty British designer Giles Deacon, who once worked at Gucci under Tom Ford.

Several elements combined to drive this evolution. The post-9/11 economic fall-out forced luxury shoppers to tighten their belts, while casting around for a viable alternative that would fool as many observers as possible. High-street shoppers, having spent years soaking up articles about Ford, Galliano, Jacobs, Prada and the rest of the fashion firmament, became design-savvy and demanding. And the retailers wanted to distance themselves from the flood of bargain-basement supermarket labels that was lapping at their heels – a tendency that has been accelerated by the end of textile-trade restrictions at the beginning of 2005 (see Chapter 19: Brave new market).

The emergence of supermarket brands and 'value-led' fashion is worth a brief detour. The reference in the sector is Wal-Mart, the world's biggest store group. When Wal-Mart acquired ASDA in 1999, the British supermarket chain was already famous for its cut-price clothing brand George, created by Next founder George Davies in 1990. Although the store didn't offer a dramatic retail environment or imaginative marketing, it sold jeans for £4 – along with other cheap and cheerful garments that, while not exactly fashion-forward, were perfectly wearable. ASDA began crowing that George now sold more clothes than British favourite Marks & Spencer.

ASDA is not alone in this growing niche. Tesco has two brands, Cherokee and Florence & Fred, which are edging ever closer to the type of 'fast fashion' items sold by the likes of H&M. These brands are given space in fashion magazines and sold in separate sections of the store, giving them an increased legitimacy. Away from the supermarkets, 'value' outlets such as Matalan, TK Maxx and Primark are nibbling away at the mid-market retailers. One of the first into the sector, Matalan has been selling discounted high-street brands for 20 years. Customers must become 'members' of the organization before they can shop at its 170 or so outlets across the UK. With a loyal customer base thus assured, Matalan saves money by locating its stores out of town, buying clothing in bulk, and selling it in no-nonsense environments.

But Matalan faces major competition in the form of TK Maxx, which stocks genuine designer brands at rock-bottom prices. It's part of the American group TJX, which was founded in 1976 and now bills itself as the world's largest 'off-price' retailer. The magazine *Management Today* explained its approach as follows: 'Like others in the sector, [TK Maxx] keeps costs low with little in the way of merchandizing or advertising, although, as its fame has spread among the more well-heeled shopper in recent years, it has started advertising in magazines such as *Heat* and the *Sunday Times Style* supplement.' ('The low-cost retail revolution', March 2005.)

In the same article, Geoff Lancaster, head of external affairs for Primark's parent company, Associated British Foods, revealed that his chain had a similar strategy: 'We don't have a glossy headquarters. . . Nor do we spend on advertising; it's word-of-mouth. But we are not cheapskates when it comes to distribution; we've invested heavily in logistics.'

As the writer of the article went on to comment, 'The tills are buzzing. Primark's prices are so low, there's simply no comparison with [Marks & Spencer].'

M&S, which prided itself for years on the fact that it never had to advertise to attract customers, appeared to be locked in a protracted and painful decline until it rejuvenated itself with a celebrity-driven ad campaign featuring swinging Sixties icon Twiggy and a handful of younger models. The understatedly chic ads hit exactly the right note for the brand's conservative consumers, who wanted to play it straight but not dowdy. 'Fashion is fickle, as Marks & Spencer knows better than most. For a few years it could do no right and was seen as dowdy and distinctly un-cool. [Now] it is set to announce a healthy sales performance with profits in the region of £745 million, a sharp rise from £90m last year.' ('Twiggy and trifle help put M&S back in fashion', *The Observer*, 9 April 2006.)

The turnaround proved that not everybody wanted to buy cheap clothing in Spartan surroundings. For fashion-led stores, the rise of bargain-basement brands represents an opportunity as well as a threat. With exciting shopping environments, creative advertising, hawk-eyed buying and cutting-edge design, they can retain customers and justify their prices. 'Masstige' is their not-so-secret weapon. A whole range of previously uninspired retailers – Oasis, Target in the United States (fashionistas have taken to giving it an ironic French inflection, as in 'Tar-jay') – have ramped up their creativity with the aid of young designers.

Topshop is way ahead of the game, in the United Kingdom, at least. Even before H&M and Zara came along, its flagship store on London's Oxford Circus was the haunt of beady-eyed stylists and model agency scouts; which led to winking 'you didn't hear it from us' references in the glossies. And although its design has been a cut above the rest for some time, Topshop now has a massluxe range, positioned at a slightly higher price point as a signal to the discerning.

However, when writing about the democratization of fashion, there's no escaping the twin titans of high-street style.

STOCKHOLM SYNDROME

'What is it with you Swedes?' I ask Jörgen Andersson, the marketing director of H&M. 'First Ikea democratized interior design; now you're doing the same thing with fashion. Are you lot on a mission, or something?'

Andersson – who is, as you might expect, tall, good-looking and fair-haired – smiles at the thought. 'It's part of our heritage. We've been brought up with a Social Democrat government. Since we were young we've always been taught that everyone should have an equal choice. It's not just a business idea, it's a political one. Ikea was born out of the theory that you don't have to be rich to appreciate good design. We have the same standpoint on fashion. You can dress from head to toe in Gucci if you like – that proves you're rich, but it doesn't prove you have taste. It's more imaginative to wear your Gucci with some H&M. That's why *Vogue* readers are among our most loyal clients.'

H&M's base at Regeringsgaten 48, Stockholm, is certainly democratic in appearance. Located in the commercial centre of the city, just up the road from an enormous H&M flagship store, it is blocky and practical. The lifts, to be quite honest, could do with a bit of a makeover. Annacarin Björne, the company's press officer, tells me that this no-frills look is quite deliberate: 'We pride ourselves in being cost-conscious, so we can pass those savings on to our customers. We don't see the point of flashy offices.'

Company founder Erling Persson opened his first store in Västerås, a small town one hour south of Stockholm, in 1947. Persson had been inspired by a trip to the United States, where he had marvelled at a new kind of ready-to-wear boutique offering fashionable garments at affordable prices. He called his concept simply Hennes, or 'hers'. In the early 1960s, the chain expanded into Norway and Denmark, and in 1968 it acquired the Stockholm store Mauritz Widforss, which specialized in hunting apparel and equipment. Crucially, the fusion allowed the newly created Hennes & Mauritz to add a masculine dimension to its collection. The first UK store opened in 1976.

In 1982, when Erling Persson's son Stefan took over as chief executive (he is currently chairman), the company entered a period of international expansion that continues to this day. At the time of my visit, H&M had just added Canada and Slovenia to the map, with Hungary and Ireland due to follow at any moment. The brand has been present in the United States since 2000. In total, it has more than 1,300 stores in 24 countries. It has an annual turnover of more than 68 billion SEK (US$ 10 billion).

H&M says that it owes its success to three factors: inventive design, the best quality at the best price, and efficient logistics.

The team of 100 designers is based in Stockholm – and Björne stresses that, contrary to popular belief, they do not copy styles that have already appeared on the runways of Paris and Milan. 'They travel all the time and pick up any number of influences, from street trends, exhibitions, movies, magazines and trade fairs. We're a bit tired of being accused of copying famous designers. If we did that, we'd be up to our neck in court cases – and that's money we'd rather save.'

The company's basic products have long lead times – from six to eight months – but it aims to have high-fashion items in stores two to three weeks after the pattern has left the designer's PC screen. The company's 21 production offices (10 each in Europe and Asia, another in Africa), with a total of more than 700 employees, are responsible for liaising with around 750 factories. About 60 per cent of these are in Asia, the rest in Europe. H&M does not own any factories, but it has a lengthy code of conduct that all its suppliers must sign, as well as a team of quality controllers who can swoop in unannounced to ensure the rules are being followed (see Chapter 21: Behind the seams).

According to Jörgen Andersson, 'Over the past 10 years, [H&M] have become preoccupied with the question of quality. We expect our suppliers to provide products of the highest possible standard at a very fair price, because that's our promise to the consumer.'

In terms of logistics, no fewer than 3,200 people are devoted to the task. The completed garments pass through a transit warehouse in Hamburg before being dispatched to distribution centres in individual markets. Only transportation is contracted out; otherwise, H&M controls every step of the process, acting as importer, wholesaler and retailer. Computerized stock management ensures that new items arrive in stores every day.

This logistics approach is at variance with Zara's centralized distribution model (see page 51), and there are other points of difference between the Swedish giant and its Spanish rival. One of them is marketing strategy. Unlike Zara, H&M has never shied away from advertising. Its simple but effective posters – showing models in casual poses against plain white backgrounds – have become a familiar part of the urban landscape. And, until recently, its Christmas lingerie campaign, featuring provocative shots of the hottest models, was a festive tradition attracting frank stares of appreciation, mutters of disapproval and free media coverage in equal measure. (A 1993 series of posters featuring the voluptuous Anna Nicole Smith in retro pin-up mode – right in the middle of the skinny-girl 'heroin chic' period – is regarded as a landmark in the brand's development.)

But all that has changed. In accordance with the new era of 'mass-clusivity', H&M is going upmarket. Jörgen Andersson says, 'What we have done very well throughout the 50 years of our existence is to keep our focus on the customer. We have a lean organization and a constant eye on the market, so, as soon as tastes change, we change with them. We don't dictate style. Our style is whatever our customers demand.'

What the customers want now, according to Andersson, is glamour: 'Fashion always mirrors society. Many people today can afford a lifestyle that was previously only available to the rich. With low-cost airlines, they can travel to places their parents only dreamed about. You want to be famous? What's fame, today? You only have to go on a reality TV show to become famous. Celebrity seems just around the corner, so why not live it out while you're waiting?'

Enter Karl Lagerfeld. A decade ago, it would have been hard to imagine H&M's young customers evincing much interest in either Chanel or its courtly, white-haired designer. The launch of Lagerfeld's collection for H&M was promoted worldwide with giant posters and a two-minute TV commercial, all of which replaced the traditional Christmas lingerie campaign. Andersson says, 'We had been running the underwear campaign for 10 or 12 years, and we felt that it had lost its relevance. We said to ourselves, "Hold on, we're supposed to be a contemporary company, a fashion company, we need to do something different." The underwear posters were very much focused on "this year's most famous model". But consumers don't care about that any more. They have become interested in design. They want to know what the new collection looks like.'

H&M linked up with Lagerfeld through the Paris-based freelance art director Donald Schneider. Andersson recalls, 'Donald created our new customer magazine and worked with us on our advertising. Through his work for *Vogue* he got to know Karl, and we had a conversation about whether Karl might be interested in doing something with us. A short time later, Donald called to say that Karl would like to meet us. So we flew to Paris and after sitting and chatting for a while, Karl said, "Let's do it – when can we get started?"'

Andersson says Lagerfeld was attracted to the 'youthful and creative' elements of the H&M brand. Lagerfeld himself confirmed as much in a flurry of interviews. He told French news magazine *L'Express*, 'One day I was in the elevator at Chanel with one of the girls who worked there. She looked very pretty in her tweed coat, and I complimented her on it. She told me, "It comes from H&M – I don't have the money to buy one here!" Obviously, I hadn't seen the buttons or the lining up close, but it had a lot of style; modern and well-cut.' ('*Karl Lagerfeld, couturier chez H&M*', 20 September 2004.)

In the same article, Lagerfeld mentions that when H&M sent him a suit for publicity photographs, 'I didn't have to make a single alteration.' He adds, 'Naturally, the fabric and the finish make a difference, but it's honest work – certainly more so than the second lines of some designers, [which are] criminal in their condescension and dullness.'

It doesn't take a marketing genius to grasp the value of quotes like that to H&M. Partnerships with leading designers have now become an important component of the retailer's strategy. Not with Lagerfeld, though, who complained to German magazine *Stern* shortly after the line's launch that not enough of the clothes had been made available, adding for good measure the suggestion that H&M's larger sizes did not flatter his designs. The statement did no harm to either party: the Karl Lagerfeld for H&M line remained a rare one-off, collectable for ever more, and Lagerfeld retained his dignity; H&M was the overall winner, in terms of publicity and prestige.

But Andersson observes that a shift in perception is not enough – the upward sweep must be visible at every intersection with the customer.

'As well as the qualitative aspects of the garments and the production process, we have been working very much with the appearance of stores. We've begun to radically rebuild and redecorate. We know that our customers love to shop – they consider it entertainment. And if the store is the main contact with the customers, we have to enhance that experience.' (See Chapter 5: The store is the star.)

Aware that its slick new image could create a distancing effect, H&M is building closer links with consumers in other ways. It has tentatively launched a web-based loyalty scheme, available in Sweden and Denmark at the time of writing. Those who sign up receive the H&M magazine – a cross between a catalogue and a traditional glossy – as well as e-mail bulletins, special offers and discounts.

In Andersson's view, 'If there's a group of loyal consumers who love H&M, we should foster that relationship. Mass communication is not always the answer – it's more efficient to address those who are the most receptive to the message.' Above all, Andersson believes it is crucially important to keep sight of the brand's core values, which he lists as 'fashionable, exciting and accessible'.

'Traditionally, fashion has been aloof and superior. You look at the advertising; it takes itself very seriously. H&M is not like that at all. I want people to come to the store because they're going out that night and they need a new top. And they don't hesitate – they buy something for 10 euros, because, let's face it, why not? For that price, you can give it to the Salvation Army the next day if you want. It hardly costs more than a couple of glasses of wine.'

VIVA ZARA

The reception at Inditex is very big and very white. It is, in fact, a glistening expanse of white tiles, with a horseshoe-shaped reception desk way over there in the distance. The walls are pale too, and entirely picture-free. I'm later told that this minimalism is for the benefit of employees: we're in Galicia, in grey and rainy northern Spain, and these spacious, pristine, light-deluged surroundings keep staff cheerful and motivated during the winter months.

Less than an hour ago, a taxi picked me up outside my hotel in La Coruña, the faintly raffish port that is the nearest large town. It feels a long way from cosmopolitan Barcelona or frenetic Madrid. This is the kind of place where fishing boats pull into the harbour every morning; where lunch is a slice of tortilla and a beer; where couples promenade in the square at dusk, surrounded by kids kicking footballs and observed by creased oldsters nursing coffees. The shopping district is a grid of well-preserved streets dotted with affordable boutiques, many of which belong to Inditex. One of them, in Calle Juan Flórez, is the first-ever Zara store.

It was in a shop window in La Coruña, so the story goes, that Zara founder Amancio Ortega and his fiancée saw a beautiful silk negligée with a barely believable price tag. Ortega, then working at a local shirt-maker, ran up a variation on the high-priced number. His fiancée loved it, and Señor Ortega started his own business producing glamorous but affordable nightwear. He later moved into general fashion, with the affirmed aim of bringing catwalk style to the street. He opened the first branch of Zara in 1975. Originally, the store was to be called Zorba, after the character played by Ortega's favourite actor, Anthony

Quinn, in the film *Zorba the Greek*. He couldn't obtain permission to use the name, so he played with the letters until he arrived at Zara, which sounded feminine and exotic. (The name should be pronounced the Spanish way: 'Thara'.)

The chain grew steadily throughout the 1980s, but did not open its first store outside Spain until 1989, when it hopped across the border to Oporto, Portugal. Paris followed, then New York. The store didn't reach London until 1998, by which time the fashion pack had carried news of the brand back from shopping excursions to Barcelona. On opening day, the place was mobbed. In May 2001, the brand launched on the Madrid Stock Exchange – and Amancio Ortega's billionaire status was assured.

Today, the Inditex group embraces Zara – which provides 70 per cent of its income – and a clutch of other brands: Bershka (young mainstream fashion); Pull And Bear (urban streetwear and accessories); Oysho (lingerie); Massimo Dutti (classic fashion); Kiddy's Class (children's clothing); and Stradivarius (fashion and accessories). Zara Home, which aims to do for interiors what Zara has done for fashion, launched in 2003 as a separate chain. The Inditex group has more than 3,600 stores across 68 countries, 69,000 employees and sales of €8.2 billion a year, with profits of over €1 billion.

The secret to Zara's appeal is that, although shopping there is cheap, it doesn't *feel* cheap. The stores are large, swish and centrally located. The clothes are given room to breathe and usually – unless it's a Saturday afternoon during the sales – so are the customers. And then there are the clothes themselves. Zara is renowned for whisking budget interpretations of catwalk styles into its stores with breathtaking speed. A designer dress photographed on a model during fashion week won't arrive in department stores for months – but something very like it can be spotted hanging in Zara in a couple of weeks. This infuriates the designers, but delights customers who can't stretch to the originals – or no longer see the point of trying.

'I am sorry, but I don't think it will be possible for you to interview any employees,' apologizes Carmen, the press officer who will be my guide at Inditex, after greeting me in the blinding-white reception area. This is not entirely surprising, as the company is famously enigmatic. Before its stock-exchange flotation, few journalists had set foot in the Inditex headquarters. Even today, Señor Ortega never, ever gives interviews. (I glimpse him during my tour, though: a sturdy, tough-looking figure with the sleeves of his white shirt rolled up, as hands-on as he has always been, even though he is one of the richest men in the world. Later, I spot him again – this time in the staff canteen.)

The company prides itself on having spent hardly a penny on conventional advertising throughout its history. No posters, no print and certainly no TV. Carmen tells me, 'The reason for not spending money on publicity is that it doesn't bring any added value to our customers. We would rather concentrate on our offering in terms of design, prices, rapid turn-around of stock and the store experience. That's why we have stores in the smartest locations and devote a lot of attention to façades, interiors and window displays. Our stores are our way of communicating.'

Everything about Zara is streamlined for efficiency. The building I'm standing in is the hub of the brand, and there are very few stages between here and the customer. Design, purchasing, pattern-making, samples and visual merchandizing are all handled in-house. More than 50 per cent of the clothes, particularly high-fashion items, are made in Zara's own factories in Spain, most of them close to its headquarters. An enormous 480,000-square-metre logistics centre is capable of handling 60,000 garments an hour, whizzing orders twice a week from the green suburbs of La Coruña to stores all over the world.

'Each order contains our latest items as well as those requested by the store managers,' Carmen explains. 'The store managers are a vital part of our strategy. They monitor the tastes and demands of their customers, and tailor stock accordingly. That's why different Zara stores in different cities – or even two stores in the same city – rarely stock exactly the same products. The clothes reflect the profile of the customers.'

Zara's product managers keep in touch with stores, seeking feedback from customers and monitoring the popularity or otherwise of items. Tills are computer-linked with headquarters, providing a constant stream of sales data: 'We know within a day or so whether or not a product is successful.'

The tour takes me through each element of the production process. In the design area, I comment on the pile of fashion magazines next to a designer's computer terminal. Carmen says, 'We don't invent trends, we follow them. Styles, colours, fabrics – we don't guess any of these things. We are a business catering to a demand, and we've never made any secret of that. But we need to know what the trends are, so we follow them through magazines, fashion shows, movies and city streets. We use trend-trackers and forecasting companies. We keep our eyes open.'

Zara has been accused of flagrant piracy, which it denies. And there's perhaps a certain amount of snobbery in the implication that a company from an obscure corner of northern Spain has no right to ape catwalk styles. In fact, the region has a strong fashion tradition, and is home to leading Spanish designers such as Adolfo Dominguez, Roberto Verino and Purificacion Garcia. It is true to say, however, that Zara specializes in 'fast fashion', cranking out some 11,000 different models a year.

As I continue my tour, we come across a visual merchandizing specialist laying garments flat on the floor, then standing to see how the colours look together. When she's happy with the arrangement, she transfers the clothes to shelves that mimic those in the stores. ('That's another reason for the white floors,' remarks Carmen.) Nothing about the stores is left to chance. Passing through a doorway, we emerge into a ghostly street of 'pilot stores', where window and interior displays are mocked up before being transmitted to branches around the world. Although it is June, the windows are dressed for winter. (I make a mental note to snap up a dandyish black corduroy jacket.) The posters inside the stores – the closest Zara ever gets to advertising – are the responsibility of the corporate image department.

Breaking for lunch in the Inditex canteen, I can't help remarking on the college refectory atmosphere. In fact, with its modernity, bustle and hordes of scrubbed, trendy young people, the entire building resembles a college campus. Carmen tells me that the average age there is 26. There are romances, relationships, even marriages. Apparently, Señor Ortega approves: 'He likes the idea of a family atmosphere. He tries to make working conditions pleasant because he wants to attract talented people, and to keep them here. After all, it's not an obvious place to live and work, compared to Barcelona or Madrid.'

We hop into a car to tour the peripheral buildings that make up the Inditex estate. Our next stop is a factory floor, where four cutting tables can cut as many as 8,000 garments a day. The highlight, though, is inevitably the logistics centre, whose immense size defies description. It works rather like a mail-sorting office, except that the envelopes and parcels are boxes or hanging plastic sheaths of garments. Each of the system's 1,200 slots corresponds to an individual store somewhere on the map. 'Everything is computerized, and there are very few errors,' says Carmen.

After what seems like half a lifetime of writing about advertising, I'm slightly numbed by Amancio Ortega's achievement: a global fashion brand with barely a photographed pout in sight. But it's not entirely accurate to say that Zara's stores are its only form of communication. There are also those dark blue paper carrier bags, dangling smartly from wrists on buses and trains and in the street, in every city, everywhere.

4

The designer as brand

'I don't follow trends. It's my job to create trends.'

A particularly well-dressed Parisian crowd packs the Fondation Cartier, a giant glass and steel art gallery designed by Jean Nouvel and created 20 years ago by Alain-Dominique Perrin, the former CEO of Cartier. That's a lot of names in a single sentence – but the star of the show is still to come. Addressing journalists in the middle of the room is a familiar figure with peroxide blond hair and a stripy sailor's sweater.

He makes playful, self-deprecating pronouncements and booms with laughter. Even somebody with a limited interest in fashion would immediately recognize Jean-Paul Gaultier.

We're standing in the French designer's first retrospective. But, this being a Gaultier show, something is out of kilter. The delicate aroma in the air gives it away: every dress on show is made out of bread. Actually, it would be more accurate to say that the designer has used basketwork, dough and armfuls of baguettes to make pastiches of dresses for a show called 'Pain Couture'.

Gaultier tells the press that he shied away from the original suggestion of a straightforward retrospective, featuring real dresses on static mannequins, because 'clothes are only interesting when they are on a body in motion'. He came up with the bread idea while recalling his childhood, when he used to go to the *boulangerie* and yearn to work behind the counter. 'There are a lot of similarities between the act of sewing and the act of baking.'

Around us, willowy girls in space-age pinafores *à la* Gaultier proffer phallic baguettes. Downstairs, an oven installed for the duration of the exhibition turns out 'designer' pastries that can be consumed on the premises – a handy metaphor for the ephemeral nature of fashion. As JPG says, 'You know, when you see a girl in a beautiful dress, you just want to eat her!'

The journalists seem to be taking the whole thing a lot more seriously than Jean-Paul himself. This is not entirely surprising, as his creativity goes hand-in-hand with a surreal sense of humour. His appearances on the vulgar-but-ironic television show *Eurotrash* endeared him to millions of British viewers – and, some say, upset the French fashion establishment.

But while 'Pain Couture' is a great deal of fun, it also does no harm to Gaultier's image. It garners plenty of press coverage and fits right in with his brand profile, which is off-the-wall but pure Parisian. And what could be more French than a baguette?

THE NEW IDOLS

Jean-Paul Gaultier was one of the first fashion designers to cross over into the realm of the pop star. Indeed, back in 1989, he actually made a record – *How To Do That* ('Ow To Do Zat'). His boundless energy and inventiveness have always appealed to the media and the public alike. The press has only just managed to stop calling him an *enfant terrible* (it had become a tradition to use the term in every article about him). But Gaultier is also a businessman, having created an array of sub-brands, fragrances and – in his latest *coup de théâtre* – a range of cosmetics for men. His company employs around 175 people and Hermès has a 35 per cent stake in it. In 2003 it announced its first loss for 12 years – blamed on the economic downturn and Gaultier's costly move into haute couture – but it expected to break even in 2005 after a restructure. ('Gaultier fashion house plans restructuring', Agence France Presse, 2 November 2004.)

All successful designers, from an icon like Gaultier to a young tyro emerging from the backstreets of New York, understand that they are running a business. Tom Ford, when he was at Gucci, took pride in it.

'I don't understand people who say that business and creativity aren't compatible,' he says in the (2001) book *Visionaries*, a collection of profiles by *Guardian* fashion writer Susannah Frankel. Ford points out that he started working in New York, where 'if the collection you designed didn't sell, you were fired the next day'. He goes on to explain, 'What some fashion designers do is art and I have an incredible respect for it, but I don't pretend to be anything other than a commercial designer and I am proud of that.'

Others have a more conflicted attitude. Miuccia Prada told the French edition of *Vogue* (not without a hint of irony), 'I want to rule the world . . . I want the name Prada to be immense. But I also want to be free to create.' Later in the piece, she explained her feelings, that '[the clothes] need to be fashionable... but also commercial. It's there that I really suffer. Because there are three fundamental questions I must ask myself: Do I like these clothes? Will they sell? And are they original?. . . If I try to transform [a garment] into something that's perhaps easy to wear, it becomes banal. . . And that's my problem. Do I make clothes that people want or clothes that I think they should wear?' (*'Drôle de Dame'*, September 2004.)

The big difference between Prada and Ford is that, by and large, Miuccia stays in the background and lets her clothes do the talking. On the other hand, during much of the time he worked at Gucci, Ford had a very public image that could not be divorced from his designs. He became fused with the Gucci brand – very successfully so. As an article in *Le Figaro* notes breathlessly, 'The standard-bearer of Gucci. . . [was] Ford himself. . . The three-day beard, the impeccable suits, the white shirt open at the chest, the burning gaze: Tom Ford inspired desire in men as much as he did in women.' (*'Quand les créateurs incarnent les marques'*, 4 August 2004.)

Ford joined Gaultier on the list of designers whose fame transcends the close-knit world of fashion. Also on the roster are Alexander McQueen, Stella McCartney, Paul Smith, Marc Jacobs, Karl Lagerfeld and, of course, John Galliano; that great showman whose runway shows are renowned for their entertainment value. Galliano's clothes are flamboyant – and so is the designer, who resembles a swashbuckling Salvador Dali.

Galliano and Ford are perfect examples of designers whose personal image has helped to transform brands. A dead or dormant brand, whose founder has passed on or ceased to be involved, often needs an identifiable figurehead to incarnate it in the eyes of consumers. The designs must be compelling, of course, but that's only part of the job. Just as Ford became linked with Gucci, Galliano breathed new excitement into Dior when he was installed as its womenswear designer in 1996. Over a decade earlier, Lagerfeld had achieved much the same transformation at Chanel. Until certain chain stores began adopting the same strategy, a glamorous star designer – parachuted in for a huge fee, like a successful soccer player – was the main factor that separated a luxury brand from a high-street one.

These days, the process has become so familiar that it is beginning to sound formulaic. With each new appointment, we read that the incoming designer has foraged in the archives of the brand, uncovering a system of codes and values that they can use to inform their own vision. In this way they don't reproduce the original designs, but reinterpret and remix them in order to arrive at something entirely new – while at the same time giving a respectful nod to the owner of the name they are about to inherit.

British designer Ozwald Boateng arrived in Paris to design Givenchy's menswear collections in 2003: 'I looked in the archives. I took inspiration from the elegance of Hubert de Givenchy. . . That's how I discovered the emblem of the tulip, a flower that could often be seen in a vase on his desk. The polka dots that you can see in the linings of suits and hats or on pocket handkerchiefs recall the motif of his favourite ties.' (*'Ozwald Boateng: Paris–Londres'*, *Le Monde*, 8 October 2004.)

After being named artistic director of Kenzo Woman in September 2003, Antonio Marras 'immersed himself in the archives of the House, discovering points of similarity with his creations, notably the taste for a *métissage* of cultures and styles'. (LVMH.com article, 23 February 2004.)

When Nicolas Ghesquière became head designer at Balenciaga in 1997, he was forbidden access to the archives by their imposing-sounding guardian, Madame Jouve. As he recounts, 'They must have thought I'd make poor use of them. I discovered [Cristobal Balenciaga's collections] by another means, in the museums of the United States and in Irving Penn's images, which at the same time meant that I was not overloaded with references, didn't end up making reproductions.' (*'Nicolas Ghesquière sort de l'ombre'*, *Le Figaro*, 28 September 2004.)

Ghesquière has since become one of the most fêted designers in Paris, praised for having turned Balenciaga back into a mega-brand by combining his own 1980s influences – the high-tech experimentation of Issey Miyake, the glamour of Versace, the daring of Gaultier – with the Spanish designer's architectural sensibilities. It doesn't hurt, either, that Ghesquière's clothes have been enthusiastically adopted by French actress and fashion icon Charlotte Gainsbourg. In 2006, Ghesquière was the only French designer to feature in *Time* magazine's annual list of the world's 100 most influential people.

When a brand decides to make the most of its designer, the media is only too happy to play along with the game. After all, in the fashion press as well as in the newspapers, a people story is a good story. When the talented Antonio Marras took over at Kenzo Woman, articles appeared establishing him as the perfect embodiment of the brand's vagabond deluxe positioning. French *Vogue* (November 2004) waxed lyrical, telling its readers that Marras has 'never imagined living anywhere but Alghero, in Sardinia, where the faces of his childhood, the smile of the sea, the colours of stone, the grace of the olive trees and the games of his sons mean real life'. We heard how the designer started out working in the family fabric store. We learned that his sources of inspiration range from the Far East to South America, embracing Japan along the way. He loves art, museum and movies, particularly Visconti, Pasolini, Kubrick and Truffaut. In short, the press office of LVMH (the group that owns the Kenzo brand) could hardly have done a better job.

However, on 3 March 2004, something happened that may call into question the wisdom of associating a designer too closely with a brand. The story in *The Wall Street Journal Europe* was headlined 'Gucci launches makeover of its designer strategy'. Underneath, in smaller type, the sub-head read 'No-name team to succeed fashion celebrity Tom Ford: can the brand alone sell?'

Can it indeed? At the time of writing Gucci remains successful, but the brand seems to lack a coherent media profile. Yves Saint Laurent, Ford's other responsibility at Gucci Group, has fared rather better. The prestigious French label never took quite as well to Ford's hard, dark and coruscating aesthetic; its elegant new designer Stefano Pilati – who worked quietly behind the scenes during Ford's tenure – has more convincingly captured the refined yet oddly provocative quality of the brand. And the lanky, bearded Pilati, with his bohemian scarves and leopard-skin loafers, knows how to play designer for the media. It all suggests that a brand can be resuscitated if the right personality comes along.

But what might happen if Galliano were to leave Dior? He's such a thorough incarnation of the brand. And what will happen to Paul Smith, the brand, when Paul Smith, the designer, decides to retire? Mulling over this question recently, Smith said, 'I always have a hard time thinking of myself as a brand, even though I occasionally talk about this entity called "Paul Smith", as if it's not my own name. I got into this business because I loved it, then woke up one day and realized I was locked into this system of marketing. I suppose we'll just have to wait and see. The business is structured so that everything is taken care of, except my own personality.'

Valentino faced this challenge in 2007 when its founder – the great Italian couturier Valentino Garavani – retired shortly after the brand's 45th anniversary. The label's new owner, a private equity fund called Permira, had to work out a way of retaining the brand's mystique without the presence of its charismatic figurehead. It was partly aided in this task by the presence of Alessandra Facchinetti, a former Gucci designer, to succeed Valentino. But Facchinetti – while an excellent designer who sustained Gucci following the departure of Tom Ford – hardly has the household name status of her predecessor. It seems that Permira will instead take the brand more mainstream with new branded stores and a closer focus on accessories.

The star status of designers has had an unexpected corollary. When, in July 2004, the US magazine *Elle Girl* asked more than 1,000 adolescent readers what they thought was the coolest profession, 'fashion designer' came out on top – ahead of film star or musician. 'For teenagers, fashion designers are the new rock stars,' said the magazine's editor, Brandon Holley. ('The coolest profession in teen dreams: designer', *International Herald Tribune*, 13 September 2004.) Adolescents are also inspired by genuine pop stars' forays into fashion: Beyoncé and Gwen Stefani both have clothing lines, and Kylie has her own brand of lingerie, Love Kylie (see Chapter 10: Celebrity sells).

But the showmanship of a Galliano and the insouciant elegance of a Ford put a smooth façade on an abrasive industry. As a choice of career, fashion designer makes even freelance journalist seem a responsible and financially secure way of earning a living. Despite Galliano's acclaimed degree collection at Central Saint Martin's College of Art, he struggled to obtain financial backing in London. Arriving in Paris, he was forced to sleep on friends' floors while he created his next collection. It was only when Anna Wintour, the editor of US *Vogue*, helped him to secure backing that his career began to take off. Ford, meanwhile, worked as an assistant to two designers in New York before moving to Gucci in 1990 – where his clothes were barely noticed until a breakthrough collection in 1995.

In the same issue of the *IHT* that mentioned the aspiring teenagers, an article by Suzy Menkes compared two very different designers: up-and-coming Zac Posen, whose backers include Cartier and music mogul Sean 'P. Diddy' Combs; and Miguel Androver, a thoughtful, multicultural designer who bounded on to the stage at the end of his New York show in a T-shirt bearing the question 'Has anyone seen a backer?'

As well as being talented, you have to be lucky, on a mission, and skilled at the art of self-promotion. Only a few have it all.

HOW TO BE A DESIGNER BRAND

A few weeks after my encounter with Jean-Paul Gaultier, I am hurrying down a street in the centre of an unexpectedly hot London, perspiring heavily and late for an exclusive interview with one of the city's favourite designers. The Gaultier event was a crowded affair, where I was one of dozens of journalists. But Matthew Williamson and his business partner Joseph Velosa have agreed to put some time aside specifically for me and my book.

Williamson burst on to the scene, as they say, during London Fashion Week in 1997. His debut collection was modelled by, among others, Kate Moss, Helena Christensen and Jade Jagger. Not bad for a start, and the press couldn't fail to notice. The show made front pages in the UK and Williamson was soon being fêted not only by the UK edition of *Vogue* – which had known about him for some time, as we'll see later – but by glossies all over the world.

These days Williamson shows in New York. His clothes are stocked in more than 100 stores worldwide, and he has his own shop in London's Mayfair, with another to come in Manhattan. A celebrity magnet, his designs have been worn by Madonna, Sarah Jessica Parker, Gwyneth Paltrow, Kirsten Dunst and Nicole Kidman. He is, perhaps, Britain's most unashamedly commercial designer. In October 2005 he added an additional, iridescent feather to his cap by being appointed as the designer at Emilio Pucci. And to top it all, at the end of 2007 the Design Museum in London staged a special exhibition celebrating his 20th year in fashion.

At the time of our meeting, Williamson's business is located in a beautiful townhouse in a street off Tottenham Court Road. It is colourful and cluttered and very neo-Bloomsbury; and the first thing I do on entering is almost trip over a small dog. 'You've met Coco, then?' says the receptionist, when the shiny-eyed spaniel follows me into her office. A few moments later, I climb the stairs to what seems like the top of the house, getting glimpses of people working in warren-like spaces; a PC here, a pile of drawings there. The walls are painted in warm, rich shades that recall Morocco or India – locations that have inspired Williamson's designs. Joseph Velosa – a dark-haired young man with a calm, measured voice – shows me into a bright and spacious office. My eye is drawn to the colourful illustrations tacked to the far wall – Williamson's next collection, which he'll be showing in New York in September. This would have started life as a 'mood board': colourful pages torn from books and magazines, images and objects, scraps of fabric... a magpie collection that defines the tone and feel of the resulting show.

Velosa and Williamson met when the designer was still at Saint Martin's. At the time Velosa was doing a philosophy degree – something that sits oddly with his obvious talent for marketing. Mutual attraction evolved naturally into a partnership, with Velosa taking care of the strategic side while Williamson concentrated on designing and giving the brand a public face. But the delineation between the two is much less strict than it appears, as Williamson is quick to point out. 'It's always presented as though [Joseph] is poring over bank statements while I'm mincing around with a pencil,' jokes the designer, whose faint Manchester accent gives him a sardonic, self-deprecating air. 'In fact I love the business side – and Joseph is very creative.'

The arrangement is not without precedents. Perhaps the most obvious comparison is the partnership between Pierre Bergé and Yves Saint Laurent. Partners in life as well as in business, they founded their company in 1961, with Bergé as managing director – the same position occupied by Velosa. The museum in Paris devoted to Saint Laurent's work is called the Fondation Pierre Bergé/Yves Saint Laurent.

Williamson is slight and energetic, and the rakish beard he has adopted can't conceal a certain boyish quality. This should not be confused with lack of seriousness or ambition, however. He is one of those rare people with a vocation: 'I always knew what I wanted to do. Even at the age of 11 or 12 I knew that I wanted to be involved in art or design, and shortly after that I realized it was fashion I was really interested in. It was instinctive, somehow. I'd been good at art all the way through school, and I was interested in clothes. I was always sketching. By the time I applied for a foundation course at Manchester Polytechnic, the woman there took one look at my portfolio and told me it would be a waste of time: I should apply directly to Central Saint Martin's.'

He did so – and was accepted after his first interview. 'I didn't think I had the slightest chance of getting in, so I must have come over as rather blasé,' he recalls, smiling. 'They misconstrued what was actually nervousness as coolness and confidence.'

He studied fashion design for four years, specializing in textiles and print. But life at the famous college – whose alumni include John Galliano, Alexander McQueen and Stella McCartney – was not to Williamson's liking. In fact, he's one of the few designers to have spoken out against the school: 'It has a phenomenal reputation, but I didn't really fit in there. They're not interested in the business side of fashion. I had the feeling you were left to sink or swim. And either you flourish and become fabulous, or you don't. I was a bit of a black sheep because I was the antithesis of what they try to promote. They're interested in fashion as art. So while I was trying to design clothes that somebody might actually want to wear, my fellow students were doing things like going to mental institutions to seek inspiration. It wasn't the greatest period of my life.'

During his third year at the school, in 1993, Williamson got a placement working for the legendary British designer Zandra Rhodes. 'I loved working in her design studio and watching the pattern cutters bring her designs to life,' he recounts, in one of the notes accompanying the Design Museum exhibition. At the end of the day he would sweep up the unused scraps of material, which he assiduously set aside for himself. A patchwork fabric made from these scraps eventually became a shift dress that appeared in his triumphant graduate collection.

After leaving Saint Martin's, Williamson went to work at Monsoon, the ethnically inspired chain store. He was there for two years as a freelance designer, dealing largely with the accessories division. 'After Saint Martin's it was an incredible release. I was doing my own thing, I was gaining experience. . . Part of my job was to go to India at least twice a year, but usually three or four times. I learned a lot through, firstly, working for a massive company – because even though it's high street, the same principles apply – and, secondly, the travelling. The trips to India were inspirational, but they also provided the first sign of a resource. Before that, I had no idea how to go about sourcing fabric.'

After two years at Monsoon, Williamson associated with two suppliers in India and started his own label. 'At first I just made scarves, because I was still too scared to make clothes. I wanted to get some publicity, so I opened a copy of British *Vogue* and scanned the editorial page. I thought going straight for the editor might be a bit over-ambitious, so I chose a writer called Plum Sykes, because I liked her name.' He laughs at the naivety, which, at the beginning of his career, turned out to be his greatest asset. 'I sent her a letter with a scarf. She was impressed by that and invited me in to the *Vogue* offices. So I took a box full of scarves and swatches and a few trinkets, and suddenly I had about 20 women around me, all *screaming*, telling me that they loved this stuff and that I had to make dresses for them all. That was my first order. I went home to Joseph in a state of shock – and told him I'd have to make some clothes. Joseph became involved organically from that moment on.'

Sykes recalls the meeting for the Design Museum show: 'I can remember a heavenly package of exotic silk scarves landing on my desk... There was a note inside saying something like, "I thought you would love these, can we meet?".' Both Sykes and Williamson postponed the meeting several times – the designer was often in India – and when the day finally came, Skyes was 'not especially excited'. She explains: 'I meet so many disappointing young designers that I was wary. I was at least ten minutes late back from lunch. But as I sauntered back into Vogue House, I noticed a beautifully tanned, blue-eyed boy wearing an emerald green silk scarf twisted around his neck. I'll admit I was mesmerized. Matthew had amazing personal style. He dressed like a glam, rock'n'roll gypsy. Not only did I want everything he was wearing, I wanted everything he pulled out of his bag and scattered all over my desk upstairs.'

Vogue told Williamson that if he could come up with some clothes and sell them to a boutique, they'd run a full-page piece on him.

Velosa recalls, 'He came home saying something like "I've got what I wanted – now what do I do?" So we sat down and worked out how much it was going to cost to produce the garments, what the mark-up needed to be in order to make it worth our while. . . and before we knew it we'd created this cottage industry.'

On *Vogue*'s advice, the pair trotted along to a Knightsbridge store called A La Mode. Although at that point Williamson had made only two dresses, the buyer immediately placed an order for several dozen pieces. Williamson says, 'I was overwhelmed, but Joseph reckoned that if we could get into A La Mode, we could get into [the temple to style on London's South Molton Street] Brown's. So we went around the corner to Brown's and got another order for 50 to 100 pieces. By then we were getting very excited with ourselves, so we started thinking about Barney's in New York and Colette in Paris.'

Fired up with enthusiasm, they got on a plane to India and started the production process. Velosa says the anecdote is illustrative of fashion's insatiable hunger for novelty: 'It shows you how little you really need to do in order to impregnate the market. As it's based on change, fashion is inevitably attracted to anything new. Clearly, Plum [Sykes] saw something in Matthew's work that appealed to her, but I don't think there is any other industry that is so accepting of this kind of approach. As you go on, of course, you realize that, while there's a certain amount of tolerance for new talent, it's actually quite a conservative industry, with almost scientifically defined parameters.'

In this respect, Williamson's overnight success has a perfectly logical explanation. Velosa elucidates: 'It's known as "confetti buying" or "confetti press". Whether you are a buyer at Barney's or the editor of a fashion magazine, it's the same principle. You have to dedicate 80 per cent of your floor space to your mega-brands, or 80 per cent of your editorial to your biggest advertisers. So you're left with 20 per cent of what's called "confetti" – the fun, new and innovative stuff that you sprinkle around to make your store or your magazine look fresh and interesting.'

The problems start when you want to hang around for a while. Velosa says that the British fashion scene, in particular, is extremely fickle; the latest big thing can turn into yesterday's news in the blink of an eye. 'Sooner or later you realize that, like any other industry, fashion is controlled by money. If you have money, you have advertising muscle, so you can control your editorial presence, which then affects how the customer perceives you, which in turn maintains the buyers' interest in your label.'

For the same reason, the label no longer shows during London Fashion Week. Velosa explains that New York was chosen because the Paris and Milan collections are dominated 'by huge advertising brands and heritage brands'. 'With the heavyweights controlling everything, it's almost impossible to get a good slot in the schedule – and if you don't, you're immediately regarded as b-list. New York is less crowded, so you can get a decent slot, yet everyone goes there. London Fashion Week is known as exciting and innovative, but it's also seen as a distraction. Because young designers receive little support in the UK beyond an initial burst of enthusiasm, few of them make it to an international level. So London has come to be seen as interesting, but not serious.'

Matthew Williamson has survived by adopting smart marketing tactics that have not, by and large, required a great deal of outlay. Most importantly, he has used his natural charm and his ability to attract supporters, mainly in the shape of beautiful young women. The first in a long line was Jade Jagger, whose papa is a Rolling Stone but who, as a jewellery designer, is these days better known for gemstones. After modelling a neon-pink Matthew Williamson dress for society mag *Tatler*, she contacted him to find out where she could get her hands on another one. Velosa, who answered the phone, told her very innocently how much it would cost her. He recalls his partner's reaction: 'When I told Matthew, he said, "Are you crazy? She needs to be wearing it! And we should give her some others too." So he arranged to see her and they had what I can only describe as a meeting of minds.'

Williamson admits that he saw the potential of the relationship – but he stresses that all his celebrity links are driven by genuine admiration. 'I am inspired by people who have a certain sense of style and way of life. So I've built this little. . . collective, if you like. But it's always a creative relationship. When I met Jade there was a spark creatively – we loved each other's work and we were drawn to the same things.'

By the time Helena Christensen, who had seen the same dress in *Tatler*, called up, Velosa had got wise to the strategy: 'I asked her whether, in exchange for a few free frocks, she'd agree to model them for us.'

Another key member of the coterie is Bay Garnett, who styles Williamson's shows. Actress Sienna Miller is also a fan. Williamson adds, 'Socializing with these girls and delving into what they're thinking has been crucial, because obviously as a guy doing womenswear you need to get some insight and feedback. But it doesn't have to be famous women – it can just as easily be my mum or my sister.'

Away from his limelight-grabbing celebrity links, Williamson has embarked on a number of business collaborations designed to raise sponsorship cash and generate PR coverage. These have included a limited-edition bottle design for Coca-Cola, a range of rugs for The Rug Company and exclusive stationery for Smythson of Bond Street, as well as a line of Williamson-designed clothes for department store Debenhams.

Williamson and Velosa maintain strict control of the brand's image, and have no desire to go on a Cardin-style licensing spree – but, at the same time, they clearly envisage a future filled with Matthew Williamson sunglasses, shoes, bags and other accessories. The store already sells scented candles, and the launch of a fragrance in 2005 – backed by an international advertising campaign – indicated that the brand was moving to the next level.

Years after that initial meeting at *Vogue*, Williamson still regularly meets up with Plum Sykes, and he works with the same two factories in India. But these days his company employs 25 people and his clothes are sold all over the world. 'On the surface it's still about me, but increasingly I'm a cog in the wheel,' he says, almost apologetically. 'Joseph always says the things we produce are at their best and most pure when they come directly from me, so I realize that I have to remain heavily involved in the design process. But as the business grows, my job becomes more fractured and I have to deal with a number of other things. It's overly romantic to think that I sit around designing 24/7. And I'm not sure I'd want to, because developing the business is important to me. I'm a businessman.'

He's certainly down-to-earth (although he claims to have a more exaggerated 'fashion' persona that he can wheel out when required). Williamson says he's not an intellectual designer 'intent on changing the way we dress'. He designs for women who want to look sexy and of the moment – and that's it. 'I don't think fashion is theatre, so my clothes aren't costume or avant-garde. A critic might say that they don't have any content other than being whimsical, feminine and decorative.

But I don't have an issue with that. I think you have to find out what you're good at and then do it to the best of your ability.'

Nor does he pay much attention to the vagaries of fashion. Like most designers at his level, Williamson is intent on creating his own style: 'I don't follow trends. If anything, I think it's my job to create trends.'

So how big could the Matthew Williamson brand be? Does he want to be a Gucci, or a Prada? He shakes his head. 'I think we're niche. But you can be niche and global at the same time. I'm particularly thinking of Missoni, Chloé, Pucci and Marni. Those four labels are international fashion brands, but they're not necessarily household names. And that's where I think our future lies, when I'm at my most optimistic.'

For now there's the shop, and the perfume. The store in Bruton Street is a strutting peacock of an establishment, embracing all the elements of the Williamson brand: colour, glamour, ethnicity, and even an unexpected Arts and Crafts sensibility. Needless to say, it sent interiors magazines into ecstasies of delight. 'Matthew Williamson's Mayfair jungle,' blazed the cover of *World of Interiors* in July 2004.

According to Velosa, 'The store is the cornerstone of why we're here today – how we can even discuss the future. We weren't an advertising brand; we were a small British designer brand struggling to break through to an international market. We thought about ways that we could stand out, and we realized we had to compete with the likes of Stella McCartney and Alexander McQueen. Even though their stores are backed by the Gucci organization, we knew we had to come in at the same level, at least in terms of perception. It was no good fading into the background with a little boutique in Notting Hill. So we raised the money through the Debenhams venture, and by re-mortgaging our own properties.'

It was a risky venture that appears to have paid off – at the time of our interview, Velosa says takings are six times higher than predicted. The formula will shortly be replicated in New York. 'It's unprecedented in that we've been able to open a retail operation without the backing of a major conglomerate, and yet be seen as almost as powerful as our neighbours. [Stella McCartney's store is two doors down on Bruton Street.] It also provides a fantastic expression of the brand and an invaluable contact with consumers.'

He points out that the fragrance works on a similar, but micro, level. 'You literally have to condense everything you stand for into a box. I think you've got a very successful brand if you can do that.'

Williamson describes creating his fragrance as 'one of the most satisfying projects I've ever worked on'. 'The man who was responsible for the bottle design was a very chic, elegant character from Paris. He sat opposite me and said almost nothing as I struggled to explain my point of view and where I was coming from. I'd cobbled together a few. . . odds and ends, for want of a better expression: a tea-cup; a Venetian mirror; various objects that had inspired me over the years. And he nodded and went away, and I said to Joseph, "That was probably the worst meeting of my life."'

Three months later, the bottle designer reappeared. This time he donned white gloves and placed eight black velvet pouches on the table. 'I opened the first one, and it was, "Oh my God!" The next one was the same. In the end, I loved all of them. The guy had not only listened to every word I'd said, but he'd perfectly interpreted my ideas.'

The fragrance launch was supported by the brand's first print advertising campaign, created by the agency M&C Saatchi. But Williamson is keen to emphasize that his approach has not changed. As he underlines, 'I've overseen every detail, from start to finish. I wouldn't do it otherwise. After all, with each product area you go into, you're still trying to express your personal vision. However big your company ultimately becomes, it's vital you keep control over that.'

5

The store is the star

'Customers today expect shopping to be a
brand experience.'

In London's New Bond Street, on a chilly November afternoon, the Asprey store is dressed for Christmas. Thousands of fairy-lights twinkle enticingly around its windows, and in the central atrium a splendid Christmas tree (could it actually be in British Racing Green?) soars almost to the ceiling. But there is nothing tacky about the festive décor, because, along with the aromas of pine and scented candles, Asprey exudes class.

'Good afternoon, sir, can I help you?' enquires a smartly suited doorman, seconds after I've stepped into the fragrant trap. I reply that I am just browsing, thank you, and he discreetly retires with a faint sketch of a bow, as if he is my brand-new butler.

Asprey has been selling luxury goods and jewellery from these premises since 1847, but in past decades it is unlikely that anybody with an eye for fashion would have paid it a visit. All that changed in May 2004, when Asprey's new owners, investors Laurence Stroll and Silas Chou, re-opened the store after a two-year, £50-million refit. The pair had acquired Asprey & Garrard from Brunei royalty in 2000. Asprey was known for selling prestigious but hardly pulse-quickening items such as silver and leather goods, watches, porcelain, crystal, rare books and gems. But Stroll and Chou promised to turn it into 'the ultimate British luxury lifestyle house' – Louis Vuitton with an English accent. When the refurbished Asprey threw open its doors, it was backed by an advertising campaign featuring the British actress Keira Knightley and styled by New York-based art director Fabien Baron. On display in the store, alongside an extravagant array of baubles and accessories, there was a line of ready-to-wear designed by Hussein Chalayan.

Once Asprey had had a chance to settle in to its spiffy new image, it became clear that the space itself was the star of the show. Before the revamp, the store was a stuffy warren formed by five 18th-century townhouses clustered around a concealed courtyard. Architect Norman Foster – whose previous, rather larger, refurbishment projects include the Reichstag and the British Museum – uncovered the courtyard, sheltered it with glass, and added a grand sweeping staircase reminiscent of a luxury liner. Interior designer David Mlinari – who refurbished Spencer House, the former home of Diana, Princess of Wales, in 1990 – retained and recovered historic elements such as decorative pillars and an 18th-century fireplace, without undermining Foster's modernity.

The 6,000-square-metre retail space feels even bigger, thanks to a mirrored wall alongside the staircase. There is an air of understated elegance that invites shoppers to linger, to wallow in the luxury. The carpets are plush underfoot; cream leather sofas beckon here and there. Various touches indicate that this is a branding concept as well as a retail one: the subtle references to the 1920s, the last period when Asprey was remotely fashionable; and, more obviously, the use of a signature hue. This colour, a purple so deep that it is almost aubergine, is seen on the banner outside the store, in the suits sported by Asprey's doormen, and in a branded fragrance called Purple Water.

'The store is absolutely the key to the brand,' confirms Gianluca Brozzetti, the CEO of Asprey & Garrard Group, and former president of Louis Vuitton in Paris. 'Customers today expect shopping to be a brand experience. As they move from store to store, they move from atmosphere to atmosphere. And Asprey has an atmosphere that is absolutely unique. Where else in London can you have a bespoke item created for you by a team of craftsmen based under the roof of the same building? It is the perfect combination of ancient and modern. Many brands today try to create a patina of history. But such a patina is not made – it is acquired.'

Asprey has since been sold once again, to a group of investors, suggesting that the revamp has not been as successful as originally hoped. But at the time of writing, its glorious flagship remains: perhaps even more seductive now it has a touch of hubris. Surveyed from the staircase, the store has a nostalgic, other-worldly atmosphere. Perhaps, long ago, all department stores were like this.

RETAIL CATHEDRALS

Buying clothes has never been a simple pleasure. In recent times we've grown familiar with the concept of the 'brand experience' – but more than a century ago retailers understood that they had to make shopping an adventure. In his book *Au Bonheur des Dames* (*The Ladies' Paradise*) Emile Zola presents a lightly fictionalized version of the Bon Marché department store in Paris, which he describes as 'devoted to consumerism'. The store's roguish manager, Octave Mouret, unhesitatingly equates shopping with lust. The sight of women scrabbling to get a look at the latest silks leaves him breathless: '[They] paled with desire and leaned over as if to see themselves, secretly fearing they would be captivated by such overwhelming luxury and unable to resist the urge to throw themselves in.' In another scene, he catches one of his salesmen laying out swatches of silk in harmonious gradations of colour, blue next to grey. Mouret pounces on the man, exhorting him to 'blind them!' with red, green and yellow. Zola portrays his hero as the best *étalagiste* – display artist – in the whole of Paris. The year is 1888.

Many of the earliest department stores are still open for business today. The Bon Marché, which opened in 1853, is generally accepted to have been the first. Its owner, Aristide Boucicaut – the model for Zola's central character – was a retail pioneer and marketing visionary. At the beginning of the 19th century, French shopkeepers were still mired in a positively medieval system. Historically, access to trades and professions had been regulated by a system of unions. Traders were required to specialize in a single product or service and could not, legally, branch out into other markets. Firms were passed from father to son, and business was done with regular customers on a one-to-one basis, often by appointment. Clients rarely ventured beyond their local vendors. Prices were not displayed, and bargaining was expected. This meant there was little need for advertising, window displays, or any other form of visual merchandizing.

The system was scrapped in 1790, but for more than 30 years traders stuck tenaciously to the traditional structure. It was only in the 1820s that a new type of boutique, called a *magasin des nouveautés*, began to appear. Grouping textiles, parasols and other items under one roof, these small shops developed revolutionary techniques like tempting window displays, clearly marked prices and the division of merchandise into aisles. It was in one of these stores that Aristide Boucicaut started his career in 1830. Some 20 years later, he formed a partnership with one Paul Videau to run a more prestigious concern. Located at the corner of Rue de Sèvres and Rue du Bac, it was called Le Bon Marché, or 'The Good Deal'. Thanks to Boucicaut's innovations, notably discounting and the rapid rotation of stock, in a few years its profits rose from 450,000 French francs to more than 7 million. At that point, Boucicaut bought out his partner and embarked on an ambition expansion plan.

Boucicaut's idea was to create not merely a 'shop of novelties', but a shopping emporium. He brought in none other than Gustave Eiffel to help him build his dream. Eiffel was an expert in manipulating iron and glass, which meant he could construct the huge display windows and open shopping spaces that Boucicaut had in mind. The new, improved Bon Marché store opened in 1870. It was a veritable cathedral of commerce, with light pouring through lofty skylights and departments accessed by swirling staircases. The structure covered 52,800 square metres and eventually employed 3,000 people. The techniques that Boucicaut used to ensnare customers were astonishing in their modernity: home delivery, reimbursement, seasonal sales, illustrated catalogues and commission for sales staff were just some of the advances he brought to the retail business.

Of course, Le Bon Marché was not alone. In the cities of Europe and America, economic growth driven by industrialization was creating an eager market of consumers, and giant stores were springing up to serve them. In 1862, AT Stewart opened New York's first department store, straddling an entire city block at Ninth Street and Broadway. Macy's – originally a smallish haberdashery – expanded in the 1900s to become the world's largest department store. In 1851 William Whiteley opened a small shop in the unfashionable Bayswater quarter of London. As his business grew, he acquired the shops around it, becoming one of the city's most successful entrepreneurs. Whiteley was murdered in

1907 by a man who claimed to be his illegitimate son. The department store that bore his name – today a shopping mall – opened in 1912. Six years earlier, an American entrepreneur called Harry Gordon Selfridge had opened his eponymous store in London. Just around the corner, in Regent Street, Liberty was closer in ambience and clientele to today's Asprey; opened by Arthur Lasenby Liberty in 1875, it catered to a craze for fabric and *objets d'art* from the Orient. Like Whiteley, Liberty gradually acquired neighbouring properties, and his emporium soon became London's most fashionable shopping venue.

For decades, the department store remained an appealing 'destination', reflecting Gordon Selfridge's foresighted philosophy that shopping should be a form of entertainment. Unfortunately, though, the stream of innovations that had originally lured customers into the stores began to dry up, and eventually trickled into nothingness. A century after their creation, the giants began to seem more like dinosaurs. Certainly, they would have looked familiar to Boucicaut and Selfridge. While bright, spirited chain stores such as Topshop began taking cues from high fashion, department stores were bogged down with dull own-brands and risk-averse buying.

Selfridges was one of the first to break out of the time bubble. It commenced a five-year overhaul in 1994, pulling in a host of cutting-edge brands and refiguring the store to target young, upmarket shoppers. Now it is described as 'creating lifestyle trends and offering a rather fun and slightly bonkers experience to its consumers'. ('The Cool Guide', *The Independent*, 30 October 2004.) At the time of writing, Harrods – one of the dustiest of the lot – had just hired Susanne Tide-Frater, who previously helped to transform Selfridges, as its creative director, and engaged advertising agency M&C Saatchi to brush the cobwebs from its image. It was pipped at the post by the John Lewis Group, which recently unveiled a £100 million renovation of its flagship Peter Jones store in Sloane Square. On the other side of the Channel, the venerable Galeries Lafayette has opened a far-from-bargain basement space targeting 12-to-25-year-olds. Called Version Originale, it features graffiti-covered walls, live DJ sessions, a nail bar, a vintage section and a café. The young, good-looking sales assistants present a sharp contrast to the stern *femmes d'un certain age* who still preside over the tills upstairs.

One UK name that has been linked with fashion since the 1990s is Harvey Nichols, which as well as its Knightsbridge flagship has stores in

Birmingham, Leeds, Manchester and Edinburgh. Affectionately known as 'Harvey Nicks', championed by the shopping- and Champagne-addicted Edwina and Patsy in the cult sitcom *Absolutely Fabulous*, the store, notes *The Independent*, 'doesn't sell washing machines or have a self-service cafeteria; 80 per cent of its stock consists of the best fashion from the best designers the world has to offer'. It is also one of the few department stores to back up its positioning with a genuinely striking print advertising campaign, which in recent seasons has resembled a collision between a model's tear-sheet and a Hieronymous Bosch painting.

Benjamin Harvey opened his linen shop in a terraced house on the corner of London's Knightsbridge and Sloane Street in 1813. In 1820, the business passed into the hands of his daughter, who went into partnership with a certain Colonel Nichols to sell oriental carpets, silks and luxury goods. The existing Knightsbridge store was opened in the 1880s. Today, the group is owned by Hong Kong-based retail entrepreneur Dickson Poon (www.harveynichols.com).

With its award-winning window displays and tempting array of designer brands, Harvey Nichols is an ideal place to examine the interplay between a department store and its customers.

CREATIVITY DRIVES CONSUMPTION

April Glassborow, senior buyer for international designer collections at Harvey Nichols, drifted into her career by accident. 'I'd left university having done a French degree and took a temporary job at Liberty, working in the jewellery department,' she recalls. 'At one point the buyer fell ill, so I took over her job for a while. Later, when she moved departments, I took over full-time. Subsequently I bought accessories; then I moved to Harvey Nichols to buy jewellery and womenswear.'

Glassborow says buying for Harvey Nichols involves something of a balancing act: 'We're expected to be a step ahead, so we are constantly looking for new labels. We take risks with young designers who may not sell a great deal for three or four seasons, until a buzz generates around them. But at the same time, we want to reflect the demands of our customers, so we stock the more commercial designers too. In general, though, I don't think our type of customer is content to blindly follow the herd.'

As well as monitoring all the usual sources – magazines, the web, mutterings on the fashion grapevine – Glassborow receives intelligence from the store's representatives around the world, who are often its first point of contact with young designers, forwarding photographs and background information. Crucially, she decides where each brand will be located in the store.

'The amount of space you are going to give to each designer clearly dictates the buying, so it's impossible to separate the two. Once again, you have to evaluate the "hot" aspect of a designer compared with the commercial reality: just how well is this label going to sell? And then, of course, the decisions you make about placing the clothes affect sales. You are aware that a certain type of customer goes for a certain type of designer, so the idea is to keep them flowing from one boutique to another, almost unconsciously, because they keep seeing things that catch their eye. I can't tell you how I do that – it becomes instinctive.'

Instinct also drives the work of Janet Wardley, the store's visual merchandizing controller, who handles window displays as well as interior mannequins and display points. 'I'm lucky because, at Harvey Nichols, the display function is separated from the marketing department, which is not the case in many places. It means there is no pressure on me to favour certain brands, or to give the entire window display over to one brand because a deal has been struck. We ensure that the Harvey Nichols brand comes out on top. That situation gives me a lot of freedom.'

To celebrate one London Fashion Week, Wardley filled the windows with 15 archive pieces from previous Alexander McQueen collections – in other words, the windows were displaying items that were not even on sale inside the store. 'Fashion students came and took pictures of it,' she recalls.

In more usual circumstances, she endeavours to evoke an atmosphere that enhances the clothes, rather than being led by them. At the time I interview her, she's just created a dark, autumnal theme with Halloween overtones, featuring giant metal insects. 'For spring I'm picking up on blue, which is going to be big next season. You have to be on-trend, not just in terms of fashion magazines and runaway shows – which of course I study – but also in terms of the general feel of the times. You're reading newspapers and listening to the radio, soaking up influences. One of the interesting things about Harvey Nichols is that it is considered a trendsetter, so we can't really get it "wrong", so to speak.'

Interestingly, Wardley never receives official feedback about whether her displays have driven sales inside the store. 'It's considered one of the last artistic professions, so to be monitored in that way would take away our freedom and the ability to take risks. It's precisely because we don't have to answer to commercial concerns that we can do something entirely different. After all, we're supposed to be the leaders in our field.'

Wardley heads a team of ten, including five prop builders and two graphic designers (who take care of signage). Harvey Nichols has its own workshop and, on the rare occasions it sources materials from outside the company, it tends to use the same trusted suppliers. Mannequins get to travel, as they are rotated around the group's stores. Occasionally they are renovated. Wardley – who rarely looks at the windows of rival stores in case she is 'inspired by someone else without realizing it' – has none the less noticed the return of the mannequin, the humble shop-window dummy, as a display device.

'There was a time when all the chain stores were using posters and bust forms in their windows. I imagine it was because they'd spent so much money on their advertising that they wanted to squeeze maximum value out of it, so they put the posters in the window, too. It was a classic case of what happens when the marketing department drives the display side. Now it seems to be swinging back the other way – you're seeing mannequins again and more creative displays.'

Of all the marketing tricks in the retail book, window displays are the oldest and, still, the most alluring. Every year in the run-up to Christmas, crowds jostle in front of breath-fogged windows in Regent Street, Boulevard Haussmann and Fifth Avenue. 'Brightly lit, they. . . exercise their powers of attraction even at night,' writes Gérard Laizé, in *Repères Mode 2003*. He adds that, historically, French fashion houses were judged by the sophistication of their window displays. In Paris, the house of Hermès on the Rue du Faubourg Saint Honoré has long been famed for its enchanting fairy-tale displays created by Leïla Menchari – who has been with Hermès since 1977 – which combine silk and leather goods with jewellery, flowers, sculptures, and even leaves and seashells. And all this from a company that claims with a straight face that it does not do 'marketing'.

But in a world where luxury is big business, even the most exclusive brands rely on marketing – and their stores are the most spectacular manifestations of their ambition.

LUXURY THEME PARKS AND URBAN BAZAARS

'Maison Hermès understands that the shop window is more than a platform for showcasing the latest bag or belt. The window... communicates what the brand represents,' writes Kanae Hasagawa in the interior design magazine *Frame* (May/June 2004). 'At the big Maison Hermès outlet in Ginza, Tokyo, the retailer has worked with no fewer than ten international artists and designers on a series of rotating displays since the store opened in 2001. Designed by Renzo Piano, Maison Hermès is a serene ten-storey edifice wrapped almost entirely in blank façades of glass block.'

As Hasagawa suggests, the communications potential of a store goes way deeper than the window. In keeping with their new status as the outriders of multinational empires, luxury brands are in competition to see which of them can open the most immense, sense-scrambling spaces. In 2005, to mark its 150th anniversary, Louis Vuitton took the wraps off its biggest store so far: more than 1,500 square metres on Paris's Champs-Elysées, previously hidden behind a colossal monogrammed suitcase while the work was being completed. This followed similarly grandiose projects in Tokyo and New York. The outlets display the entire range of Louis Vuitton products, from handbags to fashion; they are single-brand department stores.

Dior is following a similar route – its store on Rue Royale, Paris, for example, brings together its various lines on four floors In Milan, visitors to the bleached, minimalist Espace Armani in Via Manzoni can stroll through the entire price range, from suits to jeans, while pausing at a café, a bookshop, an exhibition space or Nobu, the latest branch of a restaurant venture between Armani, Hollywood actor Robert de Niro and the chef Nobuyuki Matsuhisa.

'Stores are the face of a brand,' confirms Robert Triefus, executive vice-president of worldwide communications at Armani. 'It is the entire image as we would want it to be seen. Architecture is a very important part of brand communication. When you arrive [at a store] it should conform to your expectations of the brand.'

All these stores are nothing less than brand theme parks. 'The height of the ceiling, the size of the changing rooms, the smile (or its absence) of the sales staff, the design of the columns and the name of the architect all trace the contours of the brand,' notes the French edition of *Elle* magazine. (*'Le temps des cathédrales'*, 6 September 2004.)

But the most powerful expression of architecture-as-branding comes from Prada, whose Epicentre stores perfectly express its intellectual image. The locations arc designed by the hippest architects: Herzog & de Meuron (best known in the UK for the Tate Modern art gallery) in Tokyo; Rem Koolhaas in New York and then Los Angeles. Exteriors provide no trace of the Prada name – smart Prada consumers, undoubtedly up to their ears in newspapers and architecture magazines, are expected to know where they are headed. This concept is taken to the ultimate degree in Los Angeles, where the entire front of the store is open to Rodeo Drive, taking advantage of the clement weather and tempting passers-by to drop in. A subtle wall of air keeps breezes and raindrops at bay when needs be – and at night an aluminium screen rises from the ground to seal off the space. Shop 'windows' are giant reinforced portholes set into the floor, so customers trot over the mannequins. The interior is pure science fiction. Plasma screens blink fragmentary images and clips of the day's news, and glass changing rooms turn opaque at the touch of a floor-switch. Lighting controls enable customers to see their desired garment at various times of the day. Elsewhere, laminated screens change in tone and hue depending on how many bodies are present. At the press launch, Koolhaas told journalists, 'We give people the freedom not to shop… by devising alternative sources of interest.' ('Down with shopping', *The Guardian*, 20 July 2004.)

There can be no doubt, however, that the final goal is to sell stuff. One of Prada's most important experiments is the use of interactive RFID (Radio Frequency Identification) clothing tags. The tags themselves are transparent, revealing a tiny chip inside. Their most basic function is to allow staff to keep electronic track of stock, enabling them to tell customers instantly whether a certain size or colour is available. But they offer more – oh, so much more. When used in conjunction with one of the display screens – and a scanner brandished by a member of staff – the tags can call up catwalk video clips in front of the customer, or provide information about the colour, cut and fabric used to create the garment. In the changing rooms, garments are automatically scanned by an RF detector. An interactive touch screen then allows customers to find out whether the store has alternative sizes or colours. The next step is RFID loyalty cards: when these are scanned, they will reveal an entire record of the customer's purchases, allowing sales assistants to suggest additional items that may be of interest, based on the profile in front of them.

Being 'tagged' by your favourite store is perhaps the most dramatic admission of brand loyalty. There are suggestions, however, that many consumers are veering away from one-brand shopping destinations. If clothing is an expression of identity, then shoppers require a range of brands to choose from, mixing and sampling like DJs until they've transformed their selection into something entirely personal. Such consumers wish to peruse items of the highest quality, however, so a vast department store will not do. Instead, they turn to pre-edited collections of brands, chosen for them by one-off stores such as Colette in Paris, 10 Corso Como in Milan and the more recent Microzine in London. These destinations typically also contain gadgets, furniture, CDs, books and art – the keys to a fashionable lifestyle. 'Such stores are not created, they are curated,' says Genevieve Flaven of trend-tracking agency Style-Vision.

Carla Sozzani, the founder in 1991 of Milan's 10 Corso Como, prefers to think of her operation as a contemporary European take on an oriental bazaar. Sozzani's 4,000-square-metre space fringes a shaded courtyard restaurant, and incorporates a photographic and design gallery, a bookshop, a music outlet, and boutiques selling clothing and accessories.

The ancient concept of the bazaar, or quite simply the market, is exercising the imagination of retailers at the moment. 'I have always loved the energy and anarchy of good markets,' Rei Kawakubo, the designer behind Comme des Garçons, told the *International Herald Tribune* ('Kawakubo's commune: a retail rebellion', 7 September 2004). Kawakubo was speaking at the opening of The Dover Street Market, her eclectic retail concept housed in a six-storey Georgian building in London. Along with clothing created by Kawakubo and fellow designer Junya Watanabe, there were contributions from various 'guests': furniture designed by Hedi Slimane; a white collection from Lanvin's Alber Elbaz; jewellery by Judy Blame; unique pieces from Azzedine Alaïa; the labels Boudicca and Anne Valery Hash; a vintage stand that is an outpost of cult Los Angeles store Decades.

The design of the store resembles a stage set, with boutiques housed in battered wooden huts, screened by silk curtains or standing before theatrical backdrops. There is art inspired by Picasso, and even a recreation of a French bakery. 'Shops are clothes just put in a gorgeous box. But for me, the box itself is as important as the clothes,' Kawakubo has pointed out.

It has to be said that she is more innovative than most when it comes to creating retail experiences. Running in tandem with the Dover Street venture, she has also introduced the concept of Guerrilla Stores. These hit-and-run outlets will open for only 12 months at a time, taking over semi-derelict buildings in the edgiest districts of cities. After all, if fashion is ephemeral, why shouldn't stores be equally transient? Advertised by posters pasted roughly to walls in selected areas, the stores are designed to be discovered by word-of-mouth, as their target market chatters about them in clubs and on the web. The strategy acknowledges that, being naturally suspicious of anything 'corporate', the new generation of consumers prefers to mine its information from underground seams.

Comme des Garçons' first Guerrilla Store opened in the Mitte district of Berlin in early 2004. The designer paid around €2,000 to use the site – a former bookshop with the sign still visible outside – and rent of €400 a month. There was little in the way of redecoration, and the place was run by an architecture student. It was followed by similar stores in Barcelona, Singapore, Warsaw, Helsinki and Ljubljana – all selling exclusive new pieces as well as items from previous seasons and unsold stock. As well as aiding the designer's avant-garde, art-punk image, the stores flatter consumers who take pride in discovering and inventing trends. Fatigued by the infinite buying opportunities around them, they look for the eccentric and the rare.

Whether fashion retail spaces resemble markets, art galleries or palaces, they are being forced to work harder to engage the attention of consumers. This is an era of mix and match, of experiment and personalization, not to mention web shopping. Today's shoppers don't like to stay in a box for long, no matter how gorgeous it is.

6

Anatomy of a trend

'Trends have expanded beyond fashion. What colour is your mobile phone this season?'

When a fashion-conscious friend of mine saw a poster of Uma Thurman decked out in a bright yellow motorcycle jacket and matching trousers for the movie *Kill Bill*, she turned to me and hissed, 'Shit – that means we're going to look like bananas all summer.' Actually, Uma's violent yellow outfit never quite caught on – although her sneakers, made by the Japanese brand Asics, did. Movies, particularly when they become popular culture phenomena, clearly have an impact on fashion trends, along with the music industry (see Chapter 10: Celebrity sells).

Apart from these obvious sources, though, where do trends come from? Why are the stores full of pink one season, green the next, blue the season after that? Why does cowgirl follow flapper; 1940s take the place of 1970s? Is it some kind of conspiracy? Do the fashion companies get together in a top-secret location every autumn and decide what they're going to foist on us the following year? Not quite – but almost.

'I'm not always entirely sure where trends come from,' admits April Glassborow, senior buyer for international designer collections at Harvey Nichols. 'But I tend to think they're started by the fabric mills.'

Fabric suppliers are indeed among the first links in the fashion chain. One of the most influential events of the year is Première Vision, the fabric trade show held in Paris at the end of September. As many as 800 fabric manufacturers from all over the world – Italy, France, Japan, Portugal, Switzerland and the UK are some of the most influential markets – display their wares to design teams and buyers. It's one of the few trade shows where you can spot designers like Christian Lacroix and Dries Van Noten stalking the aisles.

The fabric merchants are armed with formidable marketing skills. They have regular clients, and new wefts and weaves to sell them. Occasionally they'll be asked to come up with a specialized fabric for a designer; but they may let slip details of the product to a rival. Similarly, if an influential designer has picked up on a certain fabric, clients who arrive at the stand later may be tactfully encouraged to follow suit. Technology naturally affects trends, too: the resurgence of tweed was provoked by manufacturing developments that made the fabric lighter, more supple and easier to manipulate. Every year there's a new way of treating denim, to give jeans a look that is subtly different from the year before.

At the other end of the chain, if retailers tacitly agree to support certain colour or fabric trends, it means heightened customer demand, guaranteed sales, and less remaindered stock – which they might have been saddled with if they'd veered off-message. Hence, fuchsia one summer, lavender the next; this season linen and denim, next season velvet and corduroy.

But if the secret meeting suggested above does not actually take place, how do they know to stock similar stuff at exactly the same time?

THE STYLE BUREAU

Sitting in front of me is a man in a sky-blue V-neck sweater. He is casually yet stylishly dressed – but not particularly trendy. And yet he runs one of a handful of companies that, ultimately, have a significant impact on what we wear.

Pierre-François Le Louët is chief executive officer of Nelly Rodi, a 'style bureau' (www.nellyrodi.fr). Based in Paris, the company has offices in Italy and Japan and a network of affiliates worldwide. Its clients come from the fields of fashion, textiles, beauty, retail and interiors. They include, in one category or another, L'Oréal, LVMH, Mango, H&M, Liz Claiborne, Agnès B, Givenchy, and a clutch of brands across Asia. There are other, similar agencies, including Promostyl, Peclers and Carlin International, but Nelly Rodi (Le Louët's mother) was one of the pioneers of trend counselling in Europe. She remains chairman of the company, while he handles the day-to-day running of the business. In the early 1970s she looked after communications for the designer Courrèges, before being appointed in 1973 as manager of an organization called the International Fashion Committee, which had been created by the French government two decades earlier.

Nelly Rodi's son takes up the story: 'In the 1950s, ready-to-wear was an American phenomenon, and it was felt that the French offering was disorganized and behind the times. Following a trade mission to the United States to see how the industry was structured over there, the French government created the committee, which was essentially a state trend co-ordination agency financed by the textiles industry. Why co-ordinate trends? Simply, to reduce incertitude: if you give the same intelligence to those who sell the clothes, those who design them, those who buy the fabrics and those who supply them, there are enormous economic advantages for the fabric manufacturers, because they know what material will be in demand and where to concentrate their efforts. Similarly, if the retailers are all stocking violet that year, it inevitably creates a demand for violet, so they sell out their stock. The idea was to reduce the margin for error in the extremely risky field of fashion.'

This was the organization Nelly Rodi joined in 1973, and where she learned many of her skills before quitting to form her own agency in 1985. In 1991, she purchased the newly privatized International Fashion Committee, ensuring beyond a doubt that she would become the trend counsellor of choice. Today, inevitably, the company has a team of trend-trackers who jet around the world monitoring social phenomena, observing the emergence of youth tribes and taking note of obscure trends, which they might pluck from the streets of Rio or Tokyo to turn into global fashions. As well as supplying such information to its clients, the agency can advise on brand strategies, produce marketing materials, organize events, provide stylists, and even design entire collections (its 30-odd staff come from both design and marketing backgrounds). 'We are the mercenaries of fashion,' Le Louët smiles.

But Nelly Rodi's most celebrated products are its 'trend books'. These hefty tomes, filled with photographs, illustrations and fabric swatches, as well as explanatory texts, resemble luxurious scrapbooks. They round up the agency's predictions of forthcoming trends and act as inspirational tools – or, more accurately, as prompts – for designers looking for the next big idea. Every season, the agency produces a dozen separate trend books covering categories such as ready-to-wear, knitwear, lingerie, colours, prints, fabrics, lifestyle and beauty. It even provides a 'perfume trend box set' containing little bottles of notes, blends and scents. Each book costs around €1,400 and only about 200 are printed in each category. Retailers and the beauty industry are the biggest buyers. Le Louët says, 'The luxury brands don't often buy them, because they see themselves as trendsetters. Nevertheless, I know that photocopies can be found in many designers' studios.'

To illustrate his point, he opens a trend book at a page detailing a 'heritage' theme. It features an atmospheric photograph of a handsome tan Chesterfield sofa on a carpet with a muted paisley pattern. Then he leafs through a recent copy of *Vogue*, and shows me an ad for a well-known Italian designer label. There is the moody photography, the carpet and the Chesterfield sofa – only this time with a lithe model reclining on it. The resemblance is striking. Le Louët grins. 'And, as I say, they are not one of our clients.'

A team of independent experts helps to create the trend books. Each October, the agency rounds up 18 personalities from the fields of fashion, design, sociology and the arts for a brainstorming session. Smaller meetings, aimed at strengthening the resulting theories and synthesizing them into text, last a month and a half. As Le Louët explains, 'There is a regular core of contributors, and an outer circle that changes from year to year. We are careful to choose people who can look beyond the media of today and give us an original perspective on the future, without relying too much on their personal opinions.'

The theory is that these people are constantly creating and absorbing fashion shows, art events, exhibitions, literature and social phenomena, and can divine which of these will have an impact on consumers' appearance and lifestyles in the near future. It's like watching stones being thrown into a pond, and analysing how far the ripples will spread. As a fictitious example, let's say we know that a major exhibition about Art Nouveau will be staged at the Metropolitan Museum of Art in New York next summer. In all probability, as designers often attend such shows, we will see fashions inspired by the style of the early 1900s emerging on the catwalk a season or so later. Visualizations of the resulting fabrics and designs will appear in the trend book. Another trend could just as easily be sparked by street kids in Mexico City personalizing their T-shirts by hacking complex patterns into them.

Once all these theories and insights have been gathered, a team of photographers and illustrators brings them to life. The resulting books, as plundered by Nelly Rodi's clients, have an impact that may trickle down to consumers a year and a half later. Chain stores such as Zara and H&M, with their quick turnaround, can act on the prompts much earlier than designer brands, which is why their clothes are 'trendier' than those of their more expensive counterparts.

'I'm not saying we're indispensable – some brands are perfectly capable of anticipating or creating trends by themselves,' stresses Le Louët. 'But we're one of the many ingredients that have an impact. It's also important to note that trends, particularly colours, have expanded beyond fashion to take in beauty products, interiors, and even electronics – what colour is your mobile phone this season?'

THE NEW ORACLES

With fashion in constant flux, there is a strong argument for producing a trend book that can be updated not every season, but every day. An online service called the Worth Global Style Network (www.wgsn. com) has dramatically changed the way trends are monitored.

Created in 1998 by the brothers Julian and Marc Worth and later acquired by publisher Emap, WGSN is the Bloomberg of the fashion industry. Based in London, it has more than 150 staff, and outposts in New York, Paris, Hong Kong, Tokyo, Los Angeles, Milan, Barcelona and half a dozen other cities. As well as daily fashion business news, it delivers interviews, analyses, surveys, city reports, coverage of trade shows, and thousands of photographs of stores, runway shows and street life from around the globe. With a click of the mouse, its subscribers can see what fabrics were on show at Première Vision the previous morning, or what teenagers on the streets of Shanghai are wearing today. Not surprisingly, its extensive client list covers everybody who is anybody in fashion and retail, from Abercrombie & Fitch to Zara.

The WGSN headquarters in London resembles the bustling editorial floor of a major newspaper, with dozens of journalists tapping away at keyboards. And I'm assured that there are many others, out snapping the latest trends with digital cameras.

'It's amazing that [the traditional style bureaux] let us into the market without a fight,' observes Roger Tredre, WGSN's editor-in-chief. 'Most of them still don't have an online service to speak of, while we've been around for more than six years.'

But WGSN is no fly-by-night dotcom – it sees the web merely as a means to an end. 'We've never used the term dotcom internally,' Tredre says, 'because it has all the wrong connotations for us. We perceive ourselves as a research and information company that just happens to use the internet as the quickest means of diffusion. With the ever-changing nature of fashion, speed is of the essence.'

He adds that WGSN does not so much predict trends as provide vital intelligence for a multi-billion-pound industry: 'But of course, part of our job is to monitor cutting-edge trends, and to explain how these might be interpreted for the mass market.'

Other trend-trackers act not so much as consultants to the fashion industry, but as observers of cultural shifts that may have an impact on product development. One such agency is Style-Vision, founded in 2001 (www.style-vision.com). Alongside its bi-monthly 'mega-trends' reports, it produces surveys of individual industries (not just fashion, but also food, personal care and technology, among others) and regularly holds round-table conferences on evolving consumer trends. Usually staged at exclusive hotels or villas in the south of France, these events attract leading marketing directors, advertising creatives, designers, architects, branding experts and journalists.

Style-Vision's business development director, Genevieve Flaven, says, 'Our goal is to provide a rational analysis of societal changes, as well as forecasting developments that may have an impact on design. We're also interested in mixing consumer insights and expertise from different industries. We're very practical – there's no crystal ball, and we're not gurus. The main thing we strive to avoid is treating consumers as if they're malleable and somewhat naïve. We realize that we're all consumers – intelligent human beings with highly complex responses to the world around us.'

In fact, says Flaven, the agency is less concerned with predicting trends than in getting inside consumers' heads. 'We're interested in individuals in the context of society. Through our research among consumers and opinion-formers, we imagine future scenarios, how consumers will react to them, and what kind of products and services they might require within those scenarios.'

Ironically, though, the only people really in touch with the latest trends are those who create them – on the streets. Consumers themselves, particularly young ones, are more iconoclastic, inquisitive and inventive than any designer armed with a WGSN password and a stack of trend reports. No sooner has a marketing executive told adolescents that this is the correct way to wear a pair of jeans, than they've torn off the waistband and started wearing them differently. The classic argument runs that, once a trend has crossed over into the mainstream, it is already out of date.

The fashion industry is the ultimate fashion victim.

THE COOL HUNTER

I find the prospect of meeting a cool hunter rather daunting. After all, as somebody who mixes with rappers, graffiti artists and Mexican gang members to get a line on youth trends for a music television channel, Claudine Ben-Zenou has got to be one of the coolest people on the planet. Accordingly, I fix our rendezvous at the trendiest bar I know, and go along dressed in ancient jeans and a black T-shirt advertising the 1984 Winter Olympics in Sarajevo, as purchased on a market stall there a few months earlier.

I needn't have worried: Ben-Zenou is not some thrusting style maven in shades, but a friendly, discreetly well-dressed woman in her mid-20s. However, for somebody so outwardly normal-looking, Claudine has some very specialized areas of interest that have made her invaluable to a wide range of brands. She recently quit a full-time post as MTV's official trend-tracker to set up her own agency, called Vandal, with a colleague.

'I've always been immersed in subcultures and youth trends,' she says, without pretentiousness. 'I've been involved in the hip-hop scene for more than 12 years – I was part of a hip-hop collective called Sin Cru when I lived in London. I was also into skateboarding from about the age of 14 and had a lot of friends involved in that culture. Later I got interested in the urban music scene and the rave scene. But, while I found all this fascinating, I didn't have a clue that I could put it to any practical use.'

She studied marketing and advertising, but at the age of 19, while still at university, she got a job at a small marketing agency in Hoxton. At the time, the area was beginning to emerge after years of neglect as one of London's most vibrant districts, a veritable Petri dish of trends. 'The agency specialized in underground and youth marketing, and as I got more involved I realized that I had inside knowledge and connections that could be very useful,' she recounts. 'We were working on [beer brand] Fosters Ice and doing lots of stuff with street art and graffiti. It really opened my eyes to the possibility of using subcultures for marketing. Collaborations between mainstream brands like Nike and Adidas and underground designers are very common today, but we were among the pioneers.'

Since that first job, Ben-Zenou has acted as a consultant for global brands such as Levi's, Casio G-Shock, Pepsi and even Disney, always providing them with the inside track on street culture. 'The way I position myself is that I'm equally at home in the boardroom and on the street. I'm the connection between the two. I can talk to kids on their own level without coming across as a suit. What they're doing is not some abstract concept to me – it's very real.'

She also describes herself as 'a huge geek', and she has forged many of her underground connections via internet chat-rooms. 'A lot of the people I got close to in the early days have since become quite famous in their fields. I'm able to pick up the phone and talk to a friend who's a graffiti artist or a hip-hop MC. And, as they're my mates, I'm not trying to interpret these quite complex scenes as an outsider. Youth brands that try to connect with these communities have a habit of getting things wrong and basically getting everyone's back up. I feel strongly about trying to avoid that.'

Brands who try to target niche opinion-formers without doing their homework often find themselves exposed to ridicule. 'You can miss a step very easily. The key is to work closely with influential people within the communities, and listen carefully to what they say. Graffiti is a good example. I hear all the time about brands that've plucked some random kid off the street. If you're using somebody who's not a respected artist, the result may not be obvious to you, but it's extremely obvious to people within the scene, which undermines your credibility as a brand. It's very important to develop long-term relationships, rather than just latching on to a scene in the short term and sucking everything you can out of it in a parasitical way.'

I ask Ben-Zenou if she ever feels in danger of being regarded as a sort of double agent – a suit in hip-hop clothing. 'Most of the people I deal with know exactly what I do,' she replies. 'I've always tried to make a positive contribution, encouraging brands to create events that will bring money back into these scenes and elevate artists who might not have been able to make it in other circumstances.'

For a while, she acted as an agent for a group of graffiti artists and breakdancers, liaising with brands on their behalf. 'A common attitude among marketing executives was that they were just dealing with a bunch of kids doing graffiti, so they didn't need to pay them or even particularly acknowledge their contribution. But these people are extremely talented and often do a lot for brands, so I'm keen to get them the recognition they deserve.'

Later she worked for the MTV website, but talked the broadcaster into creating a new role after observing that 'although we were very good at mainstream research, we didn't seem to be monitoring trends'. (And yet the stars of MTV's music videos have always had an impact on trends – brands such as Tommy Hilfiger and Dolce & Gabbana swear by the access the channel provides to a young, logo-oriented public.) In addition to providing regular e-mail newsletters, she wrote a quarterly trend report called 'Switched On', which was sent to MTV's advertisers and their agencies, as well as acting as an internal primer for staff. 'It was a creative tool designed to inspire people and give them a snapshot of what's happening out there. I picked up on micro-trends rather than huge shifts in behaviour.' Following her own rule of working within cultures, she often asked hip-hop artists and DJs to write their own articles. 'I think it's important to get people to talk about their scenes in their own voices.'

The position was based in Chicago, where she is now installed at the helm of her own agency. 'I'm moving away from trend-spotting into more of a consultancy role. Lately it has become in vogue to say you're a trend-spotter. Trend-spotting has become a trend. What clients are asking us for now is not just information about emerging trends, but advice on how to use this knowledge.'

Although she's one of the global elite of cool hunters, Ben-Zenou doesn't feel part of any such group. 'I'm aware of people who do a similar job and I've met a few of them, but I always have the impression that I'm taking a somewhat different approach. They tend to come from a research background, while my training is in marketing. I suppose the main difference is that I'm not approaching it objectively – I'm deeply, passionately involved. I still go to hip-hop events, my boyfriend is from that community. . . What some people don't realize is that you can't just turn up one day and break into these scenes. I get a lot of respect because I've been involved for years. If I didn't do this for a living, I'd be doing it anyway – always reading magazines, going online, chatting to people at parties and trying to find out how they think.'

Hence her recent brush with Mexican gang members. 'I met them at a party and got talking to them. It wasn't a work thing – I just found them interesting. I'm like a cross between a journalist and a sociologist.'

Perhaps because I'm a decade older than Ben-Zenou, it occurs to me to ask if there's an age limit for being a cool hunter. Isn't there a danger that, one day, she'll no longer be able to relate to icons of hip? She says, 'I've occasionally wondered about that myself, but I think attitudes to age are changing. I've got lots of friends who are older than me and who are still very much involved in the scene. There's a graffiti artist called Futura 2000 who's 50 years old and still considered an icon of cool. He's recently done some work with Nike. Then you've got someone like Vivienne Westwood, who's still very influential. As for me – let's face it, I've got 200 pairs of trainers. I can't see myself suddenly giving up everything I love and dressing in beige anoraks.'

7

The image-makers

'There's inevitably something appealing about an imagined better world.'

The relationship between fashion brands and other product categories is rather like the one between celebrities and normal citizens: they are aware of one another's existence, they occasionally share the same space, but they rarely mingle. While other brands hire international advertising agencies such as J. Walter Thompson, Saatchi & Saatchi or BBDO, fashion brands tend to work directly with a narrow pool of freelance talents.

According to art director Thomas Lenthal, who has worked for brands such as Dior and Yves Saint Laurent, 'In fashion, there are probably only about a dozen well-known art directors, great photographers, stylists, make-up people, and so on. You don't need an advertising agency: you just need an address book with a handful of names in it.'

Many upmarket fashion brands don't have a marketing department; or even a person with 'marketing' in their job title. The designer – often known as an 'artistic director' – is responsible for advertising imagery too. For instance, while Louis Vuitton works with the advertising agency BETC Luxe on several aspects of its communications, its fashion imagery is entirely under the control of the brand's designer, Marc Jacobs.

With this in mind, a few years ago Hervé Morel set up an organization in Paris and New York called ADM – Art Direction Management. Morel does not have an agency, but he is an agent, handling a group of art directors and other creatives that includes Thomas Lenthal, Donald Schneider (H&M, Van Cleef & Arpels, *Vogue Hommes International*), Mathieu Trautmann (Oscar de la Renta Perfumes, Issey Miyake Perfumes, *Jalouse* magazine), Steve Hiett (Kenzo Perfumes), and Laurent Fétis (Cacharel Perfumes, Bless), among others. According to Morel, it was ADM that introduced Donald Schneider to H&M, which eventually led to the store's publicity-generating partnership with Karl Lagerfeld.

Morel says, 'Designer brands may employ an agency to buy their advertising space, but they don't work with agencies on the creative side. It's more cost-effective to work directly with an art director, who can then bring together the other elements – the photographer, the model and so forth. Agencies tend to put forward teams that include a copywriter. But international fashion brands, which use the same images worldwide and work purely with visual stimuli, don't need copywriters. Plus, art directors have usually gained experience on fashion magazines, so they are comfortable in that world.'

Lenthal echoes his views: 'The structure of an advertising agency makes it an unwieldy vehicle. The one thing an ad agency fears above all else is losing a client, and in order not to do that it ensures that the creative process is as risk-free as possible. There are a lot of meetings involving eight people sitting around a table with somebody making notes, so everything is agreed with back-up in writing. The agency has a huge team consisting of the creative director, the art director, the copywriter, the account director, the strategic planner. . . they try to mirror the structure of the large corporations they are working for. But a fashion house is a much smaller unit.'

Robert Triefus, executive vice president, worldwide communications, at Giorgio Armani, confirms the approach at many fashion houses: 'We decide the communication themes, the imagery and the over-all strategy at our head office here in Milan. We don't have an ad agency – we have our own graphics studio covering advertising materials as well as point of sale and store windows. We do, however, collaborate with famous photographers and art directors. It boils down to the fact that fashion is a very particular arena, and the creation of an image that is relevant and appropriate to the fashion world, given that it is a very aspirational product, requires the involvement of people who can really get under the skin of the brand. While I don't wish to criticize advertising agencies, historically fashion has not been their domain – much to their disappointment. Agencies don't necessarily have people who understand the nuances of a fashion brand. I'm sure a person from an advertising agency would have thrown your tape recorder at me by now; and certainly it's a long-running argument. They often claim we don't know what we're doing. We disagree.'

Advertising agencies say that the cliquish fraternity fashion brands work with means that their ads are often indistinguishable. And indeed it's doubtful that many fashion images could pass the marketing test that involves taking a bunch of print ads, covering up their brand names, and seeing which of them has a recognizable visual identity. Advertising for designer brands – whether clothing or accessories – is frequently sensual and elegant, but it can also be clichéd, humourless and chokingly pretentious.

In late 2004, Chanel spent a reported €26 million on a television commercial (the press office called it a 'mini movie') and print campaign to re-launch its No. 5 perfume. The TV ad starred Nicole Kidman and was directed by Baz Luhrmann, who was also behind the actress's hit film, *Moulin Rouge*. To some, the ad looked spectacular. But was it entirely a case of sour grapes when Trevor Beattie, the well-known adman, wrote in *The Guardian* that the ad 'sucks so hard it vacuumed my living room carpet'? ('The ads that stole Christmas', 6 December 2004.)

Beattie, at the time the chairman and creative director of London agency TBWA, has had considerable experience in fashion, having helped to create one of the most successful British high-street brands: French Connection UK. The acronym 'FCUK' had been used solely on internal mail until Beattie spotted and unlocked its marketing potential. 'FCUK fashion', said the store's advertising, and young consumers quickly bought into the message. Media outrage only fuelled demand. Lately, however, it seems that over-familiarity with the logo has blunted its shock appeal. Experiencing a sales slump, French Connection is downplaying its appearance on clothes and in advertising, at the same time insisting that it hasn't dumped the brand completely. Nevertheless, FCUK had an impressive run, and is a good example of what an advertising agency can achieve for a fashion brand, as long as there's a sharp creative at the helm.

And it is by no means the only example. The UK-based agency Bartle Bogle Hegarty has created consistently award-winning campaigns for Levi's in a relationship that stretches back to the 1980s. Its ability to constantly refresh the brand in the mind of the fickle young consumer – and in a highly competitive market – is certainly admirable. Diesel is another company that has worked with a series of advertising agencies. However, the brand's creative director, Wilbert Das, has ultimate control over its advertising messages, and admits that he prefers to work with 'small, energetic agencies'. 'We've worked with one large agency, Lowe Howard Spink, and, while it was an interesting process, I found their structure just too large for us,' he says. 'You should really feel that an agency is part of your brand, which is not always possible with a big international network.'

There is also a considerable gulf between a largely British chain store, a hip jeans brand, and a global luxury giant such as Chanel or Yves Saint Laurent. Here, perhaps, a more elitist approach is required.

PORTRAIT OF AN ART DIRECTOR

Thomas Lenthal has been fascinated by fashion since the age of five, when he enjoyed cutting pictures out of glossy magazines. 'Fashion is all about idealizing, and there's inevitably something appealing about an imagined better world,' he points out. In his early 20s he worked as assistant at a French fashion magazine called *Femme* (it no longer exists) with famed Swiss art director Peter Knapp as his mentor. From there, Lenthal moved on to the French edition of *Glamour*, where he formed a creatively rewarding working relationship with the editor Babette Djian.

Lenthal recalls, 'We were doing something very different at the time. The French magazine market has improved immeasurably since the 1990s, but back then publishers were determined to deliver exactly what they thought the female population was expecting. We didn't want to produce a women's magazine, but a fashion magazine. We discovered that 30 per cent of our readership was male – not just gay, but straight too. They liked the girls we used, and there was solid arts and culture coverage.'

Djian and Lenthal went on to found *Numéro*, still one of the most highly regarded French fashion magazines. In the first year of the title's existence, Lenthal was contacted by Dior, which recruited him on a part-time basis to take care of advertising, as well as related communications such as window displays. During that period, Lenthal recommended the photographer Nick Knight, 'because I felt he would be the perfect person to work alongside [Dior designer] John Galliano'.

Lenthal says that establishing a relationship with all the parties involved in a brand campaign is one of the art director's greatest challenges: 'Usually you are working closely with a designer, so it's very important that there is an atmosphere of respect and trust between you. But very often you also find that you're the liaison between the designer and the management. You become a combination of diplomat and translator, because most of the time they speak quite different languages.'

The combination of Galliano, Lenthal and Knight resulted in one of the best-known examples of the style that became known as 'porno chic'. 'Guilty as charged,' says Lenthal. 'We did a controversial campaign featuring two gorgeous models [Gisele Bündchen and Rhea Durham] embracing each other and sweating. It was almost a new start for Dior, because it was bold, extreme and arrogant – everything a great fashion house should be; or at least, needed to be at the time.'

Lenthal had already gained an insight into Galliano's style by looking at the designer's runway shows. 'I knew there was a certain stylish brashness and brutality about his designs. The campaign was overtly erotic, but it was also an exaggerated version of the interaction between French women, who are much more touchy-feely than the British, for instance. Nick's photography was sharp and luscious, which turned the image into something iconic. Dior was, after all, a fashion icon. There are clouds in the background – what you're looking at is Dior's version of heaven. Many of the elements made perfect sense.'

Lenthal's explanation brings to mind a theory I've heard often while investigating fashion marketing, which is that the brand references are extremely subtle. Although ads can look similar, codes saturate the image, and the target audience receives the message almost subliminally.

Dior's glam-trash new look was a hit. Lenthal says, 'To their credit, the management [LVMH] backed the idea wholeheartedly, even though it was outrageous, especially for Dior. Bernard Arnault was incredibly supportive. I think it was the first time John had really felt at home there. They were encouraging him to be himself, so this was his way of saying, "You want young? You want sexy? All right, I'll show you – because I guess you haven't been in a nightclub for a while."'

Later came the collection Galliano called 'Trailer Park Chic'. The related advertising imagery, says Lenthal, consisted essentially of 'tarts covered with grease on a scrap heap'. He cackles delightedly at the recollection: 'Once again, it wasn't exactly something you'd associate with a French fashion house. The consumers loved it.'

Perhaps inevitably, after leaving Dior, Lenthal ended up working with the Gucci Group's star designer, Tom Ford, on Yves Saint Laurent beauty products. 'At first I wasn't sure I could work with Tom, because his aesthetics were so well defined that I didn't know if I would have any room to experiment. The good thing was that he was already in the mood to do something different; and particularly with Yves Saint Laurent he felt that he needed to differentiate it [from his work for Gucci]. This time we stuck quite closely to the roots of the brand, as envisaged by Yves Saint Laurent himself. The interesting thing about my job is that you are reinterpreting codes and values that may have been established many years ago. And you can either decide to push the imagery a long way from the core of the brand, or hover more closely around it. The important thing is to always be aware of the brand's origins.'

Tom Ford left Yves Saint Laurent – and the Gucci Group – in early 2004. In Lenthal's view, 'He did an extremely valuable job in that he put the brand back in the spotlight, when before there was a feeling that nothing had been going on there for a while.' Since then, Lenthal has been working with the label's new artistic director, the Italian Stefano Pilati, who is deeply respectful of the Saint Laurent heritage. Lenthal feels that the brand is 'particularly rich' – starting with the YSL logo, designed by the poster artist Cassandre in 1963, which remains unchanged. He says, 'With Saint Laurent you have so much to explore, particularly the way he makes colours clash instead of trying to get them to blend together. He is famous for his daring colour palette. He also designed for a certain type of woman, so when you're doing the casting you naturally look at the kind of models he used in the 1970s. For me, today, [the model] Karen Elson is the quintessential Saint Laurent girl, with her red hair and very pale skin.' Interestingly, the actress Catherine Deneuve, who has worn Saint Laurent in a number of films, has also expressed a particular view of the typical Saint Laurent woman; she once said that the designer created clothes for 'women who have double lives'.

Lenthal believes that the same team should create a fashion brand's communications in its entirety – for clothing, accessories and beyond – even though, with branded perfumes usually licensed to large beauty companies, this is not always the case (see Chapter 13: Accessorize all areas). At the time of our interview, Lenthal has just begun to work on the fashion element of YSL, as well as the beauty side, and says it is his intention to 'try and link the two': 'I like to think that once you understand a brand, you can imagine every element within its specific world, even down to the objects. Is there a particular Saint Laurent chair, telephone, or lamp? The answer is "yes".'

THE ALTERNATIVE IMAGE-MAKER

One of the most talked-about companies in branding is not an advertising agency, a marketing consultancy, a public relations adviser, or an events organizer. It is all of these things – and none of them. With offices in London and Los Angeles, Exposure is based around the concepts of networking, leveraging influence channels, and brand advocacy. It can handle everything from getting a fashion brand into a music video or on to the back of a celebrity, to linking seemingly unrelated brands for mutually attractive partnerships, and much more besides. It was Exposure that teamed Matthew Williamson with Coca-Cola for the series of limited-edition bottles mentioned in Chapter 4.

Raoul Shah founded Exposure in 1993. He had graduated in textiles management and did a short stint at Agnès B in Paris before joining Pepe Jeans back in the UK, where he became closely embroiled in the company's marketing strategy. He recalls, 'The brand was growing phenomenally at the time. Most of the marketing was done in-house, so I learned how to do everything, from dressing windows to point of sale. It was an incredible experience; by the time I left, I knew how to market a brand in every conceivable way.'

Shah decided to use his knowledge to found his own business. His simple but effective concept was to build brands by introducing them to the right people. 'I realized that, thanks to my time at Pepe, I had this network of people that crossed fashion, music, film, clubs, the drinks industry. . . and I thought that by using my contacts and my friends, and by bringing brands together with them, I could create some extremely interesting marketing opportunities.'

Exposure's joint managing director, Tim Bourne, who came from a sales promotion background, brought an additional commercial element to the business. 'We created a dual pillar structure,' explains Shah, 'with fashion and lifestyle on the one hand, and FMCG [fast-moving consumer goods] – sales promotions, sponsorships and so forth – on the other. But the idea was that they should cross over. We saw even back then that many mainstream brands were beginning to take on the characteristics of fashion and lifestyle brands, in that they wanted to look for alternative ways of reaching an audience.'

Exposure has worked with a wide range of clients, not only in fashion (Burberry, Dr. Martens, Converse, Dockers, Levi's, Nike, Quiksilver and Topshop, to name but a few), but also in beauty, retail, FMCG, catering, movies, automotive. . . you name it. It even manages the European media coverage of the hip-hop star Damon Dash. The organization is now divided into a number of interconnected divisions, including media relations and publicity, partnerships and product placement, sales promotion and events, design and production, consumer insights and brand consulting, and digital marketing. It also has its own gallery and showroom.

A handful of Exposure case studies would take up many thousands of words (take a look instead at www.exposure.net), but the key to its success, it appears, is to shake up brands in a way that creates a surprising, media-friendly cocktail. Hence Dr. Martens boots customized by the likes of Vivienne Westwood and Jean-Paul Gaultier; or a serious museum exhibition about 'trainer culture' for sports-shoe retailer Foot Locker. Exposure asked lingerie brand Agent Provocateur to customize a Triumph motorcycle – the appropriately named Thruxton 900 was given a pink paint job featuring pin-ups in a state of *déshabillé*. Then it got the magazine *Tank* to design a coffee-table book for Oxo.

The beauty of Exposure's operation is that the elements that make up its network are constantly spinning off and re-connecting. The brands, creative talents and celebrities with which the agency has a relationship can be mixed and matched to suit the task in hand. None of this is rocket science – and other agencies have since copied the format – but Exposure seems to generate an inordinate amount of respect among the notoriously prickly fashion and celebrity community.

'The key to it all is that as a company we're very people-oriented,' explains Shah. 'We're honest about what we do, we don't over-promise, we're professional. People who work with us enjoy the experience, so they trust us the next time. We do very little of our own publicity – it's all by word-of-mouth.'

Shah seems vaguely surprised that there are still brands that haven't got the message. 'Fashion advertising is very formulaic, and sometimes I question the validity of that formula. When you consider that you can make the phone ring off the hook in a store just by placing one jacket on the right celebrity for the right party, traditional advertising is not tremendously cost-effective. The really exciting brands are the ones who take risks: I'm thinking here of Helmut Lang placing his ads in *National Geographic* magazine, or on the top of New York taxi cabs. . . We've reached a stage where consumers and the media are so saturated with demands on their time that brands have to work much harder to get noticed at all.'

8

They shoot dresses, don't they?

'The photographer has an enormous influence on the branding process.'

Flashback to June 2003. I'm standing under the portico outside the Victoria & Albert Museum, sheltering from a summer storm that has raced in from nowhere to dash the streets with raindrops the size of boiled sweets. Beside me, tourists mutter exclamations and unfurl umbrellas, or haul vivid cagoules over their clothes. Frankly, I'm grateful for the enforced pause in the day, because it gives me time to think. I've just seen an exhibition of fashion photography so disturbing – so downright weird – that it has shaken up my idea of what the alluring métier of snapping models in dresses is all about.

A couple of days earlier, the photographer's name, Guy Bourdin, had been only vaguely familiar to me. But a friend recommended the show, and I'd found the promotional poster intriguing. It was at the same time compelling and repellent, showing a girl's long white legs splayed over a sofa as if she had collapsed face down. She wore scarlet high-heels. The sofa was orange, and so was the bottom of her very tight, very short dress, which along with the curve of her buttocks was all that remained visible before she was cut off by the frame. The image was strongly ambiguous: could this be a corpse; or was she in an alcohol-induced coma? It certainly didn't look like standard fashion photography.

The other pictures reinforced this idea. They were often erotic, frequently perverse and mostly eerie; reflections in TV screens in cheap hotel rooms; the suggestion of unseen figures lurking outside the frame; latent violence. Bourdin seemed to be equating fashion with lust, and imagining its potentially terrible consequences. Elsewhere there were hints of dark satire: a group of models striding past a shop window display looked barely more human than the mannequins trapped behind the glass. Each picture was lit with the icy clarity of a crime scene; an idea taken to its logical conclusion with a picture of a discarded pair of shoes next to the chalk outline of a dead body. Some of Bourdin's work resembled that of another ground-breaking fashion photographer, Helmut Newton; but to me the images had more in common with Hitchcock and Edward Hopper.

Bourdin worked for French *Vogue* and shot a series of advertisements for Charles Jourdan shoes – a project that allowed him to give full reign to his fetishist imagery. Despite the fact that most of the pictures in the exhibition dated from the 1970s, they had hardly aged. This was not surprising, because I discovered that, although Bourdin died in 1991, his influence continues to saturate fashion advertising today. Contemporary art directors such as Thomas Lenthal and photographers such as Nick Knight acknowledge a huge debt to Bourdin. He is generally regarded as the first fashion photographer to have shifted the focus away from the product and towards the imagery. Before Bourdin, fashion advertising used fairly conventional depictions of female sexuality to sell products. Bourdin subverted the form. Instead of entire bodies, he showed fragmentary images of limbs. Models and actresses were dismembered by his lens, or mutated by make-up into ashen-faced cartoons of femininity. His fashion spreads were narratives, resembling stills from surreal thrillers. Bourdin realized that fashion advertising was not just a picture of a dress or a pair of shoes; it was an imaginary universe. In doing so, he placed the photographer at the forefront of the process that transforms a garment or an accessory into an object of desire.

BRAND TRANSLATORS

'Fashion photography is about translating a brand into a concept,' says Vincent Peters, the German-born, London-based photographer whose list of credits includes British, Italian and French *Vogue*, *Arena*, *Dazed and Confused* and *Numéro*, as well as ads for Dior, Bottega Veneta, Celine, Miu Miu and Yves Saint Laurent. 'Often, when a client comes to you, they have a product and a brand identity, but they aren't certain how to combine the two. Your job is to achieve that transition; to create the image that brings the brand to life. Sometimes the client has a reasonable idea of how you're going to do it – after all, that's why they've hired you – but in my experience they like to be surprised. This means that the photographer has an enormous influence on the branding process.'

Peters began taking pictures on a trip to Thailand in the 1980s, with the results being published in a travel magazine. In 1989 he moved to New York, where he got a job as an assistant photographer. Soon he branched out on his own, moving into fashion photography. After a while, though, he developed an ambition to become an artistic photographer, and relocated to Paris to pursue his goal. Although his work was exhibited throughout Europe and published in leading art photography magazines, he grew disenchanted with the scene and decided to refocus his efforts on fashion photography: 'I remember I had a season when it all suddenly began happening for me. I shot a campaign for Miu Miu, and that made a difference. Things evolved quite quickly after that.'

Fashion photographers have always combined commerce with art. The earliest practitioner with something of the star status accorded today's snappers was one Baron Adolphe de Meyer, nicknamed 'the Debussy of the camera'. (Although he was not from an aristocratic background, he married into nobility.) From 1913 to the early 1930s he brought an other-worldly lustre to his photographs of socialites, actresses and dancers, first for American *Vogue* and then for *Bazar* (which later evolved into *Harper's Bazaar*, picking up an extra 'a' along the way).

In 1923, de Meyer was replaced at *Vogue* by another pioneer, Edward Steichen, whose pictures already looked more crisp and modernist than the soft-focus confections favoured by his predecessor. Steichen may have taken the first colour fashion photograph, but he was far more interested in the art of photography than in fashion. In the early

1900s he'd been a friend of the sculptor Auguste Rodin, and he later co-founded, with Alfred Stieglitz, Photo-Secession, an organization whose sole aim was to elevate photography into an art form. Between 1947 and 1962 Steichen was director of photography at the Museum of Modern Art in New York.

Another founding father of fashion photography, whose background was almost as aristocratic as that of de Meyer, was George Hoyningen-Huene. Born in Russia, he had escaped the revolution with his family and pitched up in London before moving to Paris after the First World War. He started out as a backdrop designer for shoots before moving on to photography with the encouragement of French *Vogue*'s editor, Main Bocher. Hoyningen-Huene, too, was later lured away to *Harper's Bazaar*. His photographs of Josephine Baker, Joan Crawford and the model Lee Miller – eventually an influential photographer in her own right – have a frosty monochrome poetry about them.

In this respect, Hoyningen-Huene's work resembled that of his protégé, Horst P. Horst, who was inspired by Greek statues and Renaissance art. Technology had not yet freed the camera from the studio, so their pictures inevitably look stiff and enclosed, and reliant on props and backdrops for atmosphere. Cecil Beaton, the final member of this precursory quartet, used props to sometimes surreal effect, deploying sculptures of papier-mâché and aluminium backdrops. Born in London in 1904, Beaton had been captivated as a child by postcards of glamorous society women; and this influence is still apparent in his costume designs and art direction for films such as *My Fair Lady*, for which he won an Academy Award in 1964.

By the Second World War, Leica was producing cameras with faster shutter speeds – an advance that urged fashion photography outdoors and encouraged breezy spontaneity. This ushered in the era of Irving Penn, Richard Avedon and Norman Parkinson. There is the gulf of a generation between Horst's stony goddesses and Avedon's early photos of models frolicking on a beach; or Parkinson's exotic, sun-drenched location shots.

Parkinson, known to one and all as 'Parks', formed a stylistic bridge between the pre-war practitioners and the emerging generation of the 1960s, who added sexual liberation to photography's physical freedom from restraint. Working for British *Vogue*, Parks brought an impish spirit to his pictures of strong, provocative women, which did not look at all out of place beside the images being turned out by the rebellious trio of David Bailey, Terence Donovan and Brian Duffy (see Chapter 9: This year's model). With their unambiguous, cool-yet-accessible aesthetic, these photographs look as innocent now as they must have seemed decadent at the time.

In the 1970s, a seismic shift caused tremors that are still being felt today. It was provoked by Bourdin and, of course, Helmut Newton. Vincent Peters cites Newton, who died in early 2004, as one of a handful of icons who sought to change fashion photography in particular, as opposed to photography in general: 'Guy Bourdin's world was not about fashion. What makes Helmut Newton so irreplaceable is that he really was about fashion photography – he was determined to push it as far as it could go, to make it sexy and dangerous rather than cold and bourgeois. He did for dresses what James Bond did for suits. In the 1970s there were no rules, no formulas, so if you had the talent you were free to experiment.'

In the 1980s, fashion photography benefited from an evolution within the fashion media itself. New magazines such as *Blitz*, *The Face* and *i-D* – the latter started by Terry Jones, a former art director at British *Vogue* – had an irreverent, slash-and-paste style that owed far more to punk than to catwalk shows. They proved fertile ground for photographers like Nick Knight, Corinne Day, Juergen Teller and Terry Richardson, whose pictures pushed clothes – and sometimes models themselves – further into the background, relegating them to mere ingredients in entertaining tapestries. Photography took on a hyper-real, snapshot air, with the merciless light of the flashgun illuminating seedy domestic scenes, drug-fuelled nightclubs, or parties that seemed to have dragged on far too long. These pictures were personal and observational, pulling the viewer into the world of the individual who had taken them.

Corinne Day became notorious for creating the so-called 'heroin chic' look, with a series of photographs featuring Kate Moss. The pictures, which appeared in the June 1993 issue of British *Vogue*, showed the model looking wan and undernourished, clad in vest and knickers and posing in a dingy flat. The shoot, which spawned hundreds of pale facsimiles, contributed to the 'grunge' fashion trend.

Richardson's lurid, funny, blatantly sexual pictures – famously shot on an old Instamatic – continue to provoke controversy today. In an interview with online fashion magazine *Hint*, he refers to his playfully erotic advertising work for the fashion brand Sisley. 'We tried to put a picture of a girl with pompoms over her tits on a poster in Soho [New

York]. They said no, because a little of her areola was showing. . . They said it was too sexy and it would be too close to a church and a school. It's all so silly and conservative.' Despite his involvement in fashion, the photographer's attitude to clothes has a timeless ring about it: 'To me, photographs are more about people than clothes. I'm not one of those photographers who says, "Ooh, that dress is just making me crazy."' (www.hintmag.com/shootingstars/terryrichardson)

Photographers can take comfort in the existence of magazines such as *Visionaire*, a format-shifting blend of fashion publication and portable art gallery in which clothes definitely take second place to ideas. It has occasionally provided a setting for the work of photography duo Inez Van Lamsweerde and Vinoodh Matadin, who utilize digital technology to produce the kind of images Bourdin might have come up with, had he used a computer. Disturbing and disorienting, the pictures are filled with digitally contorted limbs, manipulated expressions and artificial landscapes. All of these photographers have lent their talents to advertising, as well as contributing to fashion magazines. And with their peers, they continue to blur the boundaries between art, fashion and marketing.

THE LIMITS OF EXPERIMENTATION

Other, more pragmatic industries might have shied away from the idea of artistry to promote a product. In fashion, however, it has traditionally been seen as a brand value. But Vincent Peters fears that, in the advertising field, photographers now have fewer opportunities to take risks: 'The fashion business, like Hollywood, is increasingly controlled by people who don't come from the creative tradition. It's a stock-market product.' This, he believes, encourages blandness and fuels criticism that all fashion advertising looks alike. 'Nobody wants to throw money away, so of course they're going to look at what's worked before and go down a similar route. Fortunately, there are still enough clients left who want something challenging.'

In terms of trends, he believes that fashion photography has become less narrative and more conceptual: '[Advertising clients] are looking for the big idea. This is a huge challenge for the photographer, because sometimes you're called upon to invent a brand with a single image. At the same time, it's good for us, because it makes us indispensable to the process.'

Art director Thomas Lenthal would agree. During our conversation about his work for Yves Saint Laurent, he said, 'I've always advocated the fact that if you're working for a brand, you've got to build a visual alphabet for it. Within that framework you can tell a great many stories, but I think it makes sense to link them through that visual alphabet – and the easiest way of doing that is to use the same photographer.'

Having said that, a fashion photograph is a collaborative effort, requiring the participation of art directors, stylists, make-up artists and assistants, all bustling around the central figure of the model. As Vincent Peters confirms, 'It takes an incredible amount of time and finesse, almost like making a movie. A lot of money is being spent on this one key image, so you have to get it right. Is the sun shining, is the hair and make-up the way you want it? Every detail counts. When people outside fashion say that all the advertising looks the same, they aren't paying attention to the details. But at the luxury end of the market, where I tend to work, consumers notice details.'

He adds that the life of a fashion photographer is not always an easy one: 'Don't forget, we're all freelances, and in fashion your fortunes can change very quickly. There's always somebody standing behind you. To a certain extent, you're only as good as your last piece of work. It's a delicate balance, because you want to maintain a personal style, while striving to provide something different each time. If you do three shoots in the same way, people think you're getting lazy. So we're under a great deal of pressure.'

For a while, it looked as though photographers might be losing ground to fashion illustrators. Established artists such as François Berthoud, David Downton, Charles Anastase, Jordi Labanda and Yoko Ikeno became increasingly influential, both in publishing and advertising circles. In 2002, Stella McCartney engaged the artist David Remfry to create an advertising campaign, sparking numerous articles about the trend. One of them, in *The Observer*, opined that this approach was 'valued for being warmly personal' and went on to explain that 'the expressionist, abstract aesthetic of illustration is increasingly seen as a fresh, more subtle – and attention-grabbing – alternative to computer graphics and photography'. ('Sketch show', 29 June 2003.) In the same piece, Alice Rawsthorn, director of London's Design

Museum, commented, 'It's part of the general trend towards a richer, more romantic aesthetic. We're yearning for the individuality of hand-drawing at a time when our lives are more automated.'

For now, though, the yearning seems to have passed. Although fashion illustration has rightfully regained the respect it had lost over the previous decades, it is unlikely to replace photography as the medium of choice for fashion branding.

Fashion photographers, in any case, often take their cues from artists. Although Vincent Peters' work is frequently artistic – his prize-winning 2002 ad for Dior's Poison scent, for instance, was a painstaking recreation of a 19th-century Gothic illustration – he sees no contradiction in using his skills for commercial purposes. 'Quite honestly, when I was involved in the art scene, I found it more superficial and pretentious [than fashion]. Again, I don't think people realize how much effort we put in to what we do. The people I work with have a real appreciation of beauty. It's something of a paradox. When you shoot a fashion picture, whether for an ad or a magazine, you're trying to create something beautiful. That depends, of course, on what your concept of beauty is, and we all have different sources we're feeding off. My own are quite classical, because my mother was an art teacher and I take a lot of inspiration from paintings.'

He adds that, in any case, great art has often been commercial: 'Look at Renaissance painters, or look at Mozart: their best work was commissioned by wealthy patrons.'

9

This year's model

*'A fashion picture is never a picture of a dress – it's a
picture of the woman who wears it.'*

'I can be whatever you want me to be,' Gisele Bündchen told the US
edition of *Esquire* magazine in October 2004. 'If you want me to be
the sexy girl, I can do that. If you want me to be the weird girl, I can
do that. And if you want me to be the classically beautiful girl, I can
do that too.'

The word 'supermodel' sounds a bit tired these days, but it's difficult
to find a more appropriate term for Gisele. Somewhere between
goddess and pin-up, these women are prized by designers, brands and
magazines as the perfect denizens of fashion's fantasy land. 'Almost
every other model looks ugly when you stand her next to Gisele,' says
the photographer Vincent Peters. 'Gisele is a star – she's an action
movie. But sometimes, you want a relationship movie.'

Peters confirms that choosing a model is part of the branding process. 'Most models have a precise image that either works for the
brand or it doesn't. Some of them are more couture, others are sexy. . .
And it's important to get that right for the shoot. [Art director] Alexey
Brodovitch said, "A fashion picture is never a picture of a dress – it's
a picture of the woman who wears it." When you're doing a fashion
shoot, you're creating characters.'

Models have existed for as long as there have been fashion brands. Worth used first his wife and then other women to model his designs; Poiret followed the pattern. In early editions of *Vogue*, dresses were worn by wealthy socialites – although they were gradually replaced by 'normal' girls. For many years, models were little more than clotheshorses, as their glacial expressions and disdainful poses suggested. Although some of them became famous within their profession, they were not 'stars' in the sense that many of them are today.

The London of the 1960s changed all that. Young photographers like Terence Donovan and David Bailey began to take pictures of girls in a manner that suggested there might be more interesting things going on when the shooting stopped – and there usually was. In Michael Gross's compelling (1995) book on the subject, *Model: The Ugly Business of Beautiful Women*, Donovan is quoted as saying that, until he and Bailey came along, 'in England all fashion photographers were gay'. Donovan says this was important because, as a straight bloke, he feared he didn't understand how clothes and jewellery worked together: 'And then suddenly you realized. . . all you had to do was take a strong picture of a girl.'

Bailey, meanwhile, shot stunning pictures of a girl he had fallen in love with – Jean Shrimpton, rechristened 'The Shrimp' by the tabloid press. 'She and Bailey became the archetypes of a new breed of photographers and fashion models,' writes Gross. 'By letting the heat of their sexual relationship into their pictures, by letting their models seem touchable. . . they transformed themselves into fashion's first real celebrities outside fashion.'

But Swinging London's most famous model stood at a distance from the frenzy going on around her. Lesley Hornby, a sweet girl from Neasden, was initially represented not by a modelling agency, but by her mentor and boyfriend Justin de Villeneuve. Her colt-like frame, all arms and legs, earned her the nickname 'Twig', which evolved into 'Twiggy'. When she let a hairdresser use her as a model for a new style – a short, elfin cut that emphasized her enormous blue eyes – her future was assured. She climbed quickly from the pages of the *Daily Express* to *Elle* and *Vogue*. Soon, clothing brands and car manufacturers were beating a path to her door with offers of sponsorship deals. Gross writes, 'She wasn't a model like any before her; she was a marketing miracle. . . the first model to achieve genuine international celebrity.'

But Twiggy earned only a fraction of the sums that were reaped by the stars who followed her. Kate Moss, discovered by the Storm agency in 1988 as a Croydon schoolgirl, is often compared to Twiggy. At the beginning of her career she was described as a 'waif'; and although she had been championed by iconic style magazine *The Face*, her rise to global fame was due to a landmark series of ads shot by Patrick Demarchelier for Calvin Klein's CK brand. It was the first time CK's young target consumers had seen a model with whom they could identify, somebody who – although pretty – might conceivably live around the corner.

Long after the waif era has faded into fashion's distant past, Moss has proved her adaptability. Her streetwise looks were instrumental in winning Burberry a new, young audience. The Moss style has proved as suited to the elegance of Chanel as it is to the accessible cosmetics brand Rimmel. A *W* magazine article about the Moss phenomenon suggests that her human imperfections – the scattering of freckles and ever-so-slightly crooked smile that offset her lofty cheekbones and pouting mouth – have enabled young women across the globe to identify with her. The photographer Inez Van Lamsweerde describes her as 'a generation's muse'; while the artist Alex Katz – who painted her portrait for a *W* cover – says, 'She's completely ordinary. That's what makes her so extraordinary.' In the same piece, Tom Sachs explains why he chose to photograph her in the setting of a fast-food restaurant: 'Of course her face is a brand – she's a commodity.' ('All about Kate', *W*, September 2003.)

Models grow used to regarding themselves as commodities, to expressing a set of values that can be utilized by marketers. At the beginning of Gross's book, Cindy Crawford tells him, 'I see myself as a president of a company that owns a product, Cindy Crawford, that everybody wants. So I'm not powerless because I own that product. When you start thinking that your agency owns it and you don't own it, you have a problem.'

PACKAGING BEAUTY

It's not my intention here to explore the seamier side of the modelling business, which is thoroughly described in Gross's book. (Milan, particularly, is portrayed as a morass, in which playboys circle modelling agencies like sharks.) Perhaps the profession's darkest hour was the aftermath of investigative journalist Donal MacIntyre's BBC documentary about agencies in 1999. As part of the series *MacIntyre Undercover*, the reporter used an array of bugging devices to present an industry riddled with sexual predators and drug abuse. There were recriminations and legal action – but by then the programme had confirmed what many members of the public already suspected.

The subsequent poor image of modelling agencies upsets John Horner, managing director of UK agency Models 1. 'I deplore the way the industry is represented by the media,' he says. 'In the UK, we have one of the most professional businesses in the world. [Internationally] the industry is badly let down by a few grubby agencies that sully its reputation. Most of the UK agencies are managed by women, so they're not the ones doing the damage. And men in the business have a responsibility to behave professionally. You have to be protective – I mean, most of the time these are young, vulnerable kids. When we send them to shoots in Italy – which even within the business has a poor reputation – we make sure that they are professionally chaperoned. Often their parents go with them.'

Horner, particularly, understands the value of models to marketers – after all, he worked in advertising for more than 30 years. He started out in 1965, wrapping parcels stuffed with promotional products at an agency called Dorlands. Over the years he went on to work for some of the most famous agencies in the ad industry – including Leo Burnett and J. Walter Thompson – start two businesses, sell both of them at a profit, and play a key role in high-profile mergers. In 1998 he began advising the two head bookers (modelling-speak for agents) at Models 1, Karen Diamond and Kathy Pryer, who had been offered a management buy-out by the agency's founders.

'Gradually they realized that they didn't have the necessary business skills; they weren't sure how to raise the money or write a business plan. But the future [of the agency] looked bright enough, so we did what is unfortunately called a BIMBO – a buy-in management buy-out – because I joined the team by buying into the business. And so, in January 1999, I became a model agent.'

Horner says that, as the managing director of the business, he works behind the scenes. 'On arrival, I did exactly what you'd expect a marketing guy to do, which was to re-establish the brand identity. Obviously we had a great brand name, because the agency had been going for 35 years. It also had a number of brand values, which I kept and strengthened. It's very important that we behave correctly as an agency – that's a key part of our positioning. We pay our models on time, there's no misbehaving or impropriety whatsoever. It's absolutely vital that we are second to none in that regard. It's an interesting challenge because you have to reassure the parents [of teenage models] while making the brand funky enough to appeal to youngsters too.'

Models 1 has an illustrious history. Founded in 1968, it has played an instrumental role in the careers of models such as Twiggy, Jerry Hall, Yasmin Le Bon and current favourite Karen Elson. Today it's the biggest model agency brand in the UK (in competition with Select) and has a database of 7,000 clients, some 2,000 of which are active. International clients count for 25 per cent of the business. The operation is divided into four divisions: women, men, new faces and classic. The 'classic' division handles personalities – notably Patsy Kensit and Faye Dunaway – and established or mature models. 'New faces' is obviously looking for beginners.

While he was working on the brand repositioning – a process that involved, among other things, interviewing key clients and every single member of staff – Horner discovered that the agency was known as 'reputable, but a bit dusty'. 'We had to make the place a little more dynamic. We wanted to become exciting enough so that youngsters would aspire to being part of Models 1. At the time, our new faces division was not doing as well as it should have been. It was one of the reasons we relocated from the wrong end of the King's Road to the heart of London [in offices near Covent Garden].'

Horner points out that, because the fashion industry thrives on novelty, attracting fresh faces is critical to the performance of a modelling agency. With this in mind, Models 1 ran a press relations campaign targeting the youth media, organizing a number of events that brought together journalists, photographers and representatives of the new faces division. The result is that now, when schoolgirls dream about becoming a top model, Models 1 is again among the agencies they consider approaching.

Modelling agencies are also famous for their 'scouts', the talent-spotters who cruise the gathering places of adolescents, as well as constantly keeping their eyes peeled for suitable candidates. Horner admits that this is by no means his field. 'I don't have an eye – but fortunately my job is to run the business rather than to find models. It's very instinctive: a scout "knows" when somebody has potential. We're not after a particular look – it's rare that we set out to find a redhead or a quirky look or whatever. We don't create trends. The photographers do that.'

Whether a walk-in or one of the scouts' finds, the potential model is invited to the agency, always with a parent or guardian. Polaroid photos are taken, after which the agency's experts debate the candidate's potential. If a genuine talent is thought to be present, test photography is done. On the basis of the results, a decision is made.

Models are not expected to contract to the agency for their entire working life, or even for a set period. They sign an agreement that they will not work with any rival UK outfits, but as their career develops they are free to fire their existing agency at any time. Horner says, 'If you think about it, we're taking on youngsters between 16 and 18, mothering them, looking after their careers, so the relationship between model and booker becomes very close. For them to change agencies is quite a wrench.'

In the earliest days of their new career, the young saplings are sent on 'go-sees' – they show their face at magazines and meet photographers with the hope of being hired for a shoot. For those who live outside London, the agency keeps a 'model flat', sleeping six at a time for two- or three-night periods. ('They always wreck the place,' jokes Horner. 'Don't forget – they're teenagers.') The newcomers stay in the new faces division for up to a year before moving on to what is called 'the main board'. There is also a separate 'image' division for what Horner calls 'high-profile, fast-track models' – the kind who end up in *Vogue*. But what outsiders don't realize is that they may be better off working for catalogues.

'A fast-track model can burn out quickly, sometimes inexplicably – she has such a strong image that she goes out of fashion. A bread-and-butter model working for catalogues and mainstream brands can have a solid career for years. And the simple fact is that *Vogue* only pays about £75 a day. Working for the fashion media in general, you'll only earn a maximum of £350 for a shoot. But the media know it's important for the model's career, because then she might get access to a big brand name.'

And that's when the bigger fees start – not only because the model is expected to commit to the brand for a long period of time, 'but also because she is contributing to that brand's essence'. Horner agrees that the right model can transform the fortunes of a brand. He cites the example of Christy Turlington, who became the face of the cosmetics brand Maybelline in the United States (a contract said to be worth £1.8 million a year).

A brand in its own right, Models 1 is among the best known in the fashion industry. 'In the client community, awareness is as high as it could be. But of course we keep in constant contact with our clients, by mail and telephone. My advertising background means I know roughly when clients are going to start thinking about their next campaigns. We make appointments to go and see them. Alternatively, they may ring us to say they are casting for a project, so we send them cards [photographs and statistics] either by mail or online. Each model also has a book of photographs that is constantly updated.'

The agency has about 2,000 models on its books, with a nucleus of 600 who get a steady turnover of work. The decision about which model to use can be made by various parties: the advertising agency, the art director, the photographer or the client, depending on the situation. Often, it's the photographer – and their choices can make or break careers.

Mathilde Plet, in charge of casting models at the French magazine *Numéro*, has cited celebrated photographer Steven Meisel as one of the greatest talent-spotters in the business. 'His mastery of fashion gives him an enormous influence with the agencies,' she said. (*Le Monde* magazine supplement, 20–21 June 2004.) Meisel played a key role in the 'supermodel' phenomenon, shooting Christy Turlington, Naomi Campbell and Linda Evangelista.

John Horner comments, 'Photography is a deceptive process. You can look at a girl and think "she's going to make it", but the photographs tell a different story: exaggerating a jaw, making a nose look too big. The camera is the ultimate judge.'

PERFECTION AND IMPERFECTION

'We don't wake up for less than $10,000 a day,' Linda Evangelista famously told *Vogue* in 1991. The quote was the defining phrase of the supermodel era, when the clothes faded into the background and the women wearing them became stars. Things are different now. Fees have settled down – for most models they were never that high in the first place. Dawn Wolf, of the agency IMG/France, told *Le Monde*, 'I've never read an article about the price of models that was right.'

Linda Evangelista is now on the books of Models 1, although agency boss John Horner agrees that the supermodel craze has faded. 'Versace really put supermodels on the map. He decided he'd pay whatever it took to get the best models, which started the whole inflation process. Eventually, though, they became too expensive. It began to be debatable whether they added enough value to the brand in relation to the price the advertiser was paying.'

But Horner also hints that, in terms of sheer professionalism, those few supermodels might have been worth it. 'We did a campaign with Linda Evangelista for Wallis, and it was as much about us selling her to Wallis as it was about the brand wanting a model of that calibre. They did the shoot in America. Normally you do a test day, with a fitting and so forth. But in this case they just turned up with the clothes, and she's such an amazing model that the second they were on, they looked a million dollars. Erin O'Connor is another one: quite unusual-looking, very tall; but the second you put a garment on that girl, she's instantly into model mode.'

Cindy Crawford calls her model persona 'The Thing'. The writer Michael Gross describes the process as follows: 'She fluffs her hair and strikes a pose, and suddenly The Thing is in the room.' Crawford tells him, 'I'm becoming this other character, and all of a sudden – I don't know why – all of a sudden I'm brave, I'm telling jokes, I become much more theatrical... and then I wash it off.'

Perhaps it takes a bit of pantomime to create a fairy-tale. Horner dislikes the term 'clothes-horse', but admits that models play the role of a blank canvas. 'They are there to interpret and enhance a product. The more flexible their face or body, the more easily they can create a distinctive image for the client.'

How much digital trickery goes into moulding that image is open to debate. Horner says that the very best photographers disdain re-touching, as they can achieve the desired effect through lighting, make-up and their own skill. But he admits that cosmetics advertisers and fashion magazines remove blemishes with a few judicious clicks of the mouse.

One of the things a computer can't change is ethnicity. The pages of fashion magazines are far more cosmopolitan (no pun intended) than they used to be, but black models are still a comparative rarity. Veronica

Webb, Grace Jones, Iman, Naomi Campbell, Waris Dirie and Alek Wek are memorable partly because they broke through the barrier. According to one fashion journalist, who wishes to remain anonymous, 'It's simple practicality. When you put a model on the cover of a magazine, you're promoting cosmetics as well as clothes. And if most of your readers are white, they want to identify with that image. The black community has its own fashion magazines.'

Yet L'Oreal has chosen Noémie Lenoir (who is also on the books of Models 1, along with Iman) as one of its faces, while Ethiopian beauty Liya Kebede is representing Estée Lauder alongside Carolyn Murphy and Elizabeth Hurley. 'The European market is opening up and following the American example,' said Vicky Mihaci of Ford Models' Paris office. 'In 2004 we noticed a growing demand for black models for the collections, when previously only Yves Saint Laurent systematically used them.' (*'Où sont passés les mannequins noirs?'*, *Stratégies*, 28 October 2004.)

Colour is one thing – but how about shape? In the same way that fashion models are young for practical reasons (energy, clear eyes, smooth skin), they are also skinny. When designers create clothes for their collections, they make items in one size. Therefore, models also come in a standard size. And the received opinion is that a dress is flattered by a slender frame. But John Horner strongly refutes allegations that modelling provokes eating disorders. 'Anorexia begins before modelling. We have never had an anorexic model on our books, and if we believe somebody may be veering in that direction, we send them away to get help. If models are skinny, it's often because they're born that way. They eat perfectly healthy meals. We even considered putting paid to the myth by producing a book called *Model Food*, in which they'd list all their favourite recipes. Of course, if they get overweight, they don't work. But we certainly don't want them to be all skin and bone. Some photographers like fuller figures.'

Yet various groups, from the British Medical Association to the National Eating Disorders Association in the United States (whose public face is the former model Carré Otis), have expressed concern that fashion magazines promote unrealistic body shapes. It's a case of supply and demand. In the Western world, where a growing percentage of the population is officially obese, slenderness has become idealized.

Horner observes that an agency must have, within reason, models of all shapes, sizes and racial backgrounds on its books: 'And even ages.

Some models have a short working life, often because they decide to pursue other careers or raise families. But Yasmin Le Bon has been working for 20-odd years. We also have a model called Daphne Selfe, who is in her 70s. [She featured in a Dolce & Gabbana campaign.] There is a market for different types of look.'

Lately, though, fashion brands have been favouring well-known faces over the blank canvas of models. Celebrities, while not always perfect, are undeniably powerful.

10

Celebrity sells

*'Our customers appreciate the association
with stardom.'*

In 1975, Giorgio Armani sold his Volkswagen. The money went into a pool of US$10,000 that Armani and his partner Sergio Galleoti had got together to open their Milanese fashion house. Having left medical school to enter the fashion business in 1957, Armani had worked as a buyer for the department store La Rinascente. But it was as a designer at Cerruti, which he joined in the early 1960s, that he learned the techniques that were to make his career. The charismatic Nino Cerruti was a master of marketing: he once convinced Lancia to paint a fleet of cars in the same shade as his new range of suits, and then enlisted the curvaceous actress Anita Ekberg to break a bottle of champagne over one of them for the cameras. The effectiveness of such publicity coups was not lost on Armani, who would use relationships with celebrities as the cornerstone of his marketing strategy.

Armani's clothes alone were impressive enough – although the casual deconstructed look of his suits is familiar today, it was revolutionary at the time – but it took a movie star to transfer the designs from the fashion press to the public eye. The star was Richard Gere, and the vehicle was a film called *American Gigolo* (1980). Designers had been dressing stars for years – Hubert de Givenchy was famous for outfitting Audrey

Hepburn – but this was arguably the first time a set of clothes had played such a prominent role in a film, almost becoming an extension of the main character. After Gere wore his suits on screen, Armani's sales soared. Since then, by nurturing a close working relationship with Hollywood, Armani has provided the wardrobe for more than 300 movies, always ensuring that his name appears in the credits. His marketing department has also seen to it that movie stars are regularly invited to his shows and outfitted in Armani for high-profile events – especially the Oscars. For a long stretch of the 1990s, Oscar night was Armani night.

According to Armani's communications chief, Robert Triefus, 'Certainly, Armani can be considered as having pioneered the link between fashion and Hollywood. His dressing of *American Gigolo* was a milestone that led to an enduring relationship. It's part of the brand value – our customers appreciate the association with stardom.'

Armani is not alone in developing such relationships. Designers such as Valentino and Versace have also displayed a knack for deploying star firepower. At Louis Vuitton, the brand's artistic director, Marc Jacobs, has moved on from using supermodels to pop stars and actresses in its advertising. In the UK, as we've heard, Matthew Williamson makes no secret of the fact that dressing a string of well-known young women has enhanced his profile. Male fashion is not immune, either (see Chapter 15: Targeted male). During the run-up to Oscar night, designer brands begin a mating dance with stars and their publicists, often sending racks of free clothing in the hope that a garment will make it on to the red carpet.

The benefits are as blinding as a spotlight: stars give brands a well-defined personality for a minimum of effort, and bring with them a rich fantasy world to which consumers aspire. In addition, consumers have a 'history' with stars. Even though they've only seen them on the screen or in the pages of magazines, they form an attachment to celebrities, regarding them as friendly faces and reliable arbiters of taste. Models, with their distant gazes and alien bodies, can't compete.

April Glassborow, senior buyer for international designer collections at Harvey Nichols, recalls, 'When Victoria Beckham was photographed in a green satin Chloé dress by the *Sunday Times Style* section, it created a demand. It's not a theory. When a celebrity wears something, it has a direct impact on sales.'

By now, there must be few readers of glossy magazines who still believe that, when an actress is photographed carrying the latest 'must-have' bag, she has actually paid for the item. Celebrities occasionally go shopping like everyone else, but generally they are bombarded with free gifts and offers of sponsorship deals. Designers will practically slit one another's throats to get a dress photographed on a star during Oscar night or at the Cannes Film Festival. 'When Nicole Kidman wore Pucci in Cannes, it was huge,' confirms Joseph Velosa, managing director of Matthew Williamson. Almost as huge, in fact, as the actress's engagement to be the face of Chanel No. 5.

In terms of cost-effectiveness, a public appearance that might lead to a photo in a magazine is far more desirable than a multi-million-pound contract. Agencies such as Exposure in London (see Chapter 7: The image-makers) offer brands the possibility of rounding up stars for events, or placing clothes on influential figures, as part of their service. Such deals can work both ways, too: the actress Liz Hurley's career sky-rocketed after she wore 'that dress' – a daring low-cut Versace number held together by safety pins – to the premiere of the film *Four Weddings and a Funeral* (1994).

The relationship is a delicate one, however – for both parties. The designer's marketing adviser must ensure that the chosen celebrity flatters the brand. And the stars, aware that their every move will be made in the full glare of the media spotlight, must be absolutely sure that the garment flatters them. Just as many fashion brands hire agencies to develop relationships with celebrities, the stars themselves seek the counsel of professional stylists.

Andrea Lieberman counts among her regular clients Jennifer Lopez, Gwen Stefani, Kate Hudson, Dido, Drew Barrymore and Janet Jackson. 'A star's image is today their major asset,' she told *Elle* magazine ('*Styliste de Stars*', 6 September 2004). 'With the music industry in transition and piracy undermining their income, they've expanded into other fields like designing lines of clothing, launching their own perfumes, and tours. To be credible, they have to maintain a certain style. And they're under a lot of pressure: the slightest fashion faux pas and they're skewered by the media.'

At the beginning of her career, when she left Parsons School of Design in New York, Lieberman was forced to take a job as a waitress before finding a post with the designer Giorgio Sant'Angelo. Later, after being inspired by her travels in Africa, she opened a jewellery and ethnic accessories store called Culture & Reality. Soon she found herself styling upcoming New York rock bands, and was eventually introduced to the hip-hop performer Sean 'P. Diddy' Combs. This led to a meeting with Jennifer Lopez. It was Lieberman who put Lopez into a much-photographed diaphanous green Versace dress, split to the navel, for the Grammy awards.

One stylist who has achieved star status is Patricia Field, who styled Sarah Jessica Parker for the fashion-fixated television series *Sex and the City*. Field is in fact a professional costume designer with several TV and film credits to her name. She opened her eponymous boutique in Greenwich Village in 1966 and started designing for television in 1980, creating the costumes for a series called *Crime Story*, about the Las Vegas Mafia. By putting *SATC*'s Carrie Bradshaw in a combination of designer labels and pretty thrift-store finds, Parker and Field created a bohemian mix-and-match look that resonated with consumers. How many pairs of Manolo Blahnik shoes were sold thanks to Carrie's love affair with the sleek sling-backs? At the beginning of 2004, *The Telegraph* commented, 'The fictional character. . . has had more influence on the way we dress than many designers could hope for.' ('What treats has Carrie got in store?', 20 January 2004.)

Sex and the City has finished its run, but it helped to convince image-makers that the buying public related more to the perceived 'realness' – however illusory – of actresses than to the unattainable beauty of models. Stars began to replace models on the cover of fashion magazines. Interviewed by *Time* magazine's *Style & Design* special edition (September 2003), Grace Coddington, the creative director of US *Vogue*, hinted that this might be a bone of contention: 'There are no models on covers any more. They're all actors because they're what sells. An actor often dictates what you're going to get. I find that annoying. And I'm incredibly shy, so they scare the pants off me. But I feel perfectly comfortable with the models. They're like my kids.'

Designers such as Matthew Williamson, Zac Posen and Marc Jacobs have been lucky enough to attract the attention and friendship of celebrities, who wear their clothes and attend their shows as a gesture of appreciation and support. Brands that don't have such an appeal merely dig into their wallets to ensure that the right people are seen in their front row. For upcoming and mid-range designers, however, celebrities aren't always an option.

There are signs, in any case, that the celebrity craze might be dying out. Upmarket brands, particularly, have started wondering when glitter becomes kitsch. In the view of Lanvin designer Alber Elbaz, 'The red carpet has gone from elitist to popular. Everyone has access to it, even if only on the internet or through magazines. Since fashion is an integral part of celebrities' lives, it's become a kind of permanent red carpet despite itself. But I don't think this phenomenon of identification is going to last much longer.'

WHEN CELEBRITIES BECOME DESIGNERS

As fame fatigue sets in and consumers become increasingly sceptical about the relationships between brands and stars, it has become necessary to integrate celebrities more closely with the design process. Rather than being expected to buy an item of clothing merely because it is worn by a star, shoppers are now sold products that have – they are told – actually been created by their idol.

To a certain extent, this trend grew naturally of the stars' penchant for creating their own lines of clothing. Another celebrity seems to join the list every day: Jennifer Lopez launched a fashion brand back in 2001; Beyoncé and Gwen Stefani launched their lines in 2004; French fashion model Milla Jovovich teamed up with designer Carmen Hawk to launch Jovovich-Hawk in 2003. British pop singer Lily Allen entered the fray more recently with Lily Loves. Sienna Miller and her sister created the line twenty8twelve. The Olsen twins have no less than two lines: an upmarket, adult brand called The Row, as well as a more affordable range called Elizabeth and James. And nobody was surprised when Victoria Beckham unveiled a denim collection called DvB.

It's not always easy to tell whether these projects spring out of a star's desire to further monetize their fame, or a genuine interest in fashion. Accordingly, some celebrity brands are taken more seriously by the style establishment than others. Perhaps because it is a model–designer tandem, Jovovich-Hawk has been received positively by the fashion press. In the *International Herald Tribune*, sharp-penned journalist Suzy Menkes observed: '[T]here is a significant difference between a fashion designer with an individual artistic handprint working with a licensee and those whose artistry, not to mention primary income, is not in drawing and stitch craft... Jovovich-Hawk... is an exception. Although Jovovich herself moved from modelling to movies... both she and Hawk are totally involved in the design process.'

Jovovich told Menkes: 'Carmen and I both draw – we collaborate on an equal level on anything artistic.' Celebrities with a more offhand approach, merely stamping their names on clothes they've had little involvement in designing, can expect a cooler reception. In the same article, Robert Burke of Bergdorf Goodman admitted that he found some collections 'insulting'. 'It is a little arrogant to say "I am a designer". We in the business hold the true idea of fashion closer to our hearts.'

Offering a word of warning, Menkes added: 'The stars who are making it in fashion have long-term business plans and a slow building process that puts them on a par with normal fashion designers.' ('Don't give up the day job', 13 September 2005.)

Occasionally, performing artists have been welcomed by the fashion industry because their quirky sense of style makes them genuinely interesting. This seems to be the case of Gwen Stefani, whose LAMB label (it stands for Love Angel Music Baby) has fashion journalists reaching for positive statements almost despite themselves. 'Stefani has a passion for fashion that gives a freshness and sincerity to the clothes,' allowed Menkes.

The fashion world was also intrigued by a line created in 2007 by the actress Chloë Sevigny, in tandem with hip brand Opening Ceremony. This may have been because Sevigny is a fashion industry sweetheart – regularly appearing in the audience at shows and lending her quirky personal style to photo shoots. Or it could have been because she was on familiar ground: for a while she was creative director of vintage-inspired label Imitation of Christ. *New York* magazine, at least, seemed pleased with the idea, pointing out that 'every piece in the collection had to be something she personally would want to own'. The result, the magazine said, was 'cute but also very fashion-forward and perhaps a bit too challenging for the average girl'. ('Chloë Sevigny designs the clothes of her dreams', 12 September 2007.)

The partnership with Opening Ceremony highlighted another evolution in the relationship between brands and celebrities: the recruitment of stars by existing brands.

By far the most widely reported example of this at the time of writing was the partnership between Britain's Topshop and one of the country's most visible exports, Kate Moss. The selling point here was that the collection with Moss's name on it was co-designed by the model, based on favourite items from her wardrobe. It was also extremely accessibly priced, so her young fans could dress up as their heroine for as little as £45 (around US$87): the cost of a slinky black dress.

Importantly, for marketing-savvy consumers, the alliance felt honest. 'Moss is a long-time fan of the store and has always shopped there, mixing in cheap pieces with her ultra-fashionable wardrobe.' ('Kate Moss: Topshop's new muse', Telegraph.co.uk, 20 September 2006.)

The deal with Moss was said to have cost Topshop parent company Arcadia around £3 million (US$6 million), which sounds like a bargain. Arcadia boss Philip Green told the press he expected the new label – simply called 'Kate' – to grow into a global brand. The not entirely surprising results of the partnership were straggling queues outside Topshop in Oxford Street and Barney's in New York, where the 80-piece collection also went on sale.

Commenting on the relationship in MSN Money, Verdict Research director Neil Saunders said: 'It is increasingly difficult to drive volume on [women's] clothing. The number of clothing items a woman buys each year has doubled over the last ten years, and that can't continue. That's why retailers can add value by model association.'

Not to be beaten, in spring 2007 Spanish brand Mango launched a collection designed by Jovovich-Hawk, whom we met earlier. But associations with top models may not be enough. How about teaming up with a global superstar?

Having already supplied an 'off-stage wardrobe' for Madonna and her stage crew during a 2006 tour, the following year H&M asked the singer to design a collection under the name M by Madonna. Consumers were informed that the star 'worked closely' with the company's head of design Margareta van den Bosch to come up with the resulting clothes. And Ms van den Bosch herself was on hand to assure us that '[Madonna] was extraordinarily style conscious, passionate and involved in even the smallest details.' ('Madonna becomes H&M's material girl', *Evening Standard*, 12 February 2007.)

Sometimes the more unexpected the partnership, the more it withstands scrutiny. *Sex and the City* star Sarah Jessica Parker added to her fashion credibility in the eyes of some when she joined forces with budget sportswear brand Steve & Barry's to launch a line called Bitten. The brand positioning (not a million miles from that of H&M) was that everybody should be able to afford fashion. The slogan for the collection was 'Fashion is not a luxury, it's a right.' Company owners Steve Shore and Barry Prevor said Parker 'decided to align with them because of their philosophy of offering quality merchandise at the lowest possible prices'. ('Sarah Jessica Parker to star for Steve & Barry's', *Brandweek*, 19 March 2007.) In a press release, Parker said: 'Women should be able to wear great clothes and not lie in bed at night feeling guilty about how much money they've spent.'

The Bitten line consisted of around 500 items of clothing and accessories, from shirts and cashmere sweaters to jeans and footwear – none of which cost more than US$20. The 'ethical celebrity partnership' had arrived. This may be an avenue for other stars to explore: using their fame to co-create affordable fashion for their (often) young and impressionable fans.

Aside from that, it is reasonable to assume that most celebrity-driven collections are either one-offs, or fragile structures that are unlikely to stand the test of time. Those that emerge from the spin cycle will be the most sincere and the most qualitative: in other words, striking, good-value products that are the result of a genuine collaboration between a star with a vision and a designer who knows how to interpret it.

Further down the line, with fame fatigue continuing to spread, many consumers may yearn for the return of genuine brands created by real designers. The presence of a celebrity in the strategy may one day be read as a signal that the marketing budget has taken precedence over the quality of the product.

Karl Lagerfeld shoots the H&M campaign for his own designs in one of the Swedish brand's greatest marketing coups to date

Images provided by H&M

H&M by Karl Lagerfeld

Images provided by H&M

H&M by Karl Lagerfeld

Zara's headquarters in the Galician countryside could serve as a location for a Bond film... particularly the bleached white reception area

Zara Paris

Zara Tokyo

As it doesn't use poster advertising, Zara uses its stores as a marketing tool – like these contrasting shop fronts in Paris and Tokyo – along with those ubiquitous dark-blue bags

Images provided by Zara

Shunning conventional marketing, Zara owes its success to rapidly updated stock and lightning-fast distribution from this huge logistics centre

Images provided by Zara

Diesel courted controversy with its 'Global Warming Ready'
campaign...

Images provided by Diesel

…which imagined the impact of climate change on cities as varied as Venice and New York.

The Live Fast campaign for Diesel was less provocative...

...but also played ironically on modern lifestyle trends.

Images provided by Diesel

An early Diesel ad... the executions have become more sophisticated, but they maintain a tone of dark irreverance that remains unique

Stay Young/Breathe Less

Images provided by Diesel

The vintage style craze has gone mainstream, competing with conventional chain stores for a young market.

The search for authenticity has led some fashionistas to seek vintage couture dresses. They've also been seen on the red carpet at glitzy events.

Susanna Lau of the blog Style Bubble gained legions of fans by posting pictures of herself in her latest outfits, together with fashion news and commentary.

Carlo Brandelli – photographed here by his pal Nick Knight – took a traditional English tailor and turned it into a fashion brand for men

The exterior of Carlo Brandelli's 21st-century tailor, Kilgour

Style addiction crosses cultural and geographical borders: Fashion magazines at a kiosk in Hanoi, Vietnam.

From this…

…to this.
China is the
world's leading
supplier of cheap
textiles and a
target for designer
brands … but
will it soon be
producing luxury
brands of its own?

11

Press to impress

'Fashion magazines are an extension of the marketing departments of large fashion companies.'

Marching down a steel-cold street in central Stockholm with about an hour to kill before my appointment at H&M, I end up doing what I always do in these circumstances: I find a store selling magazines. But this time, rather than simply catching up on the news and topping up my pop culture references while thawing my hands and feet, I decide to write down the names of all the fashion and style magazines on the shelf. I'm looking at the list now, scrawled in my notebook. Alongside local-language magazines, and the heavyweight bibles that can be found almost everywhere – *Vogue, GQ, Elle, Marie-Claire* – there are lots of cultish titles that none the less strive to be 'international': *Zink; V; Nylon; Oyster; Pap; Citizen K; WAD; Plaza; Squint; Rebel; Black Book; Dazed & Confused; Tank; Flaunt; Surface.* There is even a magazine called *Shoo*, devoted entirely to accessories. And this is a relatively small shop in Stockholm, not a giant media emporium like Borders in Oxford Street or the magazine kiosk at Grand Central Station in New York.

Whether all these magazines will still exist by the time this book comes out is open to question. *The Face*, the style magazine of my youth, recently closed down, having failed to age gracefully with its audience, while simultaneously losing touch with its target market of suburban hipsters. Nevertheless, my little experiment shows that despite the web – despite satellite TV, come to think of it – fashion consumers are still addicted to those glossy pages; and fashion advertisers, too.

What I'm really interested in here, of course, is the relationship between fashion magazines and advertisers. The situation warrants scrutiny. While fashion is often presented as an art form, or at least a form of entertainment, it almost entirely lacks a critical press. Movies and books are regularly disembowelled with a few strokes of the pen, but the vast percentage of fashion journalism is at best effervescent, at worst fawning. Could it possibly be because magazines need to keep their advertisers sweet? After all, following the frenzied consolidation of the last few years, which saw most of the luxury brands swallowed up by a handful of conglomerates – LVMH, Gucci Group and Richemont – fashion advertisers are wealthier and more powerful than ever.

A few days after my return from Stockholm, during fashion week in Paris, I manage to grab a few moments with Masoud Golsorkhi, the founder and editor of a magazine called *Tank*. Now that *The Face* has folded, *Tank* is possibly the best example of an edgy and intelligent style magazine.

Golsorkhi says, '*Tank* strives to provide an alternative perspective, and as such it is far more critically engaged than many of its competitors. Most fashion magazines are an extension of the marketing departments of large fashion companies. Our approach isn't about buying the complete marketing message; although we don't entirely reject it, either. We accept that fashion is not essential, but as there's clearly a sociological and psychological desire for its existence, it's a subject that merits intelligent coverage.'

So why don't other magazines have a similar outlook? Golsorkhi seems almost shocked by my naivety. 'The fashion press is very much gagged,' he says. 'This is not just about advertising cash – it's also about gifts and holidays. The connection between fashion brands and the media is based on relationships, and fashion PR people work very hard to stimulate friendships with journalists. It's very difficult to write nasty things about your friends.'

A press relations executive working for a designer label tells me a story about a training event for young PR people hosted by a leading UK fashion journalist. 'We'd all been summoned to hear this journalist tell us how we could best convince her to write about our brands. She had a list of ten do's and don'ts. The only one I remember is this: "If you must give us free gifts, give us vouchers instead."'

Golsorkhi says that *Tank*'s comparatively high cover price – an issue costs £10 – is designed to guarantee its independence. 'The idea is that the magazine survives on sales rather than advertising sponsorship. Of course we carry advertising, but we maintain the right to say what we like. And the magazine's balance is far more in favour of editorial than advertising.'

Golsorkhi believes that fashion brands are over-protected by the media, which can lead to marketing errors and ruined businesses. 'The clothes go straight out there to the biggest focus group in the world – the consumers, who have a nasty habit of rejecting a brand whose designs they don't like, even if it has spent a fortune on advertising and thus been given the stamp of approval by the fashion press. A more critical press would ultimately benefit the industry.'

He points to Versace, a brand that is increasingly described as 'troubled' by the business press, while continuing to spend a fortune on advertising in the glossies. (A recent spate of ads featured Madonna dressed as a sexy secretary.)

But perhaps it's wrong to try and separate fashion magazines from the industry they cover. Fashion is not politics, after all. It's a relatively small and self-contained community in which stylists, art directors, photographers and editors flit from magazines to advertising campaigns and back again. (This explains the common complaint that it's often difficult to tell a fashion spread from an advertisement: the same team may have created both.) Fashion editors and stylists also offer their services directly to designers at the start of the creative process, which handily enables everyone to come to an agreement on prevailing trends.

Nicholas Coleridge, managing director of Condé Nast in the UK – home to *Vogue*, *Glamour*, *Tatler*, *Vanity Fair* and *GQ*, among others – says, '*Vogue* and other fashion magazines don't exist to be overly critical; although they can criticize by exclusion. Our job is to cover trends. The editors themselves choose the clothes they want to present on the editorial pages, and the stylists have considerable room for manoeuvre. There is no pre-arranged deal in terms of editorial space in return for advertising support. The editors are as keen to show little-known designers as they are to cover the big brands. Having said that, it would look pretty strange if we didn't cover the major designers – it's what our readers expect of us.'

Carine Roitfeld, editor of *Vogue*'s French edition, confirms this opinion: 'We're not obliged to show any particular designer. In fact, due to our position in the marketplace – the power of the *Vogue* name – we have an extraordinary amount of liberty. This is not the case for everyone, and I think the readers notice when a magazine has completely sold out. I am respectful of our advertisers, but I have a duty to my readers and to myself to promote young, promising designers. And I think even the biggest advertisers accept that their clothes and advertisements look better in a dynamic environment. It can be best described as a sort of mutual understanding – a partnership.'

The methods fashion editors use to choose the clothes they feature merit a brief explanation. Most of them rely on 'look books' – a sort of catalogue sent to them by the fashion brands to present each season's collection. But Roitfeld says upcoming young designers can break through simply by being pushy. 'In my experience, American designers are far more confident and ambitious than their European counterparts. In New York, people will approach me and talk to me about their work. It happens much less over here.'

Nevertheless, small and mid-range designers with severely limited or non-existent advertising budgets complain that they feel excluded from glossy magazines. The French designer Isabel Marant states bluntly, 'To be well known in fashion today, you have to appear in the women's press. But, without buying advertising, it's almost impossible. The relationship within the fashion business is one of give-and-give: "You pay, and I'll give you some editorial. You don't pay, and I'll write about you when I have the room." Fashion journalists, rain or shine, are in the grip of their advertising departments. Advertising is a very heavy burden for a small fashion house like mine.' (*'Isabel Marant: Un bon vêtement raconte une histoire'*, *L'Express*, 6 September 2004.)

There is no doubt that glossy magazines wield tremendous marketing clout. Over the years, the fashion press has handed many designers a place in history. It was Carmel Snow, the editor of American *Vogue*, who wrote of Christian Dior's designs in 1947: 'This is a new look!' And the support of Hélène Lazareff, the founder of *Elle*, was fundamental to Gabrielle Chanel's comeback in 1954, when the designer was severely out of favour – having ill-advisedly spent the Occupation shacked up in the Ritz with a German officer.

Today, fashion fans continue to base buying decisions on what they see in the glossies. April Glassborow at Harvey Nichols says, '*Vogue* is still very influential – the photography remains beautiful. I think readers make the separation between the editorial and the advertising; but at the same time they accept that advertising is part of the package.'

Glassborow adds that some of the best fashion coverage can be found in newspapers. She cites the *Style* supplement of *The Times* as particularly effective. And, indeed, it would be churlish not to mention Suzy Menkes, the *International Herald Tribune*'s redoubtable fashion journalist, who is by no means afraid of crossing swords with designers. (Trade magazines, too, do have teeth, with a great deal of respect being accorded to *Women's Wear Daily*.)

But even some mainstream reporters don't feel entirely free of the yoke of advertising. Janie Samet, the French equivalent of Suzy Menkes, who has been writing about fashion in *Le Figaro* for many years, tells me, 'My first newspaper, *L'Aurore*, was actually owned by Marcel Boussac, the then owner of Dior. Newspapers can't survive without advertising, of course, and it's worth noting that today luxury companies are their largest advertisers, alongside automobiles. [Luxury brands] use us as auxiliaries of their advertising, in order to promote new shops and so on. Designers measure their column inches to see how much the same space would have cost them in advertising.'

A familiar criticism of the glossies is that the advertising threatens to obscure the editorial, particularly in the early sections of the magazine. In reality, there is a fairly even balance between editorial and ad pages, but the major brands all insist on prime up-front positions. A healthy advertising market also means a top-heavy product.

Nicholas Coleridge comments, 'The good thing for us is that the big fashion companies believe strongly in the power of advertising. As the likes of LVMH and Gucci have acquired more brands, they've been keen to market them. Their system is to buy a fashion or luxury business, improve the product, and then tell lots of people about it very quickly. And they've tended to do this through the pages of *Vogue* and the other glossies. At the same time, because their total advertising spend has risen, their negotiating power has increased. Related to this is the way that the competition for good positions, ie as close to the front as possible, has become intense.'

I wonder aloud whether this insistence on being 'at the front of the book' isn't indicative of a lack of imagination or advertising strategy within fashion companies. Coleridge says, 'Publishing companies are forced to perform a delicate balancing act, juggling what you might call the best seats in the house among big advertisers. You might have expected that, as media buying became more sophisticated, advertisers would begin to take up other positions – but that hasn't happened at all; rather the reverse. For example, Chanel used not to mind where it was; it minded more about price than about position. Now it cares about position. Dior cares passionately about position, so do Louis Vuitton and Gucci. Dolce & Gabbana has become very prominent. Armani is pushing for better and better positions. Ralph Lauren and Ferragamo "own" historic positions within glossy magazines, and will not let them go.'

He confirms that many brands simply refuse to advertise unless they're given an up-front position. And as fashion houses have bought one another, they've tried to move their subsidiary brands into better positions on the back of the big spenders. For example, if Gucci has an advertising spread in *Vogue*, it can argue that its sister brand Yves Saint Laurent should run alongside it. 'The most striking trend [in advertising sales] is the desire to upgrade positions. And now the jewellery companies want to push forward too. All this is exacerbated by the luxury companies' increasing use of media-buying and planning agencies, which sometimes imply that they can negotiate better positions. This can lead to short-term unpleasantness. The fact is of course that a magazine is a 3D object, so not everyone can be first.'

So what can the magazines do? Coleridge smiles mischievously: 'They pay smooth-tongued publishers to instil a sense of fairness and balance into proceedings.'

Although the clamour for high-profile positions can cause headaches for advertising sales executives, it is a sign that fashion companies still rate glossy magazines as the best way of reaching their target markets. Upmarket fashion brands have little use for television. 'Television advertising is expensive, and there is colossal waste,' observes Coleridge. 'If you take a brand like Saint Laurent, it probably has something like 80,000 potential customers in the whole of the UK. And I would suggest that the most efficient way of reaching them is through one of our magazines. Advertising on, say, Channel Four would cost many times more, and they would be communicating pointlessly to a large percentage of people who, frankly, would not be interested.'

Television, for its part, has a similar disdain for fashion. Coverage of the subject is thin on the ground, particularly outside the months of the collections. Even the successful cable and satellite service Fashion TV – which claims 500 million viewers worldwide – may make for fine eye candy in trendy bars, but it provides little in the form of commentary. Instead, it screens catwalk shows in an endless parade of nonchalant beauty – a gently sashaying shop window.

12

The collections

'For a designer, the fashion show is a way to broadcast ideas. It is a medium.'

It's both disappointing and illuminating to discover that the focal point of the Paris collections is a shopping mall. Admittedly, it's a rather grand shopping mall – a subterranean maze below the Louvre museum – but the Carrousel du Louvre is a mall nonetheless, with souvenir shops and clothing retailers and even a Virgin Megastore. Down a flight of steps, tucked discreetly away from the main drag, is the large annex that serves as a rallying point and meeting area during fashion week. The lofty hall is dominated by a huge screen flashing taped runway shows. A semi-circular reception area displays fashion magazines, brochures and flyers. To the right, a white-swathed marquee is the media centre, where accredited fashion journalists can sip coffee, juice, or Champagne, catch up on the gossip, and whizz reports back to head office.

I am not an accredited fashion journalist – I am, as always, an interloper in their world – so I wait outside, observing the comings and goings. Many of the week's most important shows will take place in the large rooms just off this central hall. Right now, a queue is forming for the Vivienne Westwood presentation, which is due to start in about half an hour. Everybody knows it will not begin on time. That would be unfashionable.

The bi-annual women's prêt-à-porter collections in Paris, which take place in March and October, are among the most important events (some would say they are *the* most important events) in the fashion calendar. This agenda also embraces bi-annual fashion weeks in London, New York and Milan, and their masculine counterparts. There are other fashion weeks around the world – in Miami, Barcelona, Sydney and Hong Kong, to name a few – but they lack the prestige of the four major spectaculars. There's a whole raft of trade shows and expos that attract little attention outside the textile industry. And then there are the haute couture shows, which these days have taken on the air of performance art. But we'll return to those later. For the moment, the circus surrounding the spring/summer prêt-à-porter collections is in full swing. This week, as many as 1,800 journalists and 800 buyers are in town. And I'm tagging along.

The hall is already very busy. People arrive and kiss one another on both cheeks, then stand around ostentatiously fanning themselves with their gold-dust invitations. Suzy Menkes of the *International Herald Tribune* sweeps regally past, unmistakable with her cresting-wave hair-do. A parasitical gaggle of hangers-on – a large percentage of them young Japanese fashion addicts – take photographs of everything that moves and pester for spare invitations. Although I, too, am a hanger-on, a residue of pride prevents me from doing the same. I already know that I don't have a chance in hell of getting in to the Westwood show.

And yet, only a few weeks earlier, I interviewed the most important figure on the Paris fashion circuit.

THE POWER BEHIND THE SHOWS

Didier Grumbach is president of the Fédération Française de la Couture, du Prêt-à-Porter des Couturiers et des Créateurs de Mode. In other words, he runs the organization that runs the Paris collections. His office is located in a discreetly elegant building on the Rue du Faubourg Saint Honoré, not far from the French headquarters of *Vogue*, as well as those of many of the fashion houses that his organization represents. Grumbach himself is not a designer, but a businessman. He helped Yves Saint Laurent and Pierre Bergé found Yves Saint Laurent Rive Gauche, and he ran Thierry Mugler until 1997, when he was elected president of the federation. He is, he says, 'completely impartial' in matters of design; which is just as well, because becoming a member of his organization – and thus gaining permission to show in Paris – is moderately harder than joining a secret society.

Although the federation is best known – to outsiders, at least – for organizing the Paris shows, it has a number of other functions, including teaching and encouraging aspiring designers; representing French fashion abroad; and combating the theft of intellectual property. It is divided into three sections, or *chambres syndicales*: haute couture and men's and women's prêt-à-porter. The Chambre Syndicale de la Haute Couture (of which Grumbach is also president) was created in 1868; the spin-off prêt-à-porter bodies as recently as 1973. Grumbach's umbrella organization oversees all three of them.

He is well aware of his privileged position. 'I could name all my predecessors stretching back to the very beginning,' he says. 'My immediate predecessor stayed for 26 years. The gentleman before him occupied the post from 1937 until 1972. I imagine this demonstrates that they were excellent politicians.' What Grumbach means is that his is an elected position, and that, 'like any president', he could be deposed at any moment. At the time of our meeting, however, he rests comfortably in the knowledge that he was unanimously re-elected in November 2003.

As far as the Paris collections are concerned, the federation's power is absolute. For one thing, it decides which journalists will be admitted. Editors must submit forms providing the circulation figures of their magazines and specifying the names of the reporters and photographers who will be covering the event. Their requests can be rejected. The final list is sent to the fashion designers and their PR representatives, who then choose which journalists they wish to invite.

Even more crucially, the organization draws up the schedule of shows and assigns locations. This dates back to the 1970s, when it was decided that all designers should show their collections in close proximity, 'in order to present the public with a general outlook of the fashion designers' creations and facilitate the work of French and foreign journalists', to quote its website (www.modeaparis.com). (Note here the rather ironic use of the word 'public', when in fact the collections are strictly off-limits to mere mortals.)

'The timetable is more or less the same each year,' Grumbach explains. 'Each member [of the *chambre syndicale*] has a specific slot, and no member can take the place of another. The exception comes when a label decides not to show for a season or so – as was the case in recent years with Kenzo and Lacroix, who returned again only last season – in which case other designers can move into their places. Generally, we reserve the first day for young brands that have begun exporting to Asia and America, meaning that they have potential. We have to place certain major designers in specific locations, because there are not many spaces in Paris that can accommodate up to 1,500 people, with all the security and organizational problems that entails.'

The Carrousel du Louvre is the administrative centre of the collections, and two rooms off its main hall can hold, respectively, 1,200 and 1,500 people. A marquee erected for the occasion in the Tuileries gardens can seat a further 1,200. Smaller locations are dotted around the city, but, ideally, they should never be more than a short taxi ride away from the Carrousel.

'There are 11 shows a day,' Grumbach explains, 'which is an enormous figure, embracing all nationalities: not just French, but English, American, Japanese, Belgian, Italian. . . Paris remains the international window for fashion design. You can be a genius in London, but to gain true international status, you must eventually show in Paris. This has always been the case, from Worth to McQueen.'

Like most decisions in the surprisingly conservative world of high fashion, membership of the *chambres syndicales* is based firmly on business performance. Those elected to the clan are judged in terms of potential or existing international sales. As Grumbach points out, 'A buyer from America doesn't travel all the way to Paris to buy something that already exists in America. So they are looking for something truly innovative. Interest from abroad is one of the key things we look for when we are considering applications for membership.'

Prospective members send a letter to the *chambre syndicale*, which then dispatches an application form. The designer must return it, along with a hefty press portfolio. 'And while a good review from Suzy Menkes helps,' Grumbach says, 'we're particularly interested in the international spread of the coverage.'

Grumbach also stresses the importance of what he calls 'the godfather figure'. Prospective members must secure the support of an established name in fashion who can state their case before the election committee. 'It is necessary to have a sponsor who can speak on your behalf, and explain why you should be admitted. This is, never forget, a club. If Christian Lacroix sends a letter insisting that you are the next big thing, it helps. And if Jean-Paul Gaultier is advising your company – bearing in mind that you are, in some ways, his competitor – we generally respect that.'

He adds that the sponsor should be the president or CEO of a fashion brand, not just a designer. Once again, although fashion is a creative industry, executives have the greatest influence.

COMMUNICATION VIA CATWALK

But it's not just the brazenly clubby nature of the Paris collections that might dissuade a designer from showing in the French capital. In fact, a number of developments have placed a question mark over the wisdom of holding fashion shows at all – not just in Paris, but in all the main markets.

The most obvious is the availability on the web of images from a show less than an hour after the designer has taken a bow. Extensive web coverage means that buyers from stores are no longer obliged to attend shows. It also plays into the hands of counterfeiters and copyists, who can have knocked-off versions of the clothes on sale before the original designers have finished taking orders from buyers. Grumbach says this is 'not just a concern – it is collective suicide'. He tempers this by adding, 'Of course, there is no rule that says designers must show in public. But they want to maintain visibility, and there is nothing like a fashion show to display their art. It is a way to broadcast their ideas. It is a medium.'

These days, most buyers place orders at private 'pre-collection' gatherings in showrooms, during which the designers present straightforward commercial versions of the garments they will later send out on to the catwalks. Matthew Williamson, for instance, holds two pre-collection events, in January and June. The brand's managing director, Joseph Velosa, says, 'The pre-collection is usually unashamedly commercial: the essence of your signature without the £3,000 dress or the £6,000 coat. The overheads and the razzamatazz aren't there, so people like me approve of it because there are no up-front costs. It's just about product, in a room, that buyers respond to. Some of the brands sell as much as 70 per cent of their wholesale stock at pre-collection. So by the time the catwalk collection comes around, if the pre-collection was received positively, the designer feels much more confident and free to experiment. Shows are therefore becoming less commercial and more theatrical. They are less and less a direct selling tool.'

April Glassborow, senior buyer for international designer collections at Harvey Nichols, agrees that attending fashion shows is no longer an essential part of her job. 'It's true that we do a large percentage of our work at pre-collection stage. You see things that are less expensive, more basic, and clearly indicative of key styles and colours. And you struggle to justify going to the collections when you can see everything on Vogue.com from your own desk. There's a lot to be said for the lights, the music, the sheer drama of the shows – but the fact is that they are more important for the media than for buyers.'

Fashion shows are, in fact, live advertisements. They are expensive and extravagant, but, according to Velosa, very effective. He says, 'People outside the industry think it's crazy: "You work for six months for something that lasts for ten minutes?" But actually those ten minutes are vital, because everyone is hyper-sensitive to what you're saying. They're all looking at your stage sets, the models you've been able to pull in, your front-row celebrities, whether [American *Vogue* editor] Anna Wintour has turned up... You are gauged hot or not every six months. And of course the product is out there on the biggest pedestal you could imagine. The product has to be right, of course, that's the cornerstone. But if you get everything around it right too, you can change it from being merely a good product into a hot product. The press write about you, the buyers see your name in magazines, and, because they're like vacuum cleaners sucking up everything new, when the next collection comes around they want to come and see you.'

Needless to say, fashion designers don't design fashion shows – not entirely, anyway. In Paris alone, a directory's worth of event organizers and set designers are on hand to help them create their spectacular showcases.

Thierry Dreyfus is a freelance lighting designer and show director working regularly with a company called Eyesight, whose past clients have included Cacharel, Chloé, Dior Homme, Paul & Joe, Sonia Rykiel and Yves Saint Laurent. In his view, 'The fashion show is not an art – it is an element of marketing. For the amount you invest in a show, you can generate between ten and a hundred times the cost in free advertising, in terms of photos in magazines and newspapers, television coverage and so forth. One designer told me that if he does a good show he doesn't have to buy advertising space for a year.'

Companies such as Eyesight and their associates have a lot on their plate. Selecting the models, organizing fittings, devising the running order, coordinating accessories, liaising with stylists, hairdressers and make-up artists, arranging sound, lighting, security, catering and seating plans are just a few of the things that must be taken care of. Occasionally, the event organizer is responsible for luring celebrities to events. 'Sometimes they want to come, sometimes they are invited, and sometimes they are paid,' Dreyfus reveals.

Perhaps the greatest of their challenges is creating the 'mood' of the show. People like Dreyfus are paid to ensure that the message the designer wants to get across is evident not just to the people sitting in the room, but also in the resulting media coverage. 'Every detail is important. For instance, because of digital photography, the way photographs are taken is changing, so we have to take account of that in the lighting. It's sort of a magic trick. Each designer wants to ensure that when you see an image from his show, you can immediately identify his particular look. The show has to illustrate the brand.'

Given the importance of accessories, runway shows are likely to have an increasingly close connection with a brand's advertising strategy. For example, Chanel's spring/summer 2005 show featured Nicole Kidman re-enacting her costly TV spot for Chanel No. 5. And Louis Vuitton's show that same season featured clashing metallic colours purposely designed to make audiences yearn for a pair of the branded sunglasses paraded by the models.

Dreyfus denies that fashion shows have become more about special effects than clothes – 'their main goal is still to show the way fabric moves on a human body' – but he admits that designers are under increasing pressure to make an impact. 'An important journalist like Carine Roitfeld or Suzy Menkes, assuming they've already been to the collections in New York and Milan by the time they arrive in Paris, could end up seeing 40 or 50 shows by the end of a season. So the trick is to be remembered.'

Dreyfus is unwilling to reveal the cost of staging a fashion show, but estimates range from £20,000 to well over £100,000. Dreyfus says, 'Certainly, if you're a young designer, my advice would be not to show. Rent a showroom, ask a couple of friends to model your clothes, try to develop personal relationships with the press. Because even if you can get a model agency to lower their price to 800 euros a girl, even if you can get sponsorship from hair and make-up companies, and even if you can find a cheap venue, it's still going to be less than professional and cost a fortune. Better to wait until you can afford to do it properly.'

Back in Didier Grumbach's office, I'm now dying to see my first show. But how do I get in? 'Well, you can't,' he says, with a laugh that may either be sympathetic, embarrassed, or merely incredulous. Perhaps registering my crestfallen expression, he adds, 'Look, you've got a press card, haven't you? Why don't you come along to the Carrousel, and we'll see what we can do.'

And so, on the first day of the Paris collections, I stroll in to the media centre and explain the situation to the beautiful girl on the front desk. I tell her that I'm writing a book about fashion, that I recently interviewed Didier Grumbach, and that the great man hinted that I might be able to get in to a show or two. She is just about to reply when a young, thrusting type with fashionably dishevelled hair appears at her side. 'Certainly not,' he says, in his clipped French accent. 'I can assure you, monsieur, that if you do not have the correct accreditation, there is nothing we can do for you.'

My fist involuntarily curls in my pocket, but I smile politely and apologize for wasting his time. Clearly I will have to resort to what the French call 'System D': the system for getting around the system.

HAUTE COUTURE LAID LOW

I dread to imagine what it might have been like if I'd tried to talk my way into an haute couture show. As you know, haute couture has its roots in the origins of fashion, when wealthy women had dresses made to measure. There were interminable fittings, and clothes were painstakingly stitched by hand. Prêt-à-porter – or ready-to-wear, to give it its more egalitarian appellation – came along much later, driven by 20th-century technology and the democratization of dress. But as ready-to-wear increased in sophistication, price and marketing support, taking on the names of designers that might previously have been associated only with couture (Yves Saint Laurent Rive Gauche was the pioneer in this field), it nudged haute couture slowly towards irrelevancy.

The haute couture shows are held in January and July. According to the rules of the Chambre Syndicale de la Haute Couture, a fashion house can only use the term if it has 'made-to-measure dressmaking activity in the Paris area'. But this humble phrase disguises the true nature of an haute couture dress, which is to fashion what a Lamborghini is to the automobile industry or a newly discovered Van Gogh to the art world. Hand-made in every detail, fused to the body of the model who displays it (and later, perhaps, to the fabulously wealthy customer who acquires it), an haute couture dress is wearable sculpture. One legendary Chanel creation, hand-embroidered by the celebrated Maison Lesage, is said to have sold for €230,000 a couple of years ago.

And there's the rub. The item above may have been exceptional, but haute couture dresses, being one-offs, are worth tens of thousands of pounds. Didier Grumbach himself admits that there are perhaps only 1,000 haute couture customers in the entire world. I have heard estimates as low as 300. In Paris today the official list of permanent haute couture designers stands at 11: Adeline André, Anne Valérie Hash, Chanel, Christian Dior, Christian Lacroix, Dominique Sirop, Emanuel Ungaro, Franck Sorbier, Givenchy, Jean Paul Gaultier and Maurizio Galante. But the schedule is padded out with young 'associate' designers. Even Gaultier, who started out in ready-to-wear and joined the haute couture clan in 1997, admits that he does it for love rather than money – and his passion has eaten into his label's profits. Lately, the French media have begun loudly wondering whether haute couture is on its last legs.

Yet there are a number of fairly good reasons for keeping haute couture alive. The first is, as ever, marketing. If a fashion show is little more than a live advertisement, then haute couture is the most spectacular commercial break of all. The sublime creations John Galliano produces for Dior, which transform women into Egyptian goddesses, are worth their weight in sunglasses and handbags. They add value to the Dior brand, and keep the Galliano buzz humming nicely.

Bernard Arnault, chairman of LVMH – which owns the house of Dior – said recently, '[Haute couture] is a fantastic tool to demonstrate the prestige of the house. Its impact on all the other lines – clothes, accessories, and cosmetics – is enormous. Of course it's very costly, but it's not our intention to cover the cost through sales.'

The second reason for the existence of haute couture is simply to push the limits of fashion. While prêt-à-porter has become increasingly commercial, fashion still wishes to maintain a shred of credibility as an art form. Haute couture is its laboratory, encouraging experimentation and generating ideas that may, one day, change the way people dress. According to Bernard Arnault, 'It is the domain in which the designer can go to an extreme... express the ultimate in quality and creativity. And this link is present in the consumer's mind when they buy prêt-à-porter.' This may explain Giorgio Armani's decision in 2005 to begin showing haute couture for the first time.

The third reason – and the most humane – is simply to preserve the craftsmanship that goes into haute couture. As well as the people who work in the designer's atelier, there are a number of cottage industries adding the luxurious touches that give these outfits their appeal. The embroidery house Lesage, the glove-maker Millau, the milliner Maison Michel, exquisite feather creations from André Lemarié and lace from Puy-en-Velay – all these traditions might be lost if haute couture were to vanish for ever.

There is, possibly, a middle ground. While haute couture customers are a rare breed indeed – limited mainly to royalty and celebrities – fashion currently has a taste for individuality. The bland uniformity of globalization means that customization and novelty are *à la mode*. With typical prescience, Prada recently identified the need for a new type of garment, somewhere between couture and prêt-a-porter – partly hand-made, adjusted to fit the customer, and released only in limited numbers. Called the 'Prada Evening Project', the collection consisted of around 30 models, each labelled from one to 100. The pieces were inspired by the regular Prada collection, but were hand-embroidered with sequins or Swarovski crystals, and produced in luxurious silk, satin and chiffon. *Vogue* pointed out, 'While allowing fashion to reclaim its artistic status, the collections also give those who buy them the idea. . . that they have acquired more than a simple product, but a little masterpiece.' (*'Prada de 1 à 100'*, October 2004.) There is more of this, surely, to come.

FRONT-ROW FEVER

The seating arrangements at Paris fashion shows are clearly defined and almost invariable. On either side of the runway, there are separate blocks of seating for VIPs, magazine journalists and buyers. French journalists get a block to themselves. The UK is lumped in with the United States. Japan is seated, inexplicably, with Italy; the rest of Europe peers out from behind the battery of TV cameras. The buyers get a block of their own. The daily newspapers, which provide the swiftest exposure to the largest audience, are given the best vantage point at the front of the room, close to Didier Grumbach. The seating plan strives to observe political sensitivities: for instance, US *Vogue* must not be placed next to either UK *Vogue* or *Harper's Bazaar*. Certain journalists – notably Carine Roitfeld of *Vogue* France and Suzy Menkes of the *International Herald Tribune* – automatically get the best seats.

The entire front-row phenomenon is fascinating. Fashion journalists will tell you that it is vital that they sit in the front row, because it enables them to see the clothes properly – including the shoes. But, off the record, they admit that it is as much about status as it is about professionalism. The further back you are, the less important you (and, by extension, your publication) are perceived to be. And if you receive one of the dreaded 'standing' invitations, reserved mainly for students, it might be better not to turn up at all.

Personally, I would be happy to stand. After my brush with the bouncer at the media centre, I return to my office and start phoning PR people. I eventually make contact with a small brand called Impasse de la Défense, created by the designer Karim Bonnet. Based on a back street of the lively 18th *arrondissement* – from which his brand gets its name – he fuses fashion with art, producing bohemian hand-painted dresses. As I live near by, I'll effectively be supporting my local designer. I get through to a young woman and explain why I want to see the show.

'Sure,' she says, brightly. 'We'll send you an invitation right away.'

It arrives the very next morning, and I note with considerable pleasure that the show will be held at the Salle Wagram, an ancient ballroom notable for its brief appearance in the film *Last Tango in Paris*. When I turn up, even though my new friend Karim is not quite on a par with Vivienne Westwood, there are plenty of people milling around outside. I even spot the requisite Japanese students begging for invitations. Clutching mine, I feel an uncharacteristic surge of condescension.

Finally the doors open, and we can escape the late-October drizzle. The theme of the show is 1960s pop music, and a psychedelic sitar band twangs merrily away in the lobby. There is a vague whiff of incense. I hand my invitation nervously to one of the two pretty young women standing at the entrance to the hall, casually mentioning that I'm a journalist.

'Oh,' she says, beaming. 'In that case, you'd better sit in the front row.'

With a sense of triumph that is utterly misplaced, I settle into my seat. I have been there for approximately five minutes when another young woman approaches.

'I'm terribly sorry,' she says. 'But I'm afraid you'll have to move back a row. These seats are reserved for the journalists from *Madame Figaro*.'

Any trace of superiority I might have felt drifts away like chiffon in a cold draught. As I get to my feet, a perfumed gaggle of forty-something ladies bears down on me. These are the representatives of *Madame Figaro*, the venerable French women's magazine. I may be supporting my local designer, but during the collections, those with a short-cut to the buying public will always have the upper hand.

13

Accessorize all areas

'The handbag is killing fashion.'

Downstairs, at a reasonably safe distance from where I am standing, a large man is waving one hand at me and making disturbing throat-slashing gestures with the other. In different circumstances, I might be concerned. However, I'm not in a Naples back alley; I'm standing on the mezzanine floor of the Armani superstore in Milan. The man is a security guard, and his urgent signals mean that I should stop taking photographs of the store's interior. No doubt he's worried that I'll do something unforgivable like publish them in a book destined to be read by potential Armani customers.

Pictures taken, I stow away the camera and wave amiably back at the security operative. He seems satisfied and leaves me to my shopping.

As well as being a Spartan, eye-achingly white example of the kind of flagship luxury store discussed in Chapter 5, the three-floor Armani space at Via Manzoni 31 is the perfect illustration of another familiar ingredient of fashion: the brand extension. In this single store, customers can sample almost every declination of the Armani brand: Emporio Armani (upmarket young fashion); Armani Jeans (casual wear); Armani Casa (home furnishings); Armani Profumi (fragrances); Armani Dolci (chocolates); and even Armani Fiori (flowers). Just about the only Armani product you can't experience here is the label's first hotel, which is due to open in Dubai by 2008.

A little while later, at Armani's headquarters around the corner in Via Borgonuovo, Robert Triefus, the company's executive vice-president of worldwide communications, explains the thinking behind such diverse branding initiatives: 'The Armani brand and its values have become understood globally. When you talk about Armani to someone on the street, they immediately have a perception of what the name means. It has almost become generic – you can talk about the "Armani look": Italian, timeless, elegant, sophisticated but understated. That concept extends very smoothly into lifestyle products, and it did so in 2000 when we launched Armani Casa.'

Unlike the Gucci and LVMH groups, which have expanded by acquiring existing brands, Armani has created its own sub-brands and diversified into new product categories, creating a coherent 'branded environment'. Triefus says the group is built like a pyramid, with the signature Giorgio Armani brand at the top 'setting the tone and style for everything that we do'. When the company moves into a new market, it always opens a Giorgio Armani boutique first, to set the standard, before any of the other brands follow. Beneath the signature brand is Armani Collezioni, a slightly more accessible diffusion line predominantly distributed through department stores; it is followed, in descending order, by Emporio Armani, Armani Jeans, and A/X Armani Exchange, a series of licensed casual-wear stores not a million miles from Gap in style. Each of these labels also markets accessories such as eyewear, watches and fragrances, produced through licensing arrangements. Although licensing was once deemed unfashionable – in the 1990s many luxury companies spent a fortune buying back licences, feeling that over-extension had corrupted the integrity of their brands – it is now sneaking back into favour. Certainly, Armani's brand-stretching does not seem to have hurt the company, which turns over 4 billion in annual retail sales, according to Triefus.

'You should be aware that the store you have just seen is a very particular environment that offered the opportunity to do some peripheral things. Armani Dolci [the chocolates spin-off] is a very small business with two or three stores in the entire world, but it works in terms of creating an addition to the Armani lifestyle in certain retail locations. The same is true of the flowers – we're not trying to compete with Interflora. Having said that, although "lifestyle" is an overused expression, I think we have been more successful than most in creating an identity that can be interpreted in diverse forms.'

The flowers and the chocolates may be peripheral, but Armani Casa is a real business, with 17 stores around the world. And the hotel operation will eventually have 14 branded locations.

'Of course you're going to ask me if we're in danger of over-extending, but I don't believe anything we have done has gone beyond the logic of the brand. It's when you go beyond the brand's logic that things start to look uncertain,' says Triefus. 'That was the problem with licences. Pierre Cardin is famous for the amount of licensing agreements he has. We have four licensing agreements worldwide. We're a very tightly controlled business, so I don't think we can be accused of pushing the brand too far.'

Armani is not the first brand to move into interiors – Ralph Lauren, the king of 'lifestyle' marketing, got in on the act around 15 years ago – but Triefus says, 'Along with Lauren, we've probably taken the most comprehensive approach. Other brands like Versace, Calvin Klein, Fendi and Donna Karan have taken a more tangential route – I refer to it as "candles and cushions" – while we have the full gamut of furniture, lighting, rugs, sheets, tableware and so forth, so it's a genuine opportunity to buy in to the Armani world.'

Brand extensions are all the rage in Italy, it seems. Rosita Missoni, having decided to leave fashion to the younger designers in her company, has launched a range of home products – and may even open Missoni-branded interiors stores. Meanwhile, Pucci, the Florentine fashion house majority-owned by the LVMH group, has produced winter sportswear in partnership with Rossignol. Pucci's glamorous, kaleidoscopically colourful prints rocketed definitively back into fashion when Nicole Kidman wore a red, pink and gold dress at the Cannes Film Festival a couple of years ago. Emilio Pucci died in 1992 and the designer behind the label is now Christian Lacroix (eminently suited to the task), while Pucci's daughter Laudomia is its 'image director'. Pucci was well known for putting his trademark print on everything from curtains to carpets (the Apollo 15 crew carried a Pucci-designed flag to the moon), and in 2001 the label launched a range of furniture in association with Cappellini. But while a Pucci ski jacket certainly stands out on the slopes, isn't it – to paraphrase Triefus – moving beyond the logic of the brand?

Certainly not, says Laudomia. She points out that her father 'lived on the slopes' (he was a member of the Italian skiing team), adding that his very first designs were skiing outfits. 'Pucci comes from a sportswear background, which is very important to point out in terms of legitimacy. We are merely going back to our roots. We have always been a lifestyle company.'

Pucci even created a one-off 300-square-metre sail for a racing yacht, perfectly underlining, says Laudomia, 'that we're Mediterranean and we're all about colour'. Sportswear seems to be a legitimate arena for high-fashion brands, with Céline, Chanel, Dior, Hugo Boss, Prada Sport and Versace Sport all venturing onto the ski slopes and beyond (Chanel has even made a branded snowboard).

The lure of brand extensions for fashion labels is obvious, given the many purposes they serve. They can be money-spinners in their own right, public relations tools for drawing attention to the brand (I mean, really, a Chanel snowboard?), or part of an overall branding strategy – another molecule in the brand universe.

But what happens when the relationship between clothing and accessories is reversed? Have clothes simply become promotional tools for branded goods?

EMOTIONAL BAGGAGE

French fashion journalist Janie Samet believes designers' insistence on brand extensions has led to a declining interest in their clothes, and fuelled the success of affordable fashion brands like Zara, H&M and Topshop.

'Naturally, [the designer labels] are keen on accessories because they provide greater profit margins,' she says. 'And customers like them because no matter what else you are wearing, if you have the right bag, you are immediately placed in a certain social context. The problem is that if you have the right bag, the right shoes and the right belt, you may decide that you no longer need the right dress. In this way, the success of bags is killing fashion.'

But fashion and handbags lead a symbiotic existence. While Dior stages fashion shows that are arguably advertising campaigns for its accessories, brands such as Hermès, Prada and Louis Vuitton began making luxury accessories, and then moved into fashion. The clothes that Marc Jacobs creates for Louis Vuitton are – like Armani's flowers and chocolates – part of a branded world. From Bottega Veneta to Loewe via Dunhill, ST Dupont and Asprey, selling accessories is no longer enough – a designer brand must touch every aspect of its customers' lives.

Louis Vuitton recently celebrated its 150th birthday, but its products are apparently as desirable as ever. Hours before the opening of its flagship store on the Champs-Elysées, dozens of Japanese tourists stand in line, convinced they will be able to acquire a prized monogrammed item at a fraction of the price they would pay in Tokyo. Other Asian visitors are here to buy bags that will later form the templates for fakes. Louis Vuitton, it almost goes without saying, is the Coca-Cola of baggage brands.

Louis Vuitton himself was born in 1821 in a small French village not far from the border with Switzerland. He grew into a natural craftsman, skilfully handling the tools of his father, a joiner. Legend has it that the ambitious young Louis walked 250 miles from his home to Paris, where he became an apprentice at a packing-case maker near the Madeleine. The age of international travel was dawning, with railway lines extending their steel fingers across France, and the first steamers traversing the Atlantic. Their wealthy passengers required a great deal of luggage – the more elegant the better. Spying a growing market, Louis Vuitton decided to start his own business.

Vuitton's first commercial premises opened in 1854 on the Rue Neuve-des-Capucines, not far from the Place Vendôme – and thus close to a steady influx of rich clients. His stroke of genius was to upholster his cases not in leather, but in durable waterproofed canvas. The classic Vuitton trunk was a glamorous monster. Made of poplar, encased in canvas, strengthened with black lacquered metal corners, it bristled with brackets, handles and crosspieces, and contained myriad trays, compartments and drawers. It was a portable wardrobe, and it was a big hit. By 1888 the design had become so widely copied that Vuitton was forced to print his surname on the canvas at regular intervals. From then on, the name Louis Vuitton was indivisibly associated with stylish travel.

Vuitton was undoubtedly an innovator (his inventions included the round 'chauffeur bag', which fitted into the centre of a pile of spare tyres; the 'aero trunk', which floated in the event of a landing on water; and the 'secretaire trunk'; a mobile writing desk), but it was his son Georges who contributed the logo that still causes all the fuss today. He designed a monogram pattern consisting of an encircled four-petal flower, a lozenge containing a four-pointed star, the same star in negative, and the initials LV, in homage to his father. The pattern is said to have been inspired by Japanese prints, which perhaps in part explains the brand's immense appeal in that market today.

Georges also created the 'Keep-all', a light canvas bag that was originally designed to contain dirty linen, and to be packed into the trunk. But it was adopted as an accessory in its own right – the first Louis Vuitton bag that voyagers kept by their side. As the years rolled on and new generations of Vuittons headed the company, its bags grew smaller and softer. At first, the family struggled to find ways of printing the monogram logo on flexible surfaces. The arrival of plastic in the late 1950s changed all that, and Louis Vuitton bags became available in all shapes and sizes. Now the iconic logo remains, and the old, original steamer trunks are collectors' items that occasionally double as coffee tables.

In 1987, Louis Vuitton merged with Moët and Hennessy. Enter Bernard Arnault, who would equip LVMH for the 21st century. Born in 1949 in Roubaix, France, Arnault was a graduate of the elite École Polytechnique in Paris. After pursuing a successful career in real estate in New York, he returned to France to apply his American-style business savvy to the country's oldest and most conservative industries: couture, Champagne and luxury goods. Arnault and a business partner from the French bank Lazard Frères and Co. raised US$80 million to buy Boussac, the textile firm that owned the Christian Dior fashion house. In 1987, Arnault was invited by Henri Recamier, the chairman of LVMH, to invest in the company. Two years later, Arnault took full control; becoming the holder of the key to what would become the world's largest luxury conglomerate.

According to Arnault's communications advisor, Jean-Jacques Picart, the secret of Louis Vuitton's continuing success was the fusion of luxury goods with fashion: 'Monsieur Arnault invented what might be called "*luxe-mode*". He devised a way of persuading customers that a luxury item was a fashion statement, and therefore needed to be renewed or replaced. In effect, he introduced the concepts of experimentation, fluidity and renewal that characterize fashion into the world of luxury products, which are by nature timeless and long-lasting.'

Arnault did this in 1997 by appointing Marc Jacobs as Louis Vuitton's artistic director. A young, acclaimed American fashion designer (he had already been named Women's Designer of the Year three times by the Council of Fashion Designers of America), Jacobs was about to open his own store in New York. Hiring a hip New Yorker to pump fresh blood into a venerable Parisian luggage firm was a typically audacious Arnault gamble. A year later, Louis Vuitton launched a range of clothing, shoes and jewellery. That same year, not at all coincidentally, it opened the first of its 'global stores' on the Champs-Elysées. Although it had existing retail outlets (more than 300 around the world), the Champs-Elysées store was the blueprint for a series of giant spaces, the largest of which have opened in Tokyo and New York. In 1912, the very first Louis Vuitton store in Paris covered some 500 square metres. The New York store offers 1,200 square metres of floor space.

Under Jacobs, the monogram pattern was transformed into graffiti (in 2001) and became multicoloured (in 2003) thanks to collaborations with artists Stephen Sprouse and Takashi Murakami. Jacobs also deployed print advertising to modernize Louis Vuitton's image: first by using well-known models such as Eva Herzigova and Naomi Campbell; later by recruiting popular-culture celebrities such as Jennifer Lopez, Scarlett Johansson and Uma Thurman. The images themselves have the gloss, superficiality and sexuality of contemporary fashion photography, owing little or nothing to Louis Vuitton's 'luxury travel' heritage.

Corinne Perez, managing director of the advertising agency BETC Luxe (part of the larger Euro RSCG group), which works alongside Jacobs for Louis Vuitton, says, 'The group's roots are clearly in luggage and travel, but since the arrival of Marc Jacobs it has a strong core of fashion, entirely created and driven by him. He succeeded in making contemporary and relevant a brand that had always been powerful, but within a very specific frame. He took the name Louis Vuitton, which incarnated a certain elegant style of living, detached it from the narrow field of luxury travel, and created around it an idea of pleasure and sensuality.'

For Perez, the campaign featuring Jennifer Lopez was the ultimate expression of Jacobs' ability to meld the apparently conflicting worlds of MTV and luxury. 'It was a controversial campaign because many people felt it would degrade the image of the brand. But Jennifer Lopez incarnates a certain notion of social achievement and wealth, as well as passion and sexuality. I think the campaign expressed the transformative power of the brand: the Jennifer Lopez we saw in those images was not just a pop star, but a sophisticated and glamorous being.'

Since Jacobs' arrival, Louis Vuitton has also moved into menswear and launched a range of watches. But alongside its more fashionable endeavours, it quietly maintains a series of branding initiatives that lie closer to its roots: the Louis Vuitton Classic car rally; the Louis Vuitton Cup yacht race; and a series of upmarket city guides and travel books. Even if Jacobs sends eccentric items on to the catwalk or creates blatantly youth-oriented advertising campaigns, in the background Vuitton keeps its traditional values polished and ready for re-appropriation when necessary.

There is a certain similarity between Louis Vuitton and that other Parisian luxury-goods house, Hermès. But Hermès is determined to retain the air of unabashed elitism that Vuitton has played down in favour of seducing the mass market. Hermès is refined and more than a little haughty. It pushes hard on terms such as 'hand-crafted' and 'artisans'. But Hermès wants to be hip, too, and hired Jean-Paul Gaultier to design its prêt-à-porter collection in 2003, as well as taking a stake in his business. Gaultier replaced the enigmatic Martin Margiela, who had been with Hermès since 1998.

Hermès started out as a saddler in 1837, and still uses equine imagery in its branding. Thierry Hermès made harnesses and saddles for the fashionable horse-drawn buggies (*calèches* and *fiacres*) that clopped along the boulevards of 19th-century Paris. Fortunately for the company, future generations of the Hermès family saw the automobile coming. Emile-Maurice Hermès diversified into luggage, hand-stitched leather goods, gloves and silk scarves. (The world-famous Hermès Carré silk scarf was said to have derived from the fabric used for jockeys' caps.) Watchbands and jewellery followed. In 1951, Robert Dumas took over from his father-in-law, and proved to have a strong grasp of marketing techniques. It was during this era that the brand launched its logo (a *calèche*, naturally) and its signature orange colour, and the window displays at its headquarters in Rue du Faubourg Saint-Honoré became increasingly opulent. Hermès goods were sought after by celebrities; something that the house encouraged by naming a bag after the actress Grace Kelly. The Kelly bag became a cult object, and a Birkin bag, in homage to the singer Jane Birkin, followed later.

The company's current president, Jean-Louis Dumas, took over in 1978. With a turnover of around €1.3 billion a year, the company (which is still 75 per cent family-owned) gains around 40 per cent of its profits from leather goods, with the rest deriving from clothing and accessories, silk, watches, perfume and tableware. It has more than 200 boutiques around the world, including a glass tower in Tokyo that offers not only the full range of Hermès goods, but also regular screenings of French films. Gaultier's first prêt-à-porter collection for the house featured cheeky ponytails, cavalry coats and delightfully perverse harnesses and riding boots.

Jean-Louis Dumas insists that 'Hermès is not a fashion house. It preserves a certain distance while at the same time being determined to remain contemporary. The notion of permanence gives us an aristocratic distinction which has, we must admit, an intimidating side.' (*'Hermès: L'oeil du maître'*, *Le Point*, 8 April 2004.)

Nevertheless, Hermès has plenty of the attributes of a fashion business – notably an interest in fragrances. The current Eau des Merveilles is the latest in a long line that began in the 1950s with Eau d'Hermès, followed by Calèche, Equipage, Amazone, Bel Ami, Eau d'Orange Verte and 24 Faubourg. Janie Samet, who is as realistic about fragrances as she is about bags, comments, 'Perfumes are the heart of the luxury war. Scent makes the cash registers ring.'

A BRAND IN A BOTTLE

Fragrances are the interface between the general public and the world of luxury. Even the most expensive scent is well within the reach of the average consumer, who, while baulking at the cost of a Chanel evening dress, may decide to splash out on a bottle of No. 5. According to market research company Mintel, perfumes and cosmetics make up 37 per cent of the US$70-billion global luxury goods market; clothes and leather goods account for 42 per cent.

Michael D'Arminio, a marketing consultant who has worked on beauty products and fragrances within the Unilever group, says, 'I've been in this field for nearly 12 years, and I have never worked with a designer who said they were just in it for the cash. However, it is 100 per cent about building the brand, communicating its values, and opening up that brand to a larger customer base. The price points within the designer fashion market continue to increase, so fragrances and cosmetics make those brands more accessible and help to build a designer's business. Clearly there are royalties at the end of it, but the process is much more subtle than "take the money and run".'

Fragrances are rarely, if ever, developed by designers alone. Instead, they are produced under licence by large beauty companies such as

L'Oreal or Unilever. Designers have neither the expertise nor the budgets to create, manufacture, distribute and market perfumes.

D'Arminio suggests that the gestation period for a fragrance is between 15 months and two years. 'Developing a fragrance and bringing it to market is a lengthy and incredibly expensive task,' he stresses. 'Normally you look to turn a profit two or three years out. Up until that time, you're still paying for the groundwork. In the United States, if you want to go into the department store market and be a top-15 player, you're looking at spending between eight and fifteen million dollars on a launch. Then you can add another eight or ten million for Europe. And the figures I've just given you are purely for media spend – I haven't included all the development costs.'

For this reason, creating a fragrance is a delicate business. The result has to be fashionable, but not a flash in the pan. It should reflect the brand's values, without being overly complex. Ultimately, no matter whose name is on the bottle, it's the juice that's being judged. And as an unsuccessful fragrance can be de-listed, ultimately damaging the parent brand, designers tend to monitor the development of their perfumes very carefully. 'In my experience,' says D'Arminio, 'the designer is involved at every stage, from beginning to end. It's like a marriage.'

This is confirmed by Valérie Sanchez, who is currently international marketing manager for Helena Rubinstein skincare products at L'Oreal, but has worked on fragrance brands for Rochas, Cacharel and, most recently, Giorgio Armani. At the time I met her, she had just helped Armani launch his male fragrance, Black Code.

She says, 'Our job is to translate the spirit of a brand into a fragrance, so it's essential that we work hand-in-hand with the designer. Working on projects for Armani, we would travel to Milan to meet with him at least once a month. The designer respects the fact that perfume is our métier and not his, but he still demands, and gets, full control.'

Before the odour comes the name. Both D'Arminio and Sanchez confirm that this is chosen at the very beginning of the process. Devising a name for a perfume is increasingly troublesome, because many of the most poetic words and phrases in English, French and Italian are already owned by somebody. This is another incentive to work with a large company such as L'Oreal to develop a perfume – as the leading company in the worldwide beauty market it has the firepower to purchase almost any name. Another alternative is to register a combination name, like Flower By Kenzo or Cerruti Sí, for instance. Often, designers are asked to provide lists of potential names. But Sanchez says that Black Code came out of a brainstorming process at L'Oreal.

'The concept for the fragrance was inspired by a midnight-blue Armani tuxedo that Denzel Washington wore to the Oscars. So we were looking for words around "ceremony", "black tie" and "dress code". "Black Tie" was not international enough: although English is now regarded as the international language of marketing, we felt some nationalities might have problem with the word "tie". So we shuffled things around a bit and ended up with Black Code.'

The fragrance itself is a team effort involving the designer, the licensing company, and a fragrance house. There are only a handful of fragrance houses in the world, and every scent on the market has been designed by one of them. The most famous are IFF (International Flavours & Fragrances), Firmenich, Givaudan, Haarman & Reimer, Takasago, Quest International and Sensient Technologies. As well as fragrances, they conjure up aromas for food companies (yes, your yoghurt smells of strawberries because somebody has perfumed it). The people who work at these houses combine the talents of chemist, musician and wine-taster.

Valérie Sanchez explains, 'Contrary to what you might have read in Patrick Suskind's novel *Perfume, les nez* [the "noses"] are not born with their talent. They may have an interest or an aptitude, but, like musicians, they are educated in their art. Odours are like musical notes – but they are also like molecules, which work together in different ways. Perfume is a science as much as it is an art. Each "nose" works with a palette of between 300 and 500 scents, which they constantly smell to keep the odours fresh in their memory. The variations are infinite. We know that certain "noses" have a particular signature, and we can ask for them by name if we have a specific type of scent in mind. But generally we brief two or three different houses, which compete for the task. Until we make a decision, they are paid nothing. But they are aware that, if their fragrance is selected, they've hit the jackpot.'

The fragrances that the houses put forward are tested by L'Oreal's in-house 'nose', as well as by the designer. As Sanchez says, 'After a while, we know what kind of scents a designer likes and dislikes; or which best reflect the brand. There is also an educational process as a designer's olfactory skills evolve. At the end of the day, although we can make suggestions or nudge a designer away from a direction that may not be commercial, they have the final say.'

Once the fragrance has been selected, there is the all-important matter of designing the bottle. A perfume bottle represents a subtle form of brand communication as well as being a beautiful object in its own right, proudly displayed on a dressing table or bathroom shelf. Again, the designer has a strong influence here; but a specialist can also be called in. The bottle for Black Code was created by New York-based art director Fabien Baron, who has collaborated with Armani on a number of projects.

The manufacturing of perfume bottles is also a specialized industry. Three-quarters of the world's perfume bottles are produced by some 60 enterprises and 7,000 workers in the Vallée de la Bresle, not far from Dieppe in northern France. The largest, Saverglass, produces a million bottles a day. (It's worth observing at this point that the production of essential oils is no longer associated with France, despite romantic images of white jasmine flowers picked and crushed in Grasse and elsewhere in Provence. Fragrances are just as likely to be constructed from Turkish roses, Madagascan vanilla; or, more often than not, synthetic substances.)

The final stage is, of course, the marketing. Increasingly, in order to ensure that the perfume slots neatly into the label's overall brand strategy, the designer tends to turn again to his regular advertising collaborators. This makes sense, as the imagery utilized to promote the fragrance, whether in the media or at point of sale, may eventually lead customers to clothes, bags, sunglasses, and other products. Sanchez says that, as well as designing the bottle for Black Code, Fabien Baron also oversaw the advertising imagery for the fragrance. And, as we've already seen, when Chanel re-launched No. 5 with a campaign starring Nicole Kidman, the actress also appeared alongside designer Karl Lagerfeld on the catwalk. The art director Thomas Lenthal, who works for YSL Beauty, observes, 'The big difference is that when you are selling a dress, you're perhaps talking to thousands of people. But when you're working on a perfume, you're talking to millions of people. So the imagery is different – smoother, more conceptual.'

Sanchez points out that marketing a fragrance is challenging because it centres on an atmosphere rather than a visible product. She says, 'Often the psychology behind the images is quite complex, because it must tempt the customer to try the scent, as well as capturing the overall philosophy of the brand. A perfume may be a product – but it's not a detergent.'

Be that as it may, the commoditization of perfume is leading some discerning (and wealthy) customers away from mainstream brands. Just as in fashion there is a move towards limited editions, vintage finds and general exclusivity, so there is a growing market for made-to-measure fragrances. In Paris, both Guerlain and Jean Patou offer 'olfactory education' courses, followed by the chance for the individual to create a unique perfume from a range of aromas. Patou customers can even spend the day with the perfumer's resident 'nose', who will lead them to chocolate shops and markets to find out exactly which smells they prefer. He can then concoct an entirely idiosyncratic fragrance based on the results. But, as usual, individuality comes at a price – in this case, between €20,000 and €50,000.

14

Retro brands retooled

'With these brands you have to feel as passionate about the heritage as about the future.'

When you stand before the urbane façade of the Gucci store in Milan's Galleria Vittorio Emanuele II – a 19th-century shopping arcade that is as far from a suburban mall as it is possible to imagine – words like 'melodrama' and 'bloodshed' don't exactly leap to mind. But as part of the brand royal family, Gucci has grabbed more than its fair share of headlines.

Along with Burberry, Gucci is probably the finest example of image turnaround in the history of fashion. So revered is the story of its reinvention that 'doing a Gucci' has become a stock phrase, whispered like a mantra by all those trying to resurrect a designer relic. After Gucci's success, everyone assumes they can take a half-forgotten label and bring it up to date in a cool, iconoclastic kind of way. Unfortunately, not everyone is Tom Ford.

The story began in 1922, when Guccio Gucci opened a company making upmarket baggage in Florence. Legend has it that the young Gucci had spent several months working at the Savoy hotel in London, where he noticed a nascent market of rich globetrotters, and correctly assumed they would be keen purchasers of luxury luggage and accessories. Italy's leather-goods savoir-faire and its instinctive adoption of family businesses favoured the growth of Gucci's empire, and Guccio soon had outposts in Rome and Milan.

In the 1950s, Guccio's son Aldo opened a boutique in New York – which was to be followed over time by branches in London, Tokyo, Hong Kong, and Paris. Rather like Hermès (see pages 156–57), Gucci profited from post-war consumer culture and the new marketing techniques that were being developed alongside it. The brand's iconic bamboo-handled bag, the 0063, appeared in 1957 and was quickly adopted by the likes of Jackie Kennedy and Liz Taylor. Gucci loafers found their way on to the feet of John Wayne. In 1964, the company produced a silk scarf in homage to Grace Kelly, which she wore in the presence of the paparazzi.

By the 1970s, the brand's distinctive interlocking double-G logo could be seen everywhere, from key-rings and T-shirts to bottles of whisky. But that was just the problem: the enterprise had split into a number of separate fiefdoms, each managed by a Gucci family member. With no logical strategy, licences were signed this way and that, and over the next decade the brand lost direction and prestige. Meanwhile, to the delight of the tabloid newspapers, the internal struggle to wrest control of the business had turned into a thriller, featuring financial mismanagement, denunciations in court and finally murder, when Maurizio Gucci – the last member of the family to run the company – was killed by a hit-man in 1995. His widow, Patrizia Reggiani Martinelli, was convicted of organizing the murder and sentenced to 26 years in prison. History will remember that the scandal almost finished off the Gucci brand for good.

Shortly afterwards, the business was fully acquired by a Bahrain-based investment company called Investcorp, which had already held a 50 per cent stake. At that stage, Tom Ford had already been working as the company's in-house designer for five years, having been hired in 1990 by Dawn Mello, then Gucci's creative director. Born in Texas in 1962, Ford had graduated from Parsons School of Design with a degree in interior architecture. But the subject was not quite to his taste. In the book *Visionaries*, he tells Susannah Frankel, 'Architecture was just way too. . . it was just so serious. Oh my god, the pretentiousness of architecture! So I realized that I was getting more excited every month buying *Vogue* and I thought, you know, this is what I love, this is what I seem to be drawn to the whole time.'

Following his instincts, Ford worked with the New York fashion houses Perry Ellis and Cathy Hardwick before joining Gucci. It took some time for him to make his mark, but gradually his contemporary twist on 1970s designs began attracting critical attention. Ford's interpretation pushed the glitzy, logo-heavy side of Gucci into the background and favoured sophistication, sex and gloss. Crucially, he understood that a brand had to have a singular vision. As well as designing clothes for men and women, he took responsibility for handbags, shoes, accessories, and two new Gucci scents: Envy and Rush. Nothing that the company produced, from an advertising campaign to a store design, went ahead without Ford's approval. 'His great genius was to reconcile creativity with coherence,' says fashion consultant Jean-Jacques Picart.

In 1995, Ford hired French stylist Carine Roitfeld and photographer Mario Testino to overhaul Gucci's advertising. It became brazen, sexual, even shocking. Celebrities and opinion-formers noticed the change and adopted the brand – and with them, of course, came the wider public. Almost bankrupt when Ford came on board, Gucci is now the lynchpin of a group with annual sales of around €2.5 billion, of which Gucci itself brings in more than half.

CLIMBING OUT OF A TRENCH

One of the British companies that has 'done a Gucci' most successfully is Burberry. Although it has experienced image problems in the UK (see Chapter 2: Fashioning an identity), its achievements should not be underestimated.

The history of Burberry is fairly well known. Thomas Burberry opened his outfitters in Basingstoke, Hampshire, in 1856. It was a modest concern until his sons joined the business in the 1880s, when it opened a second store, in London, in partnership with a company called RB Rolls. During this period, Burberry perfected the woven waterproofed yarn known as 'gabardine', which proved perfect for rainwear. The fabric caught on, and Burberry was soon exporting to the rest of Europe, as well as North and Latin America. An outlet in Paris opened as early as 1909.

The company's most significant breakthrough came when it was asked to provide rainwear for officers during the First World War; the item it came up with became known as the 'trench coat'. If anything, this iconic garment became even more popular after the war, sported by explorers, plain-clothes policemen, and members of the public with secret dreams of heroism. Thomas Burberry & Sons was floated on the London Stock Exchange in 1920. Four years later, the famous black, white and red check made its first appearance as a raincoat lining.

When Thomas Burberry died, in 1926, his second son Arthur Michael Burberry continued to run the business, remaining at its helm until the early 1950s. By the time the company was acquired by Great Universal Stores (GUS) in 1955, its raincoats were considered classics, having been worn by Humphrey Bogart and Ingrid Bergman in *Casablanca*. (It's hard to reconcile Bogart's hard-bitten screen persona with an interest in fashion, but there you go.) Audrey Hepburn later wore one in *Breakfast at Tiffany's*. The brand rumbled along through the 1960s and 70s. In the 1980s, under chief executive Stanley Peacock, the company multiplied its licences. This had the old, all-too-familiar effect of increased sales in the mid-term, but a long-term degenerative impact on the brand.

The 1990s began badly for a weary and outmoded Burberry. Its umbrellas and raincoats did well with Japanese businessmen who admired British style, but elsewhere its trademark check was no longer considered a guarantee of quality. More than 30 licensees worldwide had plastered the Burberry name on everything from watches (in Switzerland) to whisky (in Korea). In order to boost profits the company was selling its goods in bulk to cut-price Japanese 'grey-market' retailers, who undercut the prices charged by classier outlets. When the economic crisis in Asia robbed Burberry of its most lucrative market, its finances plunged into turmoil.

Stanley Peacock retired as chief executive of Burberry in 1996. A year later, GUS recruited Rose Marie Bravo from Saks Fifth Avenue as Burberry's new CEO, hoping she would be able to breathe life into the ailing brand. Briskly, controversially but effectively, Bravo took the matter in hand. She cut off the supply to the Japanese grey market, which had the immediate effect of causing Burberry's sales to slump even further. GUS was advised by analysts to sell the brand – but its management bravely waited to see what Bravo could achieve. She reined in distribution, renegotiated licences, closed a number of small stores and gave the important ones a spiffing Britpop makeover. In the mean time she recruited a new design team, headed by Roberto Menichetti (he was succeeded by Christopher Bailey in 2001). Menichetti launched the upmarket Prorsum range of womenswear (the name derives from the company's Latin motto, and means 'forwards'), which soon garnered positive reviews.

Through print advertising, Kate Moss and a host of other fresh British faces brought an unexpectedly rebellious, streetwise image to the brand. Consumers were intrigued – and what the advertising promised, the stores and the designs delivered. Burberry had not just been repositioned, but 're-imagined'. In March 2001, it announced that its sales had nearly doubled, to £425 million, while profits had tripled to £69.5 million (Adbrands.net, April 2004). Alongside men's and women's apparel, its range now includes accessories, fragrances, children's clothing and household objects. Burberry has shown, once again, that it was possible to bring a brand back from the brink.

THE ART OF PLUNDERING THE PAST

But that was just the beginning. Following in the slipstream of Burberry and Gucci, a whole host of brands have emerged from the cobwebs of history. Almost every week, it seems, we hear of another venerable label that has been given a facelift and a new suit of clothes, and then wheeled out to meet the shopping public. And the strategies are eerily similar.

In France, the luxury accessories maker ST Dupont has been re-launched with some familiar ingredients: overhauled 'concept' stores in Paris, Tokyo and Hong Kong, a flashy advertising campaign, and a new range of men's ready-to-wear. Previously, Dupont was known mainly for expensive pens and cigarette lighters – although the brand has elements in common with the likes of Vuitton and Hermès, having been launched by Simon Tissot Dupont in 1872 as a maker of luxury luggage. Later, in the 1930s, it developed a technique for applying Chinese lacquer to metal, producing a range of objects that fused Eastern ancient with Western modern. After the war, it concentrated on luxury cigarette lighters, and by the 1970s it was the reference in that market, taking a 70 per cent share. It branched out into pens, watches, eyewear and fragrances. Its first venture into clothing came in 1989, but by the beginning of the new millennium it was considered a dinosaur. Sales and profits faltered. Now, company president William Christie says that Dupont wants to reposition itself as 'a global lifestyle brand in luxury goods for men of today' (st-dupont.com, November 2004).

Dupont is by no means alone. We've already heard about the resurrection of Asprey (see Chapter 5: The store is the star), and other great British brands have also emerged from the wings. Take Mulberry, for instance. The accessories and clothing brand is unusual in that, even though it was founded in 1971, it seemed superannuated almost from the start. It was only in 2002 that CEO Lisa Montague finally decided that the doddery granny drastically needed a Burberry-style makeover. She hired designer Nicholas Knightly (who had previously worked at Ghost), and he proceeded to knock Mulberry into shape by eliminating frumpiness and adding British eccentricity. The result was an odd but alluring blend of vintage and modern, as if Quentin Tarantino had decided to film an Agatha Christie novel. 'I think of a big house in the country with chests of overflowing drawers,' Knightly said. 'You may not have the house in the country, but you can have the dress to swan about in it.' ('A Very British Coup', *The Guardian*, 23 October 2004.) Perhaps not surprisingly, Knightly has since been lured away to design leather goods at Louis Vuitton.

An equally successful transition was managed by Scottish knitwear company Pringle, for ever associated with diamond-patterned sweaters and golfers. The brand's adoption by soccer 'casuals' (read: 'thugs') had edged its status further down the road to decline. Almost bankrupt under its previous owner, Dawson International, Pringle was bought by Hong Kong millionaire Kenneth Fang for just £5 million in 2000. By 2003, sales were running at more than £100 million. 'Pringle is the new Burberry', raved *The Guardian* (24 September 2003), as the brand took the previously unimaginable step of rolling out a collection during London Fashion Week.

The turnaround was attributed to the skill of chief executive Kim Winser, previously the only female director of Marks & Spencer. Winser observed that in the 1950s and 60s Pringle had been 'an amazing, glamorous brand', and noted that advertising images from the period featured curvaceous 'sweater girls' in Pringle jumpers. In a stroke of genius, the sexy British model Sophie Dahl was recruited as a modern-day sweater girl for an advertising campaign. A revamped store in London's Sloane Street was opened by the actor Ewan MacGregor, cleverly summing up the brand's new formula of Scottish roots meets contemporary glamour. By chance, at about the same time celebrities like Catherine Zeta Jones, Robbie Williams and Geri Halliwell had begun taking up golf as a hobby; Pringle's most embarrassing association suddenly became an attribute.

Winser also had an incredible advantage in the shape of designer Stuart Stockdale, who had worked with the likes of Jasper Conran, upmarket US retailer J. Crew and Romeo Gigli. Stockdale's collections enhanced positive elements like the diamond motif and the brand's association with luxury cashmere, while running roughshod over its dullsville recent past. He showed items such as cashmere twinsets in searing fuchsia pink, strapless lemon yellow vests worn with bikini bottoms, pastel-coloured coats, sweaters made of chiffon, and cashmere knickers with buttons up the front. 'What's so exciting about it, from a technical point of view, is how innovative the company has been since it was set up in 1815,' he told *The Scotsman*. 'It started initially as an underwear company then progressed from under to outer garments and that's really how the twinset was invented in the 1930s, so it's a very interesting evolution.' ('Check mates', 9 June 2003.)

Pringle's return to grace was so remarkable that in 2003 Winser was voted Europe's third most successful businesswoman by *The Wall Street Journal*. Helpfully, she later shared some rebranding tips with the *Financial Times*. 'I think probably the most important thing is to understand the brand's personality,' she explained. 'With these brands you have to feel as passionate about the heritage as about the future. Secondly, you have to decide what is at the heart of the brand: Burberry has the raincoat, we at Pringle have our cashmere and knitwear. . . I also think it's absolutely fundamental at the early stages of taking on a brand to involve all your team – your immediate senior team, your management. . . suppliers. . . If they totally understand the vision they'll help you to achieve it. Obviously, you also have to focus on what people are spending their money on, and you have to work on your PR: if you're going to be making changes, people have to understand your changes.' ('Textbook Changes', 7 May 2004.) Winser has since gone on to work her magic for venerable British rainwear brand Aquascutum.

Of course, not all brand revamps can be as successful as those described above. Certainly, the image of Church & Co, the classic English shoe brand that Prada snapped up in 1999 – only to sell again in 2003 to a Luxembourg-based investment fund called Equinox – doesn't seem to have budged. Perhaps its owners are waiting for the right moment. Or maybe, once in a while, a retro brand with an unimpaired reputation for quality is best left alone.

15

Targeted male

'Men don't buy fashion – they buy clothes.'

Sean Connery, Michael Caine and Steve McQueen. Cary Grant and Humphrey Bogart. Maybe a hint of James Dean and early Brando. Sinatra when he was recording for Capitol. Al Pacino in *Scarface*. The guys from *Reservoir Dogs* and *Pulp Fiction*. These are the sort of men we would like to emulate, if we had the looks or the charisma. We can, at least, aspire to the clothes – which is why adult men's fashion tends towards the conservative. Most of us don't care what the male models on the catwalks are wearing; we'd much rather resemble our icons. And so, in offices and on the streets, men's fashion barely changes from season to season. A button more or less, double- or single-breasted, the colour of a shirt, the width of a tie or a trouser-leg – but that's about it. We wear suits and coats and jeans and T-shirts.

In the United Kingdom, market researcher Mintel notes that, with a total market value of £7.22 billion in 2003, the menswear sector is equivalent to only 49 per cent of womenswear sales (£14.87 billion). This proportion has remained unchanged for the last decade. In terms of distribution, women have a choice of up to four times as many stores as men. Mintel's report adds, 'It is also worth remembering that the increased popularity among men of casual clothing over formal, both for leisure and in some cases for work, may also have contributed in small part to slower value growth than would otherwise have been the case, given... the reduced volume sales of items such as suits and ties.'

Things are evolving, however – slowly and infinitesimally. At least men are paying attention to their appearance these days. They're more interested in cut and colour; they go to the gym; they buy hair gel and moisturiser. They have even been known to go shopping unaccompanied. It may sound ludicrous, but this is all quite new.

'VERY *GQ*'

In the opinion of Dylan Jones, the editor of British *GQ*, '[Men] are certainly less sophisticated consumers of fashion than women. When you look at the menswear industry in Britain, it's only about 20 years old. And when you look at the men's magazine industry, it's about 17 years old. This generation of men is the first that has been acclimatized to spending money on fashion. It started with the rise of style magazines in the 80s, when men started seeing images of themselves projected back at them for the first time. Suddenly you were looking at pictures that resembled you, rather than a model. And this, combined with the rise of menswear in Britain – which was basically kick-started by Paul Smith – made it a very exciting period for men's fashion.'

Jones speaks from experience, having edited the influential men's magazine *Arena* in the 1980s. *Arena*, a deeply stylish publication showcasing the organic graphic design of Neville Brody, was the first men's style magazine I ever saw. It was also the first time that I became aware of brands like Armani, Cerruti and, yes, Paul Smith. (But my favourite cover was still the one of Michael Caine, shot by David Bailey back in the 1960s.)

The men's magazine market has evolved considerably since then, and there are now titles serving almost every sector, from the blue-collar publications once known as 'lad mags' to the niche and sophisticated *GQ*. Jones notes with humorous pride that *GQ* has been pegged as one of the few magazines serving the 'metrosexual' market – a faintly derogatory term covering men who have more in their bathroom cabinets than a Bic razor, Gillette shaving cream, cheap aftershave and deodorant.

'Men who buy *GQ* are buying into a certain world, just as the women who buy *Vogue* are buying into that world,' Jones observes. 'Fashion is part of it, but we're also covering cars, sex, food, travel. . . In any case, it's fair to say that men don't buy fashion, they buy clothes. If you go to the collections twice a year to see what the men's fashion designers are up to, it's really just a question of tweaking. One year sportswear might be more prominent, the next tailoring. It's very difficult to reinvent the wheel every six months with menswear. *GQ* readers are probably more interested in fashion than the readers of any other men's magazine, but men in general are not as obsessive about the changing nature of fashion as women can be.'

Paradoxically, this opens a window of opportunity for fashion brands, which – if they prove their worth – can land very loyal male consumers. Jones observes, 'Men are concerned about status and they like to be confident. So if they feel good in a certain item, if their wife or girlfriend approves, and it gets a nod of appreciation from their colleagues, they're likely to go back for more.'

This explains the continuing success of Armani and Paul Smith. One might also add Hedi Slimane, formerly at Dior Homme, to the small pantheon of designers that have been enthusiastically embraced by men. With his sleek, skinny black suits that armour the body like a carapace, the rigorous Slimane was yang to that other Dior superstar John Galliano's yin. The svelte young designer joined Dior Homme from Yves Saint Laurent in 2001, and could realistically claim to have made men smarter, hipper and more dashing. His friend and adviser Jean-Jacques Picart says, 'There is an almost military discipline about Hedi's suits. They are designed in such a way that it's impossible to slump when you're wearing them. You have to hold yourself straight, or they don't look right.' Another fan, Karl Lagerfeld, is said to have embarked on his famous diet, not only for the overall health benefit, but also so that he could wear Slimane's whip-thin ensembles.

Picart adds, 'Hedi brought a sort of sensuality to the metallic and the graphic. There's nothing curved or soft about his designs. It's a dramatic contrast to the absolute glamour that Galliano is providing for women. A Dior woman could never live with a Dior man. Bernard Arnault [who hired both designers] created equilibrium via opposites. He delivered the extreme for both sexes.'

Slimane left Dior in early 2007 – apparently after a disagreement about his contract – but it's doubtful that the world of menswear has heard the last of him. He was replaced by another interesting designer, Kris Van Assche, who worked in Slimane's design team at Dior before launching his own brand. Van Assche offered new possibilities, with his blend of gangster chic and hip-hop references, as well as his liking for *trompe l'oeil* details: a tie that turned out to be part of a collar, two waistcoats that were actually one. Hard to top Slimane, though, who through his work at Dior created an entirely new male silhouette.

Another cult name in menswear is Ozwald Boateng. With his Savile Row heritage and trademark bright silk linings, Boateng makes every man look like John Steed, the indomitable hero of *The Avengers*. Both Boateng and Slimane have outfitted their fair share of icons: the suits of the former have been sported by the likes of Sir Mick Jagger, Robbie Williams, George Michael and Keanu Reeves, while Slimane dressed Alex Kapranos from the rock band Franz Ferdinand, Sonic Youth's Thurston Moore, and the singer Beck. In a market where consumers take their cues from their idols, the celebrity connection is perhaps even more important than it is in the women's fashion arena.

This explained the presence of Adrian Brody, the Oscar-winning actor, in a successful print and poster campaign for Ermenegildo Zegna. Although Brody was by no means an obvious choice, he incarnated a certain intellectual grace that fans of Zegna appreciated. In any case, the brand was already an established favourite among well-heeled, well-dressed males.

Michelangelo Zegna put down the roots of the business in Trivero, Italy, at the end of the 19th century. For the first few years it was a small-scale fabric producer, but then Michelangelo's son Ermenegildo began importing luxurious wools – fine merinos, vicuñas and cashmeres – from Asia, South America and Australia, in order to compete with the dominant English and Scottish textile markets. The firm established a reputation for providing the softest and most sumptuous fabrics, and by 1938 Ermenegildo Zegna was exporting to more than 40 different markets. Even today, the family continues to supply fabric to brands that it should, by rights, consider rivals.

Ermenegildo's sons, Aldo and Angelo, led the expansion into ready-to-wear in the 1960s, having understood that tailors were a vanishing breed. Today the label has nearly 400 stores around the world and turns over €600 million a year. As well as ready-to-wear and tailored suits, it sells accessories, a sportswear line and a fragrance. But the quality of its fabrics remains the key to its brand identity. To underline this fact, each year the company weaves its finest wools into an almost mystical yarn, with which it makes no more than 50 suits. These can be bought for €8,000 each – and there is always a waiting list. Each purchaser's name is hand-sewn into the lining. A further cry from tracksuit bottoms and football shirts is difficult to imagine.

FINE AND DANDY

But while it's easy to portray guys as a bunch of slobs whose idea of dressing for dinner is to change their socks, there have, of course, always been trends in men's fashion – and even some people who subscribe to them. The basic form of today's suit can be traced back to the 19th century, when the English gentry were proud landowners, spending a great deal of time outdoors. Anglo-Saxon style, therefore, was practical and pared down, and basically descended from riding gear. Simplicity was the order of the day – ostentation was considered bad form, if not downright suspect. The men's clothing of the late 19th and early 20th century was the sartorial equivalent of a stiff upper lip. Austere though this style may have been, it set the standard for the Western male, and ensured that Britain led the field in the textile sector.

Le style anglais was undermined in the 1920s by the Americans, who began experimenting with a new style of relaxed fashion. Voluminous trousers, short-sleeved tennis shirts, soft-collared shirts worn without ties, relaxed suits that could be worn all day. . . these developments were shockingly new. In addition, the electric razor, invented in 1928, meant that more men were shearing off their moustaches and beards. The template for the 20th-century male had been set.

American influences dominated the 1940s and 50s, as well. The young *zazous* of Paris, with their over-long jackets and greased-back hair, looked like cartoon versions of Chicago gangsters. Fashion historian François Baudot observes that the scene was closely linked to jazz, swing and the jitterbug – possibly the first example of a youth trend that combined music and dress. It was taken to extremes in the various forms of dress codes associated with rock and roll, from the timeless white T-shirt, leather jacket and jeans to the Teddy Boys, those sartorial throwbacks who took their cues from Edwardian costume. For those who didn't fit into the strange new category of 'teenager' – a creation of post-war consumerism and marketing – inspiration was to be found in Italy, with its sharp suits and Vespas. The film *Roman Holiday* (1953), starring Gregory Peck and Audrey Hepburn, still looks like a fashion plate.

It is difficult to summarize the 1960s, a period in which men's fashion seemed to go into overdrive. This was the time when ready-to-wear took the high ground, and the concept of personal tailors appeared to have been relegated to the past. While some men clung doggedly to a more classic look, it was generally a time of rejection and invention – wear anything, as long as it's something your father wouldn't have been seen dead in. The experimentation continued into the following decade, an era of androgyny and excess that made the generation gap seem far wider than a mere 20 years. The growing influence of Milanese designers was apparent in the dance-floor sheen of disco, but the Brits, doing rather better out of the deal, had saved themselves by embracing punk rock.

The term 'punk' (which derived from prison slang meaning 'delin-quent' or 'worthless trash', with catamite undertones) had been current since the early 1970s in the United States, where it was associated with the low-tech garage rock thrashed out by the likes of Iggy & the Stooges, the New York Dolls and, later on, The Ramones. In the United Kingdom, though, punk rock was a pure creation of marketing. It owed its genesis to Malcolm McLaren and Vivienne Westwood, who ran the Sex store in London's King's Road. McLaren was a former art student who had been inspired by 1960s radical politics, notably the Situationist movement in Paris. Westwood, meanwhile, had moved on from making clothes for die-hard Teddy Boys to something altogether more original, running up quasi-fetishist garments daubed with arcane political slogans.

Both McLaren and Westwood were well versed in subculture and understood the mechanics of the media. In order to give Sex a live, physical presence, McLaren brought together the Sex Pistols as a promotional vehicle for the store. Key to the band's runaway success was the energetic presence and aggressive sartorial style of John Lydon, with his green hair and ripped, safety-pin-adorned T-shirts. At the time, Britain wallowed in deep recession, and punk provided the perfect outlet for its unemployed, disaffected youth, who literally spat frustration. With McLaren's management, Westwood's designs and the Pistols' own anarchic enthusiasm driving it, punk rock took off. As McLaren had calculated, an outraged mainstream media was delighted to cover the phenomenon. By the time the Pistols split, in 1979, they had spawned dozens of imitators and spearheaded a movement that traversed Europe and the United States.

By the mid-80s, however, it seemed as though punk had never happened. An economic boom meant that Wall Street brokers became the new fashion avatars, with their double-breasted suits, shoulder pads and wide ties. Movies and even literature provided archetypes: Gordon Gekko, as portrayed by Michael Douglas in the movie *Wall Street* (1987); and Sherman McCoy, the callow yuppie anti-hero of Tom Wolfe's bestseller, *The Bonfire of the Vanities* (1988). Like a slightly later book, *American Psycho* (1991) – also a critique of yuppie culture – *Bonfire* obsessively cited the brand names of its characters' clothes. The conceit was designed to highlight the materialism of the age – but it also provided a handy shopping list.

The following decade saw the inevitable backlash. Sportswear, which had been gaining ground at the tail end of the 80s, thanks in part to the hip-hop community, elided almost completely with mainstream fashion – the two sectors are now virtually indistinguishable. A mass rejection of yuppie values led to an inevitable relaxation of workplace dress codes. For a while, it looked as if the suit might disappear for good. But classics are never entirely suffocated by trends; the suit not only made a return, but did so in its most elitist and luxurious form.

A TAILOR-MADE OPPORTUNITY

When Carlo Brandelli took over the venerable Savile Row tailor Kilgour, French & Stanbury, he already had one of the greatest fashion icons in cinematic history on his side. The tailor made the suit that Cary Grant wears throughout the Hitchcock film *North by Northwest* (1959). Whether he is being pursued by a malicious crop duster or seduced by Eva Marie Saint, Grant remains impeccably smooth; and so do his threads. Brandelli also discovered that Kilgour had made suits for Rex Harrison. Unfortunately, a fire in 1982 destroyed the patterns, almost taking the building with them. Despite this disadvantage, Kilgour is once again a reference for the sartorially discerning.

Brandelli – his heritage, as one might guess, is Italian – always had an eye for the bespoke. Growing up in Parma and Milan, before moving to London, he recounts that he was surrounded by tailors and craftsmen, and learned many of his skills directly from a generation whose lifestyle seemed to be in peril. It was almost inevitable that he would become a designer.

In 1992, at the age of 24, Brandelli launched a menswear brand called Squire, based in a former art gallery in Clifford Street, Mayfair. Working with the art director Peter Saville and the photographer Nick Knight – both legends in their own field – Brandelli invented what he terms 'a new visual identity and language for a contemporary menswear brand'. The idea was to create a world where art and fashion collided. It worked so well, he recalls, that the brand was soon dressing celebrities in both the entertainment and design fields.

Eventually, though, the tide turned – Squire spawned too many imitators, and Brandelli grew disenchanted with the mainstream fashion business. He became a freelance designer for brands in Japan and Italy before arriving at 8 Savile Row, the home of Kilgour, French & Stanbury, in 1998: 'The move was born out of a craving to go back to my roots, to rediscover tailoring. It was only when I got here that I realized it had this chic, cinematic reputation. As well as dressing stars like Cary Grant and Rex Harrison, it had worked with Tommy Nutter [the maverick tailor of the 60s and 70s], so it had always been a forward-thinking firm.'

Secretly, though, Brandelli yearned to run his own business – and to make his mark, once again, on men's fashion. He didn't know whether it would be possible to take over Kilgour, but, as he says, 'I asked the question, and the answer turned out to be "yes".' He acquired the business with a group of backers in October 2003, with the ambition of creating a 'luxurious, elegant, English menswear brand'. He adds, 'I didn't want to return to the past – I wanted to bring the past back to life in a contemporary way.'

In reality, bespoke had been moving back into favour for some time, thanks to a new generation of tailors led by Timothy Everest, Ozwald Boateng, Mark Powell, John Pearse and Richard James. They had already attracted the attention of fashion editors and stars; Everest, for example, outfitted Tom Cruise for the film *Mission: Impossible* (1996). In short, through skill and luck, Brandelli found himself in the right place at the right time.

The brand name was shortened to Kilgour, and Peter Saville's design studio re-drew the logo. But this was by no means the least of the changes. The elegant 1920s Portland stone façade of the premises was renovated, while the interior was overhauled to Brandelli's speci-fications by interior architects Cenacchi, who had also worked on stores for Yves Saint Laurent and Chanel. 'One of my inspirations was the French architect Jean-Michel Frank. I wanted a combination of minimalism and art deco,' explains Brandelli. 'I felt that the brand identity should take its cue from the look of the store.'

So what is the brand identity? Brandelli feels that it is a contemporary look at what he calls 'correct' British style: 'I was under the impression that the traditional English look had been usurped by the French and the Italians, so to a certain extent I wanted to bring it back home.'

Just as a Scot and an Irishman provided the best incarnations of that very English agent, James Bond, perhaps it takes an Italian to show the Brits how to dress. Brandelli says his trademark suit is single-breasted and charcoal grey. 'It's a look you can wear any time. I also like the idea of a garment whose history you can trace in its design.' He adds that the 'correct' colour palette for the English male is charcoal grey, navy, white and sky-blue. Anything else smacks of the trendy. 'Men have a conservative approach to clothes. They often live difficult and complex lives, with a lot of stress, so in clothing they look for simplicity. I also think that many of them have become resistant to being spoon-fed with marketing imagery. They like to make their own choices, which is where bespoke comes in. They can be part of the process.'

Nevertheless, Kilgour was obliged to devise some marketing imagery of its own. Brandelli turned once again to Peter Saville and Nick Knight. The resulting image was a suited figure reflected in a circular mirror on a plain floor. The suit-wearer's face was not visible, but we could tell from his nonchalant pose and the way he lightly held a pair of specta-cles that he was distinguished. 'Nick's idea was to play on the theme of narcissism, hence the mirror,' says Brandelli. 'We didn't want to be overt or obvious. We also wanted to avoid showing the man's face: we felt that our target customers would put themselves in the picture. Overall, we wanted an image that suited our clientele. They are well travelled and creative. They are thinkers.'

Customers can have suits hand-made on the premises, if they are willing to pay more than £2,400. Other suits are cut by Kilgour and then assembled off-site. This keeps the cost down to around £1,500. The method gives aspiring males access to cutting-edge Savile Row tailoring and a contemporary British fashion brand in one affordable package. 'Even my prices,' says Brandelli, 'are correct.'

As a result, Kilgour is now considered one of the most influential British fashion brands. But quite apart from being a re-branding case study, the transformation of 8 Savile Row suggests that men's clothing is reflecting an overall trend: the search for the unique. Retaining the services of a tailor has become a statement of independence.

GROOM FOR IMPROVEMENT

Even so, men who cherish the idea of a suit made by Kilgour or Ozwald Boateng remain rare indeed, as do those who have developed an iron resistance to marketing. When questioned by the Textile Federation in France, 46.5 per cent of male respondents listed their favourite brand as Levi's, followed by Zara, H&M and Adidas. It's certainly no coincidence that these brands are highly visible and (with the exception of Zara) have large communication budgets.

On a more upmarket level, the German brand Hugo Boss is a male fashion reference to rival Paul Smith and Armani. The original Hugo Boss founded his work-wear garment business in 1923. He died in 1948 and the company has long been out of family hands. Since 1991 the brand has been owned by the Italian group Marzotto (which also snapped up Valentino in 2002).

Boss relies heavily on marketing. Advertising images are created every season at its headquarters in Metzingen and positioned by external agencies, which place an emphasis on international business publications. Like Armani, the brand has a long-standing relationship with the film industry. In addition, since the 1970s it has sponsored a wide range of sporting events, including Formula 1, sailing, boxing, golf and tennis. These are all chosen to 'reflect the values of the core Boss brand: internationalism, perfection, and success' (www.boss.com). Boss has maintained its high profile in the menswear market (it launched womenswear only in 1998) by courting the business community and sticking to time-honoured male values in its communications. Hence it is seen as a 'safe bet', free of ambiguity. Even the revelation in 1997 (by the Austrian magazine *Profil* and *The Washington Post*) that Hugo Boss provided German army uniforms during the Second World War failed to dent the brand's popularity.

Creating brand imagery that appeals to men is a delicate business, according to the fashion photographer Vincent Peters: 'In men's fashion the boundaries are stricter. There's a lot of sensitivity around issues of sexuality. Many American brands, in particular, are fearful of projecting an image that might be considered too gay. The other problem for the photographer is that masculinity is a more psychological concept than femininity. I would argue that it's easier to capture femininity visually.' This explains the frequent use of established male role models as brand reference points.

One important area of male fashion is the wrist-watch, a man's most prominent accessory. Watch brands have also had recourse to male icons, including the late Steve McQueen for the Tag Heuer Monaco. According to Dylan Jones, 'Watches play a similar role for men that shoes and handbags do for women; although a watch is often a much larger investment. It's obviously a status symbol. You may not have the suit you want, the car you want, the woman you want... but you can have a great watch. It says something about your taste, as well as expressing your personality and your aspirations. When you think about it, men have far fewer ways of communicating those things: we can't really do it through our hair or our shoes or our bag, so the watch becomes a communication tool.'

If men's fashion is still a growing industry, then skin products for men – often referred to as 'grooming products' – have barely registered on the radar. 'The sector is in its infancy,' confirms Dylan Jones. 'We're buying skin products, but nowhere near as many of them as we will in the future.'

Researcher Datamonitor predicted that men's usage of personal care products in Europe and the USA would grow from US$31.6 billion in 2003 to US$37.6 billion in 2008. Its report, Evolution of Global Consumer Trends (2005), suggested that 'role anxiety' among men was becoming more apparent, with pressure on them to look younger and fitter at work. Among European and US men, the report found that 73 per cent of men felt that spending time on personal appearance was 'important or very important' to them.

But the market is still very much focused on personal hygiene, which covers almost 70 per cent of sales. More sophisticated products such as anti-wrinkle creams, while growing in popularity, have yet to make a significant impact. This puts Jean-Paul Gaultier's Tout Beau Tout Propre line of cosmetics for men at the farthest side of the cutting edge.

In Dylan Jones's view, 'Make-up for men is never going to be enormous, but it's certainly going to be bigger than it is now.'

Moisturized, wrinkle-free, blemishes disguised and wearing a bespoke suit – say hello to the 21st-century man.

16

Urban athletes

*'One of our greatest successes was to get sports shoes
and apparel out of the gym and on to the street.'*

The obfuscation begins very soon after you have made contact with
one of the sportswear brands. 'I'm not sure how much we can help
you with your book,' says a European spokeswoman from Nike, with
whom I am not officially having this conversation. 'You see, Nike isn't
really about fashion, it's about sports. Our focus is on technology.'

The chat that isn't happening is taking place in a loft-style open-
plan space called the Nike Studio, tucked away in an obscure corner
of Paris. I had trouble finding it, because the exterior is discreet to the
point of enigmatic. The only indication that it belongs to Nike is a single
Swoosh, no bigger than the radius of your palm, beside the door. There
are other outposts of the Nike Studio in Milan, London and Berlin,
and similar concepts in Los Angeles and New York. They are used
for product launches and achingly hip multimedia events designed to
federate young opinion-leaders around the Nike brand. Nike describes
them as 'a meeting point between culture and sport'. The company
doesn't talk about them much, because it wants to keep them exclusive.
It all sounds suspiciously like fashion branding to me.

On the other hand, it's true that most sports brands occupy a very
different place in the fashion universe from, say, Yves Saint Laurent.
While designer labels shy away from mass communication, brands such

as Nike and Adidas retain the services of global advertising agencies and use the full gamut of promotional tools, from costly TV campaigns to guerrilla marketing. Nike, the leading name in the market with an estimated 35 per cent share, has a turnover of more than US$12.3 billion a year. Its annual spend on advertising is around US$300 million and rising (Adbrands.net). Add sponsorship and endorsement deals into the equation, and the figure tops US$1 billion. The figures mustered by the designer brands are minuscule in comparison. But sportswear is a commodity. While designer brands are keen to retain their air of elitism, it's fair to say that Nike has much more in common with McDonald's than it does with Chanel.

My friendly but anonymous spokeswoman disappears back to base, having assured me that 'a senior Nike marketing executive' will respond to my questions by e-mail.

Here is my first question: 'When did sports shoes and other sportswear start crossing over to become streetwear? Did Nike and its competitors encourage this, or was it a creation of the street itself?'

And here is the answer, from Phil McAveety, vice-president of marketing for Europe, Middle East and Africa: 'Our approach has always been based first and foremost on the product. If a product does not perform, there is a problem. Performance technologies have therefore always been at the heart of Nike, right back to when Bill Bowerman and Phil Knight founded the company, and Bill Bowerman took his wife's waffle iron and poured rubber into it to make an outsole for a running shoe. . . This quest for functional innovation has never stopped and the company has been synonymous with product innovations.'

The response may not be the one I was looking for, but it certainly tells us a lot about the positioning Nike has established in order to market its products. Tom Vanderbilt's excellent *The Sneaker Book* (1998) observes, 'Statistics routinely claim that roughly 80 per cent of athletic-shoe wearers will not use them for any kind of sporting pursuit. Still, sneaker companies strive to have top athletes as their standard-bearers and work to develop technologies that sound reasonably advanced, yet make sense to the consumer.'

Vanderbilt points out that sportswear companies have sound economic reasons for taking this approach: 'The image of athletic integrity can imbue an entire line with a positive aura; a "fashion" perception, meanwhile, can spark a trend or draw new customers, but is perceived as risky in the long term.'

Nike's stance is a shining example of this philosophy. Adidas, the second-largest brand in the market, has flirted with fashion more overtly; Puma has fully embraced it. In any case, whatever the sportswear companies might claim, their products are a key element of fashion. All of us wear sports shoes – to work, to clubs, to pubs. They are collected and cherished. They are status symbols. Their wearers have occasionally been shot dead for them. Sports shoes have become an integral part of our lives – and sportswear has developed alongside them. To find out how this happened, we need to go back more than 150 years.

GETTING ON TRACK

At school, we used to call them 'plimsolls'. It was a wonderfully onomatopoeic word, evoking the squeak of rubber on a gymnasium floor. Later on, when we got older, they became 'trainers'. Americans call them 'sneakers' or 'kicks'. In France, they're known as *baskets* (italics obligatory), because of their association with basketball. In historical terms, at least, we British kids got it right the first time. According to Vanderbilt, in 19th-century England the soft shoes used for tennis and other lawn sports were nicknamed 'plimsolls' because the line bonding sole to upper resembled the mark on a ship – named after the British parliamentarian Samuel Plimsoll – indicating correct cargo weight.

The sports shoe was made possible by the American inventor Charles Goodyear's 'vulcanization' process, patented in 1839, which involved mixing rubber with sulphur and heating it. This transformed sticky, easily malleable raw rubber into a substance that was both flexible and impervious, springing back into shape when bent. The early 20th century saw the launch of two sports-shoe brands: Reebok, produced in England by Joseph Foster from 1900, and Converse, founded by Marquis M. Converse in Massachusetts in 1908. In 1923, the Converse All-Star shoe became associated with semi-professional basketball player Charles 'Chuck' Taylor. In addition, Taylor was a salesman for the company, so he was able to tour the States demonstrating the shoes and selling them at the same time. These days, sports stars are not expected to go on the road and physically sell the products they are associated with, although the principle remains the same.

Also in the 1920s, the term 'sportswear' was already beginning to enter the fashion lexicon. In the United States, items previously associated with tennis and yachting – flannel trousers, short-sleeved shirts, jerseys and caps – began to infiltrate everyday wardrobes. For the leisured classes, they expressed nonchalance and liberty. Soon they found their way into the collections of designers like Chanel and Schiaparelli. To this day, many designer brands include a 'sport' line in their range.

In general, though, sportswear brands grew out of the early sports-shoe market. The leading names have proved as resilient as the soles of their products. Adidas can trace its roots back to 1926, when the brothers Adolf and Rudi Dassler established their sports-shoe business in Herzogenaurach, Germany. In 1928, their shoes were worn by athletes at the Amsterdam Olympics. In 1936, track and field champion Jesse Owens won four gold medals in them. (The black athlete famously scuppered Hitler's plans to use the German games as a showcase for 'Aryan' superiority.)

At the outbreak of war, the brothers' factory was commandeered for the manufacturing of army boots. While Adolf Dassler struggled to keep a hold on the family business, Rudi joined the army, eventually being captured by the Allies. He was repatriated in 1947, by which time his brother was doing a brisk trade providing boots to the occupying US army. The pair's wartime experiences are said to have caused the split that pushed them to go their separate ways. Adolf (Adi) created the Adidas brand (from the first syllables of his given and family names) while Rudi founded Puma. The two brands became fierce rivals.

While Puma struggled for years, Adidas went from strength to strength, eventually dominating both soccer and the Olympics. Its success on the football field stemmed from its development of the first boots with screw-in studs, which provided better control, and were worn by the West German team during the 1954 World Cup. By the 1960s Adidas was the only global sports brand, having expanded smoothly into sports clothing, bags and equipment. In 1970, its branded football became the official ball of all international tournaments – a position it has yet to relinquish.

At around the same period, the sports shoe was continuing its slow evolution into lifestyle accessory, first as an accoutrement of rock and roll, then as a cooler alternative to stiff traditional footwear. The movie industry, as usual, helped. Tom Vanderbilt points out that the Jets and the Sharks of *West Side Story* (1961) were clad in sneakers. Later, he adds, Dustin Hoffman wore them to the office in the film *All the President's Men* (1976).

The 1970s was the decade when jogging came to the fore as a leisure activity, helping to nudge sportswear further into the mainstream. It was a market in which Puma's products proved especially popular, enabling it to gain ground on Adidas for the first time. But trouble had materialized for both brands in the form of a brash young upstart called Nike.

Phil Knight, a former member of the University of Oregon track team, started out selling Japanese Onitsuka Tiger running shoes from the back of his car. While still at university, Knight had written a paper describing how the market dominance of Adidas could be broken by importing lower-cost sports shoes from Japan. He teamed up with his former coach, Bill Bowerman, to set up Blue Ribbon sports. With the Tiger shoes selling reasonably well, the pair opened their first retail outlet in 1966. Five years later, wanting more control over his inventory, Knight paid a design student called Caroline Davidson US$35 to come up with a logo that he could put on shoe boxes. 'I don't love it, but it will grow on me,' he said of her 'swoosh' design.

However, as Nike's website is careful to set straight, the pair's collaboration didn't end there. Davidson continued to work for the company until it hired a full-time advertising agency. Later, she was presented with an envelope containing Nike stock. 'How much stock remains a secret between Knight and her,' the site adds (www.nike. com/nikebiz).

The Swoosh would begin its rise to omnipresence when Andre Agassi won the men's tennis championship at Wimbledon in 1992. Nike had been experimenting with baseball caps and other clothing that bore the logo alone, dispensing with the brand name. Pictures of Agassi wearing just such a cap appeared on front pages around the world, creating an instant trend. Nike's designers quickly became conscious of the fact that the Swoosh transcended language barriers – it was the perfect global branding device.

Knight and Bowerman ended their deal with Tiger and began making their own trainers in 1972. Their first shoe, the Nike – named after the Greek goddess of victory – proved such a hit at the US Olympic trials that it prompted them to change the name of the company. Another early success was the waffle trainer, born out of the anecdote recounted earlier. By 1980, when Nike went public, the company had snatched more than 50 per cent of the American sports-shoe market. The strategy of delocalizing production to Asia had enabled it to undercut Adidas's prices. And in a foretaste of technological claims to come, Nike also promoted an air-cushioning system, designed by a former NASA engineer, which supposedly gave the wearer extra bounce. Nike's rivals were squeezed between the pincers of cheap labour and expensive branding – although it didn't take them long to catch on (see Chapter 21: Behind the seams).

The market changed for good in 1984, when Nike beat Adidas to sign up basketball star Michael Jordan to wear its shoes. Tom Vanderbilt explains his appeal: 'Freshly bedecked with Olympic gold, likeable and telegenic, Jordan seemed capable of delivering basketball to the entire country. With this possibility in mind. . . [his agent] was able to wring from Nike the largest basketball endorsement then signed – roughly US$2.5 million over five years.'

Nike Air Jordans entered sports-shoe mythology. In 1987, Nike's advertising agency Wieden & Kennedy launched the 'Just do it' campaign. Combined with Jordan's charismatic presence and a series of high-impact TV ads – diffused by an ever-expanding international media – the slogan turned Nike into a global brand. The company was the first to blend MTV-style imagery, pop music and sport, creating a real buzz when it set a commercial to the Beatles song 'Revolution'.

Vanderbilt adds, 'From Jordan on, the creation of a persona with strong, readily identifiable characteristics would be as important to the shoe companies as it was to the NBA. Since most basketball-shoe consumers did not play basketball, the shoes clearly had an appeal beyond their functional attributes – a fact that shoe companies were slow to pick up on, but then pursued with abandon.'

The 1980s were as unkind to Adidas as they were kind to Nike. Adi Dassler had died in 1978, at the peak of his company's success, and his son Horst had taken over the running of the business. Adidas now found itself locking horns not only with Nike, but also with British outsider Reebok, which was gaining market share in giant strides. Reebok proved particularly adept at spotting and capturing the emerging aerobics market, which even Nike had failed to anticipate due to its male-oriented, sports-star culture.

Horst Dassler died in 1987 and the Adidas company was bought by French entrepreneur and politician Bernard Tapie. Tapie soon became embroiled in a corruption scandal, and he was forced to let go of the ailing sports brand. In 1993, crippled by debt, Adidas found itself in the hands of the French bank Crédit Lyonnais. It was bailed out by Robert-Louis Dreyfus, former chairman of the advertising agency Saatchi & Saatchi.

With an ad-man's flair for enhancing brands, Dreyfus slowly nursed Adidas back to health. He restructured the company, closed expensive European production plants, and placed the design emphasis back on the three-striped logo and accompanying 'trefoil' device, which had been inexplicably abandoned. Over the past few years, the brand's three-pronged strategy has focused on professional sports footwear, consumer-oriented sports heritage ('vintage'-inspired styles), and fashion, hence its partnerships with Yohji Yamamoto and Stella McCartney (see Chapter 2: Fashioning an identity). While it still lags behind Nike with worldwide sales of about US$5.5 billion, Adidas has none the less achieved a phenomenal comeback.

Difficult though it may be to believe, Nike has also had its share of ups and downs. The 1990s began promisingly enough, with the opening of the first Niketown superstore, selling the full range of clothing and shoes, in Portland, Oregon. It signed up an unbeatable team of celebrity endorsers – including, in 1995, Tiger Woods – and moved aggressively into soccer, a sector strongly associated with Adidas, by setting up a sponsorship deal with the Brazilian national team. Then, unexpectedly, Nike was hit by a triple whammy. In 1998, France symbolically beat Brazil in Paris in the World Cup. During the same period, the press was filled with stories criticizing labour practices in Asia, where workers in appalling conditions were paid minuscule sums to make shoes that sold for over US$100. Proof that Nike shoes were more about fashion than sport came when youngsters began abandoning them in favour of sturdy work boots. Sales in the United States plummeted, and when the Asian economy stalled, Nike was hit by another broadside.

Nike was not prepared to lie down and die, however. It made highly publicized efforts to clean up its Asian production issues, it reshuffled its management team, and it modernized and streamlined its distribution process. When Michael Jordan retired from sport in 2000, Nike refocused on the consumer, with brand communication stressing that even an everyday slob could be a hero. This strategy also enabled the brand to place more emphasis on its apparel, something it had viewed purely as a second-string business a few years earlier. While it still retained the services of athletes such as the basketball star LeBron James (signed up in 2003 for a staggering US$90 million, according to press reports), its award-winning advertisements – 'Tag', 'Musical Chairs' and 'Hotdog' – featured ordinary people, whose Nike footwear gave them an edge in urban environments. As a key line on Nike's website reads, 'If you have a body, you are an athlete. And as long as there are athletes, there will be Nike.'

There will be Converse, too. In summer 2003, Nike snapped up the 95-year-old footwear brand for US$305 million. Converse had dominated the basketball-shoe market from the 1920s to the 70s, but by the end of the 1990s it was regarded as little more than a charming relic: low-profile ownership, zero celebrity endorsement, no flashy advertising, and minimal sales. The company filed for bankruptcy in 2001 and was briefly acquired by private investors before being sold to Nike.

The news upset remaining Converse fans, because its 'All-Stars' shoes had traditionally been seen as the footwear of the American counter-culture, having been passed down from the early rockers to The Ramones, Nirvana, and a whole new generation of black-wearing, guitar-clutching wannabes. The fact that Converse had failed to keep pace with modern marketing or design initiatives only endeared it to these rebels. Discovering that Nike had bought Converse was 'like hearing Elvis Costello had started writing jingles for Microsoft', wrote Rob Walker of online magazine Slate. But, with low-tech retro styles back in fashion, Nike had made a typically deft move, buying itself a slice of history. 'Converse really does have an authentic heritage, and the company is smart to make that a selling point,' Walker admitted. ('What's up, Chucks?', www.slate.msn.com, 15 September 2003.)

A few months after the purchase, Converse released an advertising campaign narrated by the rapper Mos Def. The shoes were seen on famous feet, and fashion editors began to write about how they'd been wearing Converse for years. In the background, those in the know could hear the roar of a marketing machine getting into high gear. Before long, the shoes were everywhere again.

Nike owns other brands, too, including Nike Golf, Bauer Nike Hockey and, most surprisingly of all, smart formal-shoe brand Cole Haan, which it acquired more than 15 years ago.

In December 2004, Nike founder Phil Knight stepped down as head of the company after 32 years, bringing an era to a close. Although he remains chairman, he was replaced as president and chief executive by William Perez, the former chief executive of S C Johnson & Son, a company best known for furniture polish. Under Knight's watch, the humble sports-shoe market had been transformed into a global multi-billion-dollar industry combining elements of sport, entertainment and fashion. 'He created an entire industry [of sports merchandizing] basically on his own,' commented Marc Ganis, president of Sportscorp Ltd, a Chicago consulting firm, in *The Washington Post*. 'By and large he's made athletes richer, he's made athletic footwear and athletic clothing a luxury item, and he has turned a small company in Oregon. . . into an international goliath.' ('Father of Nike, marketing guru, gives up post', 19 November 2004.)

EXPECT A GADGET

Take a look at the following comment from Phil McAveety, VP marketing EMEA at Nike: 'Because of what they stand for. . . products can sometimes become iconic. For example, the Dunk made its debut in 1986. . . The Dunk was designed specifically with the awe-inspiring basketball move after which it is named [in mind]. It features a unique low-profile sidewall that reduces weight to enable players to focus on their game. The concentric-circle-patterned forefoot with flex grooves incorporates maximum traction for better grip, flexibility and ease of rotation during pivoting. The Dunk. . . went on to inspire other product developments in sports outside basketball, like skateboarding.'

The key to the comment lies in the language: 'Concentric-circle-patterned forefoot with flex grooves incorporates maximum traction for better grip, flexibility and ease of rotation.' It's a typical example of the techno-speak that sportswear brands, particularly Nike, use to seduce consumers. Even though we're only going to wear our sports shoes to the supermarket, we could, if we wanted, make a leap for that cereal packet on the top shelf.

According to Tom Vanderbilt, 'Athletic shoes are to other shoes as sports utility vehicles are to other cars: large, loaded with impressive but rarely-used options, a statement less of need than of desire.'

Phil Knight's oft-quoted comment that 'the design elements and functional characteristics of the product itself are just a part of the overall marketing process,' originally made to *The Harvard Business Review* in 1992, clearly still holds sway.

Despite the mind-scrambling jargon used to describe the shoes, technological advances basically amount to little more than adjustments in weight and cushioning. But experts have determined that cushioning might actually be bad for runners, as if they're constantly struggling against soft sand, ultimately damaging their knees. Help is at hand, though, because Nike has come full circle with a product called the Nike Free. It's a shoe that – wait for it – mirrors the advantages of *running with bare feet*. Or, as McAveety puts it, 'mimics the benefits of barefoot training'. He adds, 'It's an amazing development that took many years of research and will challenge the way we think about footwear.'

One's mind reels at the presumptuousness of the idea: sports shoes that feel like you're not wearing shoes at all. But you pay for them, all the same.

STARS AND STREETS

Two trends that were prominent in the late 1980s and early 1990s – sports shoes without laces and oversized jeans worn so low that the wearer's underwear waistband is visible – have something in common. They were both started by criminals. When you're flung in jail, you're forced to hand over your belt and your shoelaces, in case you feel like committing suicide in your cell, or maybe strangling one of your cellmates. Since a spell in the joint was considered mandatory by many rappers, the style became a sign of fellowship.

This kind of cool, hard, urban imagery was useful to sports-shoe companies – but at the same time they couldn't be seen to be placing too much emphasis on it. Tom Vanderbilt writes, 'As companies targeted the urban market, they were also reaching out to certain segments of the suburban market that, in a twist on the aspirational brand theory, often emulated the tough, urban culture beamed by satellite to the most pastoral settings. For the shoe companies it was a tightrope... The shoes had to be "black", but not "too black".'

Sports companies sent 'cool hunters' into the grimmest districts of American cities to find out how their latest shoe designs were being received. Other executives were encouraged to distribute free shoes to influential youth groups. But the urban audience and their heroes had already made up their own minds. Free of white establishment associations but imbued with status, kicks were an established hip-hop accessory, a trend underlined in 1986 by the Run-DMC song 'My Adidas'. The band was later repaid for its unofficial promotional work by being invited to sign a sponsorship deal with Adidas. In 1989, a pair of white Air Jordans played a key role in Spike Lee's slice of urban cinematic poetry, *Do the Right Thing*.

By the end of the decade, the association of sports shoes with street culture was getting out of hand, with media reports of urban teenagers being slain for their expensive branded shoes. Along with claims that, in Asia, children were being paid peanuts to make sportswear, the stories contributed to a brief downturn in the sector's fortunes.

Today, though, trainers are back on top – and the urban market remains crucially important. Generally, sports-shoe brands have found that the most effective approach is to target icons, and then let the influence trickle down. Adidas, for instance, has established relationships with personalities as varied as David Beckham, Missy Elliot and The Beastie Boys. But the brand is equally skilled at more oblique approaches. It has a 'global entertainment and trend marketing department' that is responsible for non-traditional branding. An article in *The Independent* explains: '[The department's] educational, permissive approach to communicating the brand and its heritage takes many forms, ranging from localized ambient campaigns, such as the step-risers outside the South Bank that immortalized the Olympic medallists around the Sydney Games of 2000, to shop window displays at Savile Row's Oki-Noki on the evolution of the Predator football boot. The aim. . . is to assist discovery of details about the brand, rather than to directly coerce consumers into parting with their cash.' ('Stars in stripes', 13 December 2004.)

In the same article Gary Aspden, the brand's global head of entertainment promotions, says that the idea is to 'look at ways to communicate the brand to a more fashion-minded, design-oriented consumer'. The piece also points out that, as a result of his pioneering work in the field, Aspden is considered one of the 100 most influential people in fashion.

And fashion, in theory much disliked by the sports brands, has been the saving grace of Adidas's traditional arch-enemy, Puma. Although the brand's sales, at €1.3 billion, are a fraction of those of its competitors, Puma (this week, at least) has an enviably cool image. 'One of our greatest successes was to take sports shoes and apparel out of the gym and get them, at the same time, on to the streets,' the brand's CEO, Jochen Zeitz, told French magazine *Le Point* (*'Puma: le fauve en forme'*, 2 September 2004). He added, 'Today, the sports shoe. . . is an indispensable fashion accessory.'

Puma even has a chimerical name for its strategy: 'Sportlifestyle'. When Zeitz took command of the company, at the age of 30, back in 1993, the brand had changed its leadership four times in two years. After he had radically overhauled the enterprise – closing several factories and slashing staff numbers by as much as 36 per cent – the operation went into profit, the very next year, for the first time since 1986. Over the last decade, Puma has managed to differentiate itself from its competitors by charging higher prices, creating regular limited editions (only 888 pairs of its collectible Shudoh Tang shoe were ever made), and pulling models off shelves before they become too widespread. It has also rolled out a global chain of concept stores. Its decision to sponsor the Jamaican Olympic team – a group which managed to be cool, idiosyncratic and talented at the same time – for the 2004 Athens games was typically smart. Similar thinking lies behind its decision to develop strong links with the world of motor sport, a sector that had remained under-exploited by sports-shoe brands.

But more than anything, Puma has unhesitatingly pushed the fashion button. For both its clothing and footwear, it has collaborated with designers such as Jil Sander, Neil Barrett – formerly of Gucci and Prada – and Philippe Starck. It launched a line of yoga wear, Nuala, in association with the supermodel Christy Turlington. In addition, Puma's range of urban wear, 96 Hours, designed by Barrett, aims to combine sporty ruggedness with pan-European chic. (The sub-brand takes its name from the duration of the average business trip.) In 2003, a series of non-product print ads, called the 'Hello' campaign, was shot by fashion photographer Juergen Teller. The light-hearted, apparently candid images were calculated to provide an impression of quirky accessibility – marketing that pretended it was not marketing.

Puma, the David of sports-shoe brands, has challenged its Goliath-like competitors by adopting some of the characteristics of a designer label: elitism, iconoclasm and artistry. Jochen Zeitz says, 'Our clients are individualists who like to distinguish themselves from the mass.' This is one sports-shoe company that would certainly not wish to be compared to McDonald's.

17

Virtually dressed

'It's a fashion magazine where you can click to buy the things you like. What could be more fun than that?'

It does not seem so very long since the heady days of the dotcom boom, when swathes of young internet entrepreneurs were transformed overnight into the new yuppies, drunk on venture capital and conspicuous consumption. Drunk on vodka and Red Bull, too, at the parties I used to attend in London while covering the scene for a media magazine. It was the first time I'd met company directors who were younger than me – and more decadent. One article described the sector as driven by 'three Cs: caviar, champagne and Concorde'. Then it suggested throwing cocaine into the mix, too.

Like all great times, it couldn't last forever. I'm probably not the only one for whom the collapse of Boo.com was the definitive sign that the party was over. Although I'd only observed it from a distance, Boo seemed to be the ultimate dotcom. It was run by a bunch of good-looking young people who appeared on the covers of magazines, it sold urban fashion, and it had millions of dollars' worth of backing.

There wasn't quite enough backing, though. Boo collapsed through lack of funds just six months after it had launched. According to reports at the time, 'Boo fell apart after investors failed to stump up an additional US$30 million' ('Top web retailer collapses', BBC.co.uk,

18 May 2000). This was pretty shocking, given that the company had already managed to burn through some US$120 million from investors such as Bernard Arnault of LVMH, Benetton, and the investment banks J P Morgan and Goldman Sachs.

Boo's failings were many, but they can be summed up as 'over-ambition'. With offices in London, Stockholm, Paris and Munich, it aimed to be a global brand from day one. It spent a fortune marketing Miss Boo, the online character who would help customers navigate the site and choose their clothing. The distribution and tax issues that came with trying to dispatch items across the globe tied the company's management in knots for months. Even more crucially, although the site itself looked great, it was too advanced for the technology that most of its target customers were using. The company wasn't doing nearly enough trade to cover the cash it was spending. In addition, like many start-ups of the era, Boo had become 'as famous for its sybaritic lifestyle as for its. . . attempts to sell urban sportswear over the web' ('From Boo to bust and back again', *The Observer*, 26 August 2001).

According to the same article, Boo's liquidators sold its technology for about £170,000, and its brand name for roughly the same sum. Its founders, Ernst Malmsten and Kajsa Leander, became consultants and regular public speakers, having recovered from their virtual rollercoaster ride.

THE SUCCESS STORY

Malmsten and Leander were, quite simply, ahead of their time. Fashion addicts now regularly buy clothing over the web – via eBay. Various sources suggest that the auction site now makes around US$2 billion a year from clothing and accessories alone. Certainly, it is considered an essential hunting ground for rare and collectible items. It even has its own online fashion magazine, Personal Style.

But there is at least one fashion-specific e-commerce service that deserves our attention. It's called Net-A-Porter, and despite its virtual status the British Fashion Council recently voted it the best shop in the country, selecting it from a list of possibilities that included Asprey and Matthew Williamson. Surprisingly, it was launched around the same time as Boo.com.

Net-A-Porter's founder is Natalie Massenet, an American fashion journalist. She was West Coast editor of *Women's Wear Daily* before moving to London in 1986, when she joined *Tatler*. She recalls that, foreshadowing later events, 'when I wrote an article telling people to buy something, I always wondered how many of them actually went out and bought it'. Now she knows, because her website, deliberately designed to look like an online fashion magazine, has an estimated 300,000 customers, with an extra 1,500 coming on board every month.

Massenet says the spark of inspiration that led to Net-A-Porter came when she left *Tatler* in 1998 to go freelance: 'I went online for the first time, to research a piece, and it was a revelation – I was instantly hooked. Being a girl, I wondered whether there was anything I could buy. I was surprised to discover that it wasn't really possible. There were a few American brands online, but they weren't shipping outside the States. And the design of the sites wasn't so great.' At that point, says Massenet, 'the online community was largely male. Now fashion is one of the largest categories in online retail, and there are more women than men online.'

With the seed of an idea growing in her head, Massenet had lunch with several key people in the fashion business to sound them out about the potential of an upmarket internet retail site. 'Plenty of those I spoke to told me I was absolutely crazy, but because I like to prove a point, I thought, "Right, I'm going to do it anyway." I picked up a brochure called "Are You an Entrepreneur?" from Barclays Bank and ticked all the boxes.'

Choosing a name proved surprisingly difficult. '[The site] was originally going to be called "What's New Pussycat?". But my lawyers naturally advised against it. I went to the *Women's Wear Daily* site and in the dictionary of fashion terms I found prêt-à-porter. A light went off, but for days I thought it was too good to be true. I kept turning the idea around in my mind. And then I woke up one morning thinking, "What am I doing? Of course it's got to be Net-A-Porter!"'

Once the brand name was in place, the look of the site came into focus. 'It was such a great, classy brand name that I felt we had something to live up to. The site should deserve the brand. So it would be upmarket, global, black rather than pink, simple but elegant. I was convinced it would work, because we were just beginning to see the globalization of fashion: women in New York and Hong Kong wanted the same jeans from Chloé and the same bag from Dior.'

Around the same period – by now we're in 1999 – Massenet picked up a copy of the *Financial Times* and read about the launch of something called Boo.com. Her heart sank, just for a moment. And then she thought, 'Well, you know, there's more than one store in a city.'

The site was launched in June 2000 by five women with no experience in retailing – although they did know about finance, technology and fashion. The initial investment was £190,000 from a selection of family and friends. At launch, the site offered 35 of the hottest fashion brands.

'As we were all women, we based the service on what we'd want it to be. We were our target customers. That's why we designed the site to look like a fashion magazine. We didn't see why we had to make it more complicated than that, when it was a format that our customers loved. Even today, we've stuck to editorial iconography. It's a fashion magazine where you can click to buy the things you like. What could be more fun than that?'

One criticism of fashion on the web is that it robs designer brands of one of their key selling points – the brand experience. When you're not buying your expensive shirt in a sleek retail hub attended by gorgeous staff, is it worth the same amount?

Massenet says, 'We took care of that by providing our own brand experience, which is the service. In a way it's quite revolutionary, because the internet tends to be associated with discounting and no-frills. But this is a luxury service, offering not last season's fashions, but next season's fashions. And you should see the gorgeous packaging it arrives in. Today, the one true luxury is time. And we save you time by enabling you to shop 24 hours a day.'

When the site was being conceived, Massenet and her colleagues would sit around for long evenings, discussing the details of the offering. 'We'd be shrieking and saying, "Wouldn't you just *die* if…", or, "Wouldn't that just make you *cry*…." Basically, there was a lot of shrieking and dying and crying. We launched the business in a frenzy of happiness, and I think a lot of that communicated itself to the consumer.'

These days, the original core of five staff has expanded to over 100. The site ships products to more than 50 countries – on the same day in

London, within 72 hours to Europe, the United States and further afield. Taxes and duties are calculated in advance by a proprietary system, so the customer only pays the price indicated on the site.

Interestingly, Massenet says the site sells more clothes than accessories. But what about the size issue – surely that presents problems? Massenet says, 'If something doesn't fit, Net-A-Porter will come and pick it up from you, at our expense. Of course we realize people want to try things on. The difference here is that you get to try it on at home.'

The fact that Net-A-Porter is thriving long after the collapse of Boo. com, the interloper that gave Massenet such a fright back in 1999, justifies her simple, understated approach to thc web. 'I think Boo would still be here today if they'd had a smaller team and less money at the beginning. They were under a lot pressure to go public in six months, and there was a lot of hype. We've only started getting media attention in the last 18 months.'

With the Boo case study now losing its relevance in the face of success stories such as Net-A-Porter, traditional fashion retailers may soon have to face up to competition from the web. 'They're building huge flagship stores in cities all over the world, a strategy that costs them billions of dollars,' says Massenet. 'We're saying you only need one store, and you can get people from all over the world to come to you – a much more efficient way of doing it. Think about it: what would an alien think if you explained the concept of a fashion store to him? "You have to get dressed, drive somewhere in your car, get undressed in front of a bunch of strangers, try something on, then get undressed again. . . ." Our way is much less stressful.'

INTERACTIVE CATALOGUES

And Net-A-Porter is by no means alone. Other fashion retail sites are springing up across the web, from eluxury, Yoox and Chic-N-Unique, right through to Walmart.com, which has reintroduced its apparel category after abandoning it a couple of years ago. Amazon. com launched an apparel and accessories section in November 2002. Forrester Research estimates that the online retail market will be worth US$316 billion by 2010.

Nicole Heidemann, the e-commerce director of web-based fashion and trends service WGSN, says there are simple reasons for this expansion: 'The most obvious one is that people are much more at ease with the web than they were in the era of Boo.com. And of course there has been the arrival of broadband, which means you don't have to wait ages for a picture to download, as you did not so long ago. This in turn has led retailers to design more imaginative and attractive sites. A lot of people who might have been catalogue shoppers before are now turning to the internet.'

This theory is confirmed by Eva Jeanbart-Lorenzotti, who started her own luxury retail site, Vivre.com, as a spin-off from her existing catalogue business. 'I wanted to create another way for people to have access,' she told the *International Herald Tribune*, adding that internet sales would soon outpace the catalogue. ('Online luxury comes of age', 10 August 2004.)

Luxury brands, surprisingly, are in a good position to take advantage of the web, says Heidemann. 'A large percentage of their customers are in high-powered jobs which mean they don't have time to go shopping. Convenience is a major selling point for the web. These sites also provide advice, and edit the vast range of fashion choices down to the most essential items.'

Unlike the vast majority of glossy magazines, the sites may also provide a valuable means of expression for up-and-coming designers. 'Yoox, which is based in Milan, makes a point of promoting young designers it thinks are interesting. As most sites combine retail with journalism, they can offer the best of a store and a fashion magazine in one interactive package,' explains Heidemann.

Net-A-Porter's Natalie Massenet believes her former employers, the glossies, will have to compete more effectively with their online rivals: 'Fashion trends are speeding up. The internet is the only medium that can keep pace, while the glossies still have three- to four-month lead times. Over time, their only choice will be to evolve into big, beautiful coffee-table books.'

Certainly, the most innovative things in fashion media are happening on the web. Apart from neoteric online magazines such as Hint and Into the Storm – cannily published by the Storm modelling agency – there is photographer Nick Knight's genre-bending SHOWstudio. The site was launched in November 2000 as an online space enabling creatives to present interactive and mixed-media work. As the site itself explains, it has developed into 'a high-profile fashion broadcasting initiative with over 200 contributors including Kate Moss, Hussein Chalayan,

Alexander McQueen, Björk, Julie Verhoeven and Yohji Yamamoto'. Get any hipper than that and you implode. For the mere spectator, SHOWstudio is an electronic tapestry of fashion news, cutting-edge design, experimental film, and interviews with leading industry names. The latter are increasingly broadcast live – and free of charge, to boot. In addition, the site has its own studio space where staffers and invitees stage live fashion-related events, from straightforward runway shows to surreal performance art. It's probably no exaggeration to suggest that SHOWstudio is the fashion medium of the future. (*Tank* magazine is also part of this evolution, having launched Tank TV, a subscription film site.)

But while journalists, photographers and free-wheeling designers seem determined to push ahead, there is evidence to suggest that the mainstream fashion brands are lagging behind. Few of them offer a comprehensive online shopping service – as Massenet discovered way back in 1998, they can't deliver across borders – and many of them don't even seem to know how to tackle the medium. Trapped between the dual necessity of appealing to customers and providing corporate information for reporters, investors and job-hunters, they end up fulfilling neither function effectively. The typical result is a jumble of Flash animation and ugly downloadable PDF files.

A survey by New York branding consultancy Brand Keys (www. brandkeys.com) in late 2004 highlighted the issue. It stated that, while most fashion brands understood the power of a pretty picture to sell their product, they got stuck when they were obliged to make that picture interactive. According to the survey, many top fashion retailers failed to communicate their image effectively over the web – and even risked generating negative attitudes among consumers. The consultancy hinted that fashion brands took a rather snobbish attitude towards the internet, regarding it as a 'below-the-line' medium, akin to junk mail, or merely a tedious necessity. Which is a shame, because the internet is actually a 'high consonance' brand-enhancing vehicle – meaning that it has a high impact among upmarket consumers, like cinema and niche cable and satellite TV channels.

The Brand Keys survey questioned 1,500 women about 15 fashion brand websites. Brands whose sites were rated positively included Armani, DKNY, Nike, Gap and Ralph Lauren. Those that were thought to undermine the brand included Versace, Dior, Levi's and Wrangler.

The results were almost duplicated in a study released the same year by Ledbury Research, a British organization specializing in the luxury market. Having analysed the sites of 25 luxury brands, Ledbury found them, almost without exception, 'slow and difficult to navigate'. Gucci, which offered an internet shopper, and Louis Vuitton, which provided advice via an instant messaging service, were highlighted as exceptions. Ledbury pointed out that the luxury brands were missing a trick, as affluent consumers were 'three times more likely to spend more than £250 on a single purchase than mainstream consumers, and more likely to recommend good sites to friends'. ('Luxury brands need online strategy', WGSN News Service, 11 June 2004.)

Since that time, however, there have been signs of improvement. Despite their almost paranoid need to retain control over every aspect of their brands, some designers have begun outsourcing their web operations. Armani, for example, appointed Yoox to create its online boutique. The process was not a smooth one, however, as Giorgio Armani himself oversaw the project and wanted to ensure that the site captured the luxurious experience of shopping at the brand's flagship store in Milan. 'Mr Armani wasn't satisfied with the results and sent back the early drafts with changes. He wanted the site to look three-dimensional, and he wanted a spotlight to shine on each product as it moved across the screen, a technique used in his stores to impart elegance. Yoox had never used such a visual effect, and it had to invent a new software code.' ('Fashion's Trend: Outsource the web', *Wall Street Journal*, 12 September 2007.) Armani was also displeased with the product images that Yoox planned to use, and demanded reshoots. But he has a sound reason for being so demanding: the internet boutique is expected to become one of his brand's biggest stores within a few years.

In 2007, Louis Vuitton appointed the advertising agency Ogilvy & Mather to inject some modernity into its advertising – and more importantly, into its internet strategy. The brand wanted to recapture its travel heritage, which had become obscured by the images of models and actresses with handbags that have characterized the Marc Jacobs era. The initial result of Ogilvy's appointment was a trio of print ads featuring very different personalities – Mikhail Gorbachev, Catherine Deneuve and the golden couple Andre Agassi and Steffi Graf – on their 'personal voyages'. Seeing Gorbachev cuddled up to a Vuitton bag was a little surprising, but other than that the ads seemed perfectly banal

– even a touch retrograde, although they were immaculately shot by Annie Leibovitz.

The online element was far more unusual. A series of microsites could be accessed from the main Louis Vuitton homepage. Through a beguiling blend of photography, narration and music, each personality featured in the advertising campaign shared their personal vision of a favourite city, transporting the user on a magical voyage with them. The fact that the microsites used photography rather than the expected video in this new medium added to their elegance and allowed them to stand out from the crowd. Thanks to Ogilvy, Vuitton had finally found a way of transferring its high-end brand values onto the web.

Other luxury brands are now working hard to decode the web, and it seems unlikely that it will remain a mystery to them for much longer.

18

Rise of the bloggers

'I'm hacking fashion, I suppose.'

Every April, in the verdant grounds of an angular art deco villa not far from Saint Tropez, the French fashion pack gathers to determine the future of the industry. The focus of the event is a series of catwalk shows – held in a tent down on the beach – featuring the work of young designers from fashion schools around the world. In between shows, the hopefuls install themselves in makeshift ateliers and share their vision with buyers, reporters and, most importantly, a judging panel that will later award the festival Grand Prix. Alongside the fashion competition is a parallel category for photographers. The event also embraces seminars, networking – and some pretty fabulous parties.

The Hyères International Festival of Fashion and Photography used to be a rarefied, exclusive event, attended only by the happy few who worked in the industry, wrote for the right magazines, or knew the right people. In recent years, though, a new tribe has been spotted stalking across the villa's immaculately barbered lawns, staking out the best places at the shows and helping themselves to finger food and champagne. They are the fashion bloggers, and they are assailing the elitist world of glossy magazines.

One of them is British blogger Susanna Lau, whose blog Style Bubble attracts more than 10,000 visitors a day. A minor celebrity among UK fashion fans, Lau occasionally gets spotted when she's out shopping. This popularity with everyday consumers is what makes blogs increasingly attractive to brands – and subsequently gains bloggers access to fashion events.

Not that it was Lau's goal when she started out. She's always considered fashion a hobby, and although she did 'a bit of styling for student magazines' at university, she actually studied history. At the time of writing, she works for a digital advertising agency in London. Increasingly, however, she finds herself being approached by fashion brands for styling and consultancy advice. Not bad for somebody who only started blogging in March 2006.

'I was partly inspired by leading fashion blogs like Fashionologie and A Shaded View on Fashion [by Paris-based commentator Diane Pernet],' she explains. 'And I was always chatting with other fashion fanatics on forums like Fashion Spot. I wanted to express myself, and I thought a blog would be a much easier platform than a website. My idea was to get back to the basics of blogging, which is to express a personal viewpoint. Some blogs have begun to approach fashion in a rather cold way, with newsy posts about dresses you can't afford. But I want to raise issues and provoke debate.'

Their provocative, often irreverent, approach to fashion is exactly what made blogs seem daunting to big brands, which were used to the criticism-free environment of the glossies. But readers quickly realized that blogs were an alternative, refreshing source of news and opinion. And smaller designers saw a promotional opportunity: after all, you can't dismiss 10,000 visitors a day.

'As we all know, glossy magazines devote an extremely limited amount of space to designers that don't have an advertising budget,' says Lau. 'On the other hand, I'll enthusiastically support and promote a designer whose work I find interesting.'

In addition, hyperactive bloggers are arguably more in sync with the changeable spirit of fashion than the traditional glossies. Fashion magazines are planned up to three months in advance – a blogger can report on a show ten minutes after the designer has left the runway.

BLOGS AND THE PRESS

The organizers of catwalk shows in London, New York, Paris and Milan all report an increasing presence of bloggers. But their gradual acceptance by the fashion community has also eaten into the bloggers' independent status. Well-known fashion bloggers are now sent gifts, invited to launch parties and taken on press junkets just like glossy magazine journalists.

Some have crossed to the other side on a more professional basis. Lau dabbles in fashion journalism and admits she may eventually take it up full time. Another popular blogger, The Sartorialist – Scott Schuman, who wowed the fashion crowd with his razor-sharp street photography and pithy commentaries – was given his own column in the US edition of *GQ*, after stints taking photographs for the Condé Nast website Style.com.

'I could see from the statistics on the site that they were watching me for a while,' says Schuman, who started his photo-blog in September 2005. 'I think what they noticed was consistency: I wasn't shooting someone with good taste one day and bad taste the next. They also noticed an eye for detail.'

Schuman had an advantage in that he'd already worked in the fashion business for 15 years, including running a showroom for designers. The blog sprang out of his observation that a certain kind of well-dressed male was not represented in men's fashion magazines. 'I'd be out on the streets of New York and I'd see these ordinary guys who nonetheless had a very distinct sense of style. Some of them were quirky; others were wearing beautiful Italian suits. I thought other guys would be inspired by them, but you never saw pictures of them anywhere.'

He initially toyed with the idea of setting up a website, but it seemed overly complicated, as well as requiring a whole team of people. 'It was only when I found out about blogging that the whole thing clicked. This was a platform that was easy to set up, virtually free, and enabled me to express my ideas.'

Less than a year after his blog had gone online, Scott got a call from Style.com, which dispatched him to Milan to take pictures of the guys attending, or merely hanging around, the men's fashion shows. That's when the media really began to notice him, he says. 'I was dressed stylishly, so I didn't look like just another photographer. I didn't blend in. I looked more like a fashion editor with a camera. Before long, people asked me what I was up to, and we got talking. Then one time I was at a Prada show and [*GQ* editor] Jim Nelson called me over.'

As the site evolved, The Sartorialist began to take photos of women as well as men. This broad appeal – combined with media coverage

– drove his site's figures up to 45,000 visitors a day. With Condé Nast handling his ad sales, he began to reap genuine income from the blog. He also signed a book deal with Phaidon, and the James Danziger gallery in New York staged an exhibition of his work. Schuman admits that his rapid ascent has left him slightly breathless. 'I could never have imagined that things would move this fast. To use an English expression, I'm chuffed.'

But he doesn't believe that blogs will one day take over from magazines as the fashionista's medium of choice. 'It's a totally different thing. My photos are a slice of life, while a magazine makes you daydream in another way. But I do think blogs are a great source of talent for the mainstream media. And at the same time, the people who run blogs have a certain amount of power. A blogger who is recruited by a newspaper can maybe negotiate a better contract because they have an audience of thousands of people that they're bringing with them.'

Inevitably, the bloggers who have been adopted by the mainstream fashion press did not ape it, or fantasize about being part of it, but set out to express their own unique visions. Fashion has a vampire-like lust for novelty.

This new collusion between the outlaw world of the blogs and the fashion establishment is generally perceived as a good thing – injecting a much needed dose of fresh air into the industry media. In New York, it helps harassed PRs ensure that fashion shows will be packed out, despite an over-supply of shows and an over-stretched press corps. But it can also create some abrasive moments. In early 2007, media news website Mediabistro reported on a fashion show encounter between blogger Julie Fredrickson – of the site Coutorture – and *Vogue* supremo Anna Wintour. Spotting Wintour 'minding her own front-row business', Fredrickson gamely began to interview the powerful editor. Much to her credit, Wintour politely began to answer the questions – until her publicist appeared and sent the blogger packing. ('Bloggers in tents: fashion warms to new media', 6 February 2007.)

For readers – and, of course, for the bloggers themselves – this new media is another stage in the democratization of the fashion industry, enabling them to pierce the façade of this notoriously elitist business. Even the backstage of catwalk shows is no longer out of bounds to the general public, thanks to blogs like the one begun by Anina, a model. Using her mobile phone, she started snapping backstage scenes, parties and images from her travels and posting them on her blog with breezy commentaries. She's since gone on to create 360 Fashion, a network of blogs from around the fashion industry.

'I blog using my mobile about a hundred times a day because, in my work, I'm absolutely not anywhere near a computer,' she told *Wired* magazine. 'Fashion is a mystery to many people. Now, like voyeurs, they can see what's happening in the industry.' Hardly conforming to the clichéd image of the fashion model, Anina learned how to write computer code at school. 'I like to see how systems work... I'm hacking fashion, I suppose.' ('Le chic shall inherit les blogs', 6 December 2005.)

Understandably, the rise of blogs has inspired many mainstream media to start their own versions. Among the most respected establishment bloggers is Cathy Horyn of *The New York Times*. Horyn noted the rising power of blogs back in 2005, when she wrote: 'Although fashion, like politics, is still an insider's game, with its own addicts and agenda-setting editors, nothing, it seems, can compete with the authentic judgement of bloggers and web viewers.' ('The Paris 6', 28 April 2005.)

Forget 'authentic': a positive judgement is what brands are hoping for when they dispatch a freebie to a blogger – or summon them to an exclusive launch event. Some bloggers are easily seduced. Others, though, are determined to remain outspoken and untarnished. 'I still think my first duty is to my readers,' says Susanna Lau of Style Bubble. 'I was recently invited on a trip to Paris by Chanel, to cover the launch of their latest advertising campaign, but in my posts I was absolutely transparent about what the deal was. I certainly won't accept money from brands for posts, which I know some bloggers do. And although I receive at least 30 e-mails a day asking me to promote some product or another, that's not what I'm here for.'

Apart from a single banner – for Net-a-Porter – she does not yet accept advertising. 'I know I should monetize the site, but as a digital media planner I'm not convinced that a blog is the right place for brands. British readers tend to find advertising invasive and the click-through rate is very low.'

Not all bloggers – or advertisers – share her view. While it's difficult to unearth any concrete figures, anecdotal evidence suggests that a handful of bloggers are making a great deal of money out of advertising. The creator of Manolo's Shoe Blog – who is no relation to designer Manolo

Blahnik – is apparently a 'six-figure blogger'; while an irreverent site called Go Fug Yourself – which lashes dodgy celebrity dress sense – has enabled its creators to give up their day jobs. ('Flashy and tailor-made: rag trade blogs', *International Herald Tribune*, 17 September 2007.)

The market is becoming overcrowded, however, and it's now almost impossible to quantify the number of fashion blogs on the web. In April 2007, the website Fashion IQ compiled a list of the top 50 fashion blogs in the United States, based on unique visitors (audience), traffic (page views) and the number of other blogs that linked to the site (influence). The top five were Go Fug Yourself, Young Black and Fabulous, Purse Blogs, Fashion Tribes and Shoewawa. But the list was inevitably controversial, and it's certain that the hierarchy of fashion blogs has changed many times since then.

Some bloggers have professionalized by becoming part of branded networks run by web media companies. The results resemble online magazines. Yet they don't create, they merely curate. Typical of these is Glam Media, whose network of women-oriented sites is led by Glam.com, an aggregation of fashion, beauty and lifestyle blogs. Officially launched during New York Fashion Week in September 2006, just over a year later its staff had swelled from 25 to 100 and it had become the most popular women-oriented site in the United States, according to ComScore Media Metrix.

Glam's vice-president of product marketing Bernard Desarnauts says: 'Today there's no question that the internet has become an additional form of entertainment. And within this new medium you have a new and authentic voice – the voice of bloggers. It's the voice of the people, if you like. Consumers have no problem differentiating between an "official" medium like a newspaper and an independent voice that's not moderated or edited.'

Glam.com founder Samir Arora noted that many bloggers were evolving into independent publishers: their blogs had become full-time occupations. And yet they were unable to make a decent living out of their work. Glam allows them to do this by placing their blogs on its network and splitting advertising revenue 50/50, based on page impressions. It also works with the bloggers to create microsites and promotional content for brands. All this has changed the lives of many of the site's 400-plus 'indie publishers', as Desarnauts calls them. 'We've got people who were only making two or three hundred dollars a month out of advertising on their sites before – and are now making as much as five thousand dollars.'

In addition, Desarnauts says that Glam is going after big advertisers: 'those who really want to use the internet to build brands, rather than seeing it as a way of getting people to click through to a transactional site'. Based in San Francisco, with a sales and editorial office in New York, Glam is rapidly expanding worldwide.

Its rival is FabSugar, run by San Francisco-based Sugar Inc. In 2006 the company raised investment of US$5 million from investment fund Sequoia. It also has backing from establishment media company NBC. This has enabled it to expand its blogging empire – it bought Coutorture, a network of more than 200 blogs, for an undisclosed fee in October 2007. ('Sugar Publishing buys fashion blog network Coutorture', Paidcontent.org, 8 October 2007.)

More and more bloggers, it seems, are tempted to sell out to this new generation of media companies.

But not Susie Lau, who says, 'It's not my ambition to be bought out. I want to retain control of my blog. I'm more likely to develop it by adding video material. I can use the fact that it's now fairly well known to gain access to exclusive events and report on them. And then I can imagine having a sort of parallel career in mainstream fashion journalism.'

One question that springs to mind when looking at Lau's blog is: how does she find the time? After all, she's posting every day – often more than once – and holding down a full-time job. 'Basically, I don't need much sleep,' she reveals. 'I come from Hong Kong and I think that's part of my heritage. We're always awake. I can get by on about three hours a day.'

Aspiring bloggers, take note.

19

Brave new market

*'China has the potential to become the biggest luxury
goods market in the world.'*

The glowing jade numbers flash up on the screen of the cash register:
615 Hong Kong dollars. Even with my poor grasp of arithmetic, I can
work out that I'm about to pay less than £45 for two pairs of jeans,
a leather belt and a sweater. And far from being a bargain-basement
seconds outlet, the store where this transaction is taking place is part of
a young, modern retail chain called Giordano, which resembles Gap in
almost every respect – apart from the price.

I suspect my label-conscious new Hong Kong friends – who prefer
Dior, Prada and Louis Vuitton – might sneer at the functional Giordano.
But I rather like the idea of buying a brand of jeans that does not exist
back home – we all have our own version of snobbery. In any case,
it's a handy metaphor, as the conflict between cheap clothing from
China and luxury labels from Europe will soon be played out on a
much bigger scale, and it will have a profound effect on the future of
the fashion business.

I'm in town for a luxury branding conference called The Lure of
Asia, organized by the *International Herald Tribune*. Everyone who
is anyone in the luxury business is here: Bernault Arnault of LVMH;
Matteo Marzotto of Valentino; Umberto Angeloni of Brioni; Ferruccio

Ferragamo; Ralph Toledano of Chloé; Santo Versace. . . I could go on. The doyenne of fashion journalism, Suzy Menkes – who is hosting the two-day event – describes the line-up as 'brand royalty', and she is by no means exaggerating.

So what has brought these busy, glamorous chief executives all the way from Europe to Hong Kong? What's the big attraction? Well, let's just say it's no coincidence that this chapter begins with an image of a cash register.

Even more than Shanghai, Hong Kong is considered the gateway to the most important emerging market for luxury brands. There are others, of course, contained within the acronym the fashion industry uses to describe its juiciest targets: BRIC – Brazil, Russia, India and China. But it's telling that, during a conference that is supposed to be identifying opportunities for luxury brands in Asia as a whole, everyone wants to talk about China. Trade barriers have been lowered and the rule that required foreign companies to partner with local businesses has been scrapped, leaving the market wide open. Dickson Poon, the Hong Kong entrepreneur who owns Harvey Nichols, says, 'China definitely has the potential to become the largest luxury-goods market in the world.'

With a population of 1.3 billion and an ever-growing middle class, China makes retailers' pulses quicken and their palms sweat. Poon says that the number of Chinese with the wherewithal to buy mid-priced consumer goods has reached 300 million. The market is already worth an estimated US$550 billion. The new wealth is clustered around Beijing, Shanghai, Guangzhou and Shenzhen; but there are also rich citizens in so-called 'second-tier' cities such as Chengdu, Dalian and Shenyan. And these people frequently travel – not only to Hong Kong, but also further afield. In Paris, luxury stores are advertising for sales assistants who speak Mandarin. China, effectively, is the new Japan.

While retail developments are undoubtedly progressing apace in Shanghai – notably the luxury emporium Three on the Bund – Hong Kong's lust for upmarket brands is dizzying. The fear that accompanied the SARS outbreak in 2003 was nowhere to be seen when Dior opened its two-floor flagship store in Hong Kong the following year, fireworks popping over the heads of local VIPs. Not a sign, either, of the gnawing doubt that lingered after the handover to China in 1997. Today, Western brands cluster around classic Hong Kong shopping districts Causeway Bay and Central like bright tropical fish nibbling a coral reef: Armani,

Prada, Jean-Paul Gaultier, Chanel, Louis Vuitton, Hermès, Tod's. On the waterfront, the soaring IFC (International Finance Centre) is the location of the revamped Lane Crawford, venerable Hong Kong department store turned superbrand paradise.

The fashion titans are using Hong Kong as a base for their push into mainland China. Armani plans to open up to 30 new stores in China by 2008. Prada is reportedly investing US$45 million in the country, opening at least 30 outlets. Louis Vuitton has long been committed to the market. During the *IHT* conference, LVMH chairman Bernard Arnault said, 'We believe we can double in size and profitability over the next five years, because we have taken time to invest in markets with potential.'

Smaller designer brands have also begun looking hopefully at China. In November 2004, a group of French designers including Stéphanie Coudert, Anne-Valérie Hash and Marc Le Bihan embarked on a mini trade delegation to Beijing, with an eye to 'raising their profile and making contacts'. (*'La Chine recrute'*, *Le Figaro*, 30 November 2004.)

China is particularly attractive to elitist brands, because its consumers have not yet developed the cynicism that is beginning to infect shoppers in the west. Bernard Arnault believes China's middle class identifies with European notions of luxury: 'European products still make people dream, whether it's fashion and fancy leather goods from France and Italy, wine and spirits from Bordeaux, Cognac and Champagne, or whisky from Scotland. People from all around the world still flock to the beaches of the Riviera and the slopes of the Alps.'

The Economist notes, 'In China, attitudes to luxury have changed dramatically from just a few years ago, when any form of ostentation was frowned upon. Today's Chinese, above all, love to flaunt their status. . . [They] favour prominent logos that shout, "Look, I'm rich."' ('Luxury's new empire', 19 June 2004.)

When I compliment a friend's charm bracelet over dinner, she tells me not merely that it is 'vintage', but specifically that it is 'vintage Céline'. During the same evening, I ask a group of people if there's a sport that Hong Kong citizens enjoy above all others. They answer in unison: 'Shopping'.

A PROMOTIONAL TIGHTROPE

The likes of Armani, Prada and Vuitton are by no means the first Western brands into the Chinese market. Pierre Cardin has been selling branded goods in China for years, having organized the first fashion show in Beijing in 1993. Hugo Boss opened its first store in 1994 and now has more than 60 outlets there. At a different level, Etam has no fewer than 1,200 points of sale. Esprit, which started life as an American brand, is now headquartered in Hong Kong.

A similar story lies behind a brand called Ports 1961. Unlike Esprit, it is little known in Europe, but it's very familiar to the Chinese. Launched in Canada over 40 years ago, the brand hit hard times in the 1980s, when it was bought by a Hong Kong family. It is now one of the most popular fashion outlets in China, with stores in all major cities.

Alfred Chan, managing director and CEO of Ports Design, has a realistic view of the market. 'China's per capita income is less than US$200 a month in cities – much less in rural areas,' he observes. 'Many of our customers regard our products as a "once-in-a-lifetime" purchase. For this reason, it's very important that we spread the message of the brand as widely as possible.'

This is no easy task. Ports runs poster and print campaigns featuring international supermodels, but fashion magazines in China have a circulation of around 100,000, which, as Chan points out, 'is a drop in the ocean in a market of this size'. So, alongside these activities, it sponsors television broadcasts that some Western consumers might regard as sexist and out of date – tacky, even. The Miss Universe China competition, for example, featured prominent Ports branding. Think what you like about this, but the broadcast reached 25 million viewers.

Dickson Poon agrees that marketing to Chinese consumers is tricky: 'Irrespective of how liberal China may be with its financial reforms, I believe it will maintain strong control over the press and the media for a long time to come. This means. . . one will not be able to buy into the market through effective and appropriate advertising. Therefore, even if the market may not yet be totally ready, the opening of shops may still be the best way to introduce and to educate the Chinese consumers about the image, lifestyle and products of a luxury brand.'

He points out that the Chinese are no strangers to luxury goods: 'Excavations have uncovered gold pendants and earrings dating back to over 3,000 years ago, and luxury products from China, such as silk, would travel west on camel caravans via Persia as early as the seventh century.'

Handel Lee, co-chairman of Three on the Bund in Shanghai, suggests that, with this in mind, approaches to shopping in China are different from those in the west. In his view, 'Aspiring Chinese do not necessarily embrace the ways [foreign] retailers are presenting themselves: it is too formulaic, too condescending. That's why we've designed our space as a sort of art gallery, displaying fashion items as beautiful objects. We're not overtly trying to get our customer to buy an item – we encourage them first to look at it, savour it, and appreciate it. We believe they'll buy something not because of the superficial satisfaction of the label, but because they are in some way touched by it.'

And quality will not go unnoticed. It's worth remembering that the Chinese are skilled at producing fake versions of luxury goods that are, at least to an untrained eye, indistinguishable from the real thing. (For more on this, see Chapter 20: The faking game.)

Simple respect for cultural differences can pay dividends. Recalling his first forays into a similar market, Japan, in the early 1980s, Paul Smith recalls, 'Many people were going into Japan during that period, but their attitude was generally disrespectful. But I went there, personally, and I loved it. I got involved in the culture, I opened an office there. . . and my business was successful because I was good at communicating. We've been in Japan since 1984 and now we have 200 shops there and wholesale sales of £161 million.'

It would certainly be foolish to patronize Chinese consumers, no matter how brand-crazy they might seem. Nike came unstuck with a television spot featuring basketball player LeBron James laying waste to an array of animated combatants, including a white-bearded kung fu master and a pair of dragons – considered sacred figures in China. Chinese regulators banned the ad, saying that its depiction of violence against cultural symbols 'caused great anger among viewers' and that Nike had violated broadcasting rules with its 'blasphemous' disrespect for 'national dignity and Chinese culture'. ('Nike kowtows over LeBron ad in China', *New York Post*, 10 December 2004.) Given the apparent sophistication of Nike's marketing department, it's surprising that they did not see this coming.

Nike, Adidas and Reebok are pushing hard in China in the run-up to the Beijing Olympics in 2008. But Western companies can also assume they will be in competition with home-grown brands. One of Nike's greatest rivals in China is Li-Ning, which sells US$200 million worth of sports shoes a year. It takes its name from its founder, Li Ning, a former gymnast and winner of several Olympic gold medals. Its scything logo is as dynamic as the Nike Swoosh, and its slogan is 'Anything is possible'. Its advantages are that it is a trusted local brand, and that its products are not beyond the pocket of the average Chinese consumer.

In response to the influx of foreign names, Li-Ning has started producing Nike-style products such as the Free Jumper, boosted its investment in marketing, and recruited Chinese athletes for endorsement campaigns. Abel Wu, Li-Ning's marketing director, comments, '[Western brands] have a good image. They have lots of sports stars as sponsors. However, they don't know how to survive in these tough conditions.' ('China shoe firm tries to fit in at home', *Los Angeles Times*, 1 January 2005.)

FROM CHINA WITH CLOTH

Just as sweeping changes to trade regulations have given Western fashion brands unfettered access to China, they have also allowed Chinese textile merchants to import their goods to Europe in even larger quantities than before.

Midnight on 31 December 2004 saw the end of the 30-year-old Multifibre Agreement, a quota system maintained by the World Trade Organization to protect textiles industries in developed countries from overseas competition. China, with its huge supply of cheap labour and easy access to raw materials, was already the world's biggest exporter of textiles before the scrapping of the agreement. Ironically, investment from Western brands has enabled its factories to modernize machinery, increase output and experiment with desirable new fibres. Euratex, the European Apparel and Textile Association, says that since China became a member of the WTO in 2001, imports have soared and prices have plummeted. Now China threatens to dominate the world market, increasing its share from 20 per cent in 2002 to as much as 50 per cent before the end of the decade. India, another large textile producer, also stands to benefit from the end of the quota system, but the change may be devastating for producers in smaller markets, notably Bangladesh

– previously a frequent recourse for importers when India reached its quota limits – Poland and Turkey.

Shortly after the Multifibre Agreement ended, the Chinese government attempted to calm the situation by saying that it would impose its own taxes on exports, charging by volume. This would lessen the bulk of material coming out of China, while ensuring higher quality.

In the meantime, China's competitors would do well to play the quality card. For the time being, the label 'Made in China' does not exactly equal prestige, either in terms of fabric or design. The standards of the latter are set to change, however; several sources in Hong Kong told me that China was luring talented young designers from fashion schools in London and Paris with the promise of a bountiful job market. It may not be long before China is producing its own designer brands.

For Western fashion companies, the situation benefits only those with the strongest brands. Mid-market chain stores are feeling downward pressure on their prices, thanks to the increased availability of cheap merchandise in the form of cut-price casualwear sold in supermarkets. Upmarket labels, however, can continue charging high prices for their name and logo, while reaping the rewards of higher profit margins. At the top end of the market, luxury brands will continue to emphasize their use of local 'artisans' and the finest materials. In other words, they'll employ the same brand-positioning techniques that they'll use to seduce a new generation of rich Chinese consumers.

20

The faking game

'The biggest factory of fakes in the world.'

There are two good reasons to visit the Temple Street night market in Hong Kong. The first is the steamed prawns with garlic sauce and fried noodles at the Tak Kee Seafood Restaurant. The second is to marvel at the vast array of counterfeit branded goods on sale (without actually buying any of them, of course). Bags bearing the Louis Vuitton monogram and the Burberry check are everywhere: lined up in neat rows on aircraft carrier-sized trestle tables, or hanging from hooks on fences of wire mesh. There's plenty of Dior, too; not to mention Gucci, Fendi and Coach. When I finger some 'Omega' watches on one stall, a young man hands me a ring-binder full of photographs – a catalogue of fake luxury timepieces.

There are other markets like this in Hong Kong – and, indeed, in other major Chinese cities – where Western visitors snap up copies of luxury goods, half-hoping that they might pass muster back home. They see it as a bit of fun, one of the obligatory tourist experiences. In the past, I doubt that the sight of all these fakes would have bothered me. The trouble is that, just a few hours earlier, I'd been listening to some of the leading names in the luxury market debating how to stamp out counterfeiting.

The global counterfeit goods market is worth €500 billion a year, according to the International Chamber of Commerce. Interpol puts the figure at US$250 billion. (Both sums are based on what the goods would be worth if they were sold at full retail price.) And the problem is growing. In 2002, investigators seized 85 million articles in the European Union alone. A year later, the figure had topped 100 million.

It's thought that between 80 and 90 per cent of all the world's fakes are made in China. Luxury brands are watching closely for concrete proof that the Chinese government intends to back up its promises to stamp out counterfeiting. Judging by my visit to the night market at Temple Street, any existing crackdown hasn't yet begun to bite.

The previous morning, at the *International Herald Tribune*'s luxury branding conference, I'd heard LVMH boss Bernard Arnault confirm that crushing the counterfeiters is one of his group's biggest challenges. Louis Vuitton has its own anti-counterfeiting squad, and in conjunction with various police forces around the world it claims to have staged more than 4,000 raids in 2004, leading to almost 1,000 arrests. It spends an estimated €15 million a year on its copyright protection efforts.

Arnault stated, 'Counterfeit goods now represent 10 per cent of world trade. Such fakers live off the hard work and creativity of others. As well as working with the police to stop counterfeiting at its source, we are calling on [the media] to send out the message that when you buy a counterfeit product, you are funding crime, misery and hardship.'

As the traditional home of luxury goods, France has long been a victim of the counterfeit trade. Associations such as the Union des Fabricants, established way back in 1877, and the more recent Comité Colbert, founded in 1954 (its glittering list of members runs from Baccarat through to Yves Saint Laurent), have battled to raise international awareness of the problem.

It seems ironic that China, the country that luxury brands so dearly want to penetrate, is causing them such a headache. But in developing countries, high import taxes encourage the production of fake luxury goods. And by marketing their products to consumers who can't afford them, the brands themselves may be exacerbating the problem. A familiar conspiracy theory suggests that, while brands are forced to tackle counterfeiting, they are secretly aware that it has certain advantages: it means that their logo carries a cachet, and the fakes act as moving billboards, all the while provoking a desire for the real thing. This comment is only ever whispered.

During the conference, Tan Loke-Khoon, international partner at the legal firm of Baker & McKenzie – which helps brands to combat the theft of intellectual property – said, 'Counterfeiting can tarnish the image of a brand for ever. Companies need to factor the cost of fighting fakes into their businesses. They also need a strong long-term strategy.'

He described China as 'the biggest factory of fakes in the world'. Counterfeiting had not been a small-scale business for some time, he added. Sometimes, the same factories that produced legitimate branded goods during the day would pump out copies after hours. This rise in expertise has led to the 'super fake', an item almost identical in quality to the real thing. He went on to say that investigators frequently went missing.

Apart from the tourists in places like Temple Street, who's buying all these fakes? Not all the purchasers live in developing markets. According to a report by the WGSN News Service ('Counterfeiting and luxury goods', 20 October 2004), Italy is a major market. The Italian consumers' association Intesa dei Consumatori says the country consumes an annual €3.13 billion worth of fake clothing and footwear. Luxury brands have occasionally sent teams to airports to warn travellers that they will be fined if they return with fake branded goods. But Italy is a production centre, too; counterfeit items made up 20 per cent of all clothing produced in Italy in 2003.

Consumers of fake goods are occasionally innocent dupes. In markets where brands have their own stores, this is rarely the case. In countries where items are sold by third parties, there is less certainty that shoppers are getting the genuine article. But the truth is that most purchasers of fakes know exactly what they're doing.

Interpol says counterfeiting is generally perceived by society as a victimless crime. And it's true that buyers of fakes are often proud of their acquisitions, having got one over on Big Brand. They see it as a form of bargain-hunting. Interpol would disagree, as it says professional counterfeiters belong to criminal organizations that are involved in drugs and prostitution, and may be funding terrorist groups.

The United States has a big problem with counterfeit goods. According to the International Anti-Counterfeiting Coalition in Washington, DC, fakes cost the country's businesses US$350 billion in annual sales. There have been frequent raids on New York's Canal Street, which resembles a black-market bazaar. And yet any visitor to the city will see fake Burberry scarves and Prada bags spread across the sidewalk on blankets, which are swiftly bundled up and whisked away when a cop appears. Such scenes normally take place just a few blocks away from Barney's or Bergdorf Goodman. Elsewhere 'purse parties' have replaced Tupperware parties as a leisure pursuit, with women buying counterfeit bags from dealers and selling them in suburban homes at a profit.

The internet has been a boon for fakers and their customers. As well as sites aimed at those who are looking specifically for fakes, goods are traded over e-commerce and auction sites. Research from internet monitoring company Envisional suggests that, of all spam measured worldwide, 23 per cent relates to the sale of counterfeit goods.

WGSN says counterfeiters have devised various elaborate ploys to send fakes through the mail undetected. One involves camouflaging counterfeit Louis Vuitton bags with zip-up vinyl covers, which can be removed when they reach their destination. Mostly, though, rip-off goods arrive in bulk. In May 2004, Italian customs investigators found 9,000 fake Nike shoes (around €800,000 worth) on a Chinese container ship.

What all this highlights, of course, is the pervasiveness of branding in fashion. Heavily logo-ed items, such as bags from Coach, Gucci, Burberry and Louis Vuitton, seem to be begging to be copied. It's much harder to fake a Bottega Veneta bag, whose authenticity is announced via its supple woven leather rather than any visible logo. (Indeed, the brand's marketing mantra is 'When your own initials are enough'.) Louis Vuitton claims that it seeks to stay ahead of the fakers through constant product innovation, but only a customer with the highest degree of loyalty could keep track of every single model it releases.

The prevalence of fakes is one – although by no means the only – factor that is nudging fashion away from logos. Rather than making any Naomi Klein-inspired gesture, the self-proclaimed stylish have eschewed branded products simply because they are afraid of looking cheap.

For a real fashion snob, God now lies in the details that only initiates can detect. Martin Margiela's labels are simply numbers, although each signifies a specific line. Udo Edling's jackets are identifiable to aficionados via a series of visual codes: one pocket (on the right), darts above the shoulder blades, and the reverse of the collar in Alcantara microfibre rather than in felt (a different colour each season). Let the mass brands and the fakers play their games, these designers are saying to their customers; we'll just keep ourselves to ourselves. Despite the migration of 'luxe' to 'mass' – and vice versa – fashion is still not entirely democratic.

21

Behind the seams

'The shops always need to be full of new designs.
We pull out all the stops to meet the deadline.'

The possibility that their factories in developing markets might be knocking out fakes on the side should be of minor concern to the fashion brands, in the light of a more serious problem. When I told a friend that I was going to write a book about fashion, he asked, 'So what's the angle – gorgeous models; or underpaid women in sweatshops?'

Although the labour issue has been discussed ad infinitum, it is one that no writer on fashion can afford to ignore. Those who have gone before me have done a good job; brands are so worried about the PR repercussions of the word 'sweatshop' that they now have extensive 'codes of conduct', designed to reassure their customers that they are closely monitoring the situation.

The reality is far from edifying, as two separate reports from the anti-poverty and aid organization Oxfam suggest. The original exposés of exploitative labour practices at the end of the 1990s particularly targeted the sportswear companies. Nike and its rivals have since worked hard to give the impression that they are tackling the issue. But Oxfam's report *Play Fair at the Olympics* (www.fairolympics.org) is unequivocal: 'If labour exploitation were an Olympic sport, the sportswear giants would be well represented among the medal winners. Whilst the industry can boast its commitment to some impressive principles, enshrined in codes of conduct, its business practices generate the market pressures that are in reality leading to exploitative labour conditions.'

As with the counterfeiting problem, the labour controversy has been caused by the brands' own marketing strategies. The voracious, constantly changing nature of fashion means that it does not lend itself to heavy mechanization, because the costs involved in updating the machinery would be untenable. What fashion boils down to, then, is lines of women at sewing machines: lots of them. In China's Guangdong province, one of the world's fastest-growing industrial areas, Oxfam claims, 'young women face 150 hours of overtime each month in the garment factories – but 60 per cent have no written contract and 90 per cent have no access to social insurance'.

In Oxfam's report on sportswear, not one of the major brands escapes criticism. In the second report, the garment industry as a whole is eviscerated. Two quotes from *Trading Away Our Rights: Women Working in Global Supply Chains* (www.maketradefair.com) bring the situation into sharp relief. One is a comment from a production planning manager at a factory in Morocco: 'The shops always need to be full of new designs. We pull out all the stops to meet the deadline. . . our image is on the line.' The result, according to Oxfam's report, is a seven-months-pregnant girl working ten hours a day, 'and as she has to make a lot of pieces per hour, her employer won't let her go to the toilet'.

The reports can be dismissed as anecdotal, but they have a ring of truth. At the head of the supply chain are a handful of global, marketing-led fashion brands under pressure from their shareholders to increase sales. The brands have in turn educated consumers to expect a fast turnaround of high-fashion, low-priced garments. With fashion cycles shortening and the demand for new items rising, the brands put pressure on their suppliers to deliver to increasingly tight deadlines. The exigencies of the clients are pushed back down the chain to the workers.

Over the past decade or so, the falling cost of sea and air transportation has made it practical for retail brands to delocalize production to Asia. In turn, Asian governments have lured foreign investors with promises of tax exemptions, investment allowances and union-free workforces. Advances such as the internet and barcode-driven stock control have drastically improved communications and efficiency. As Oxfam explains, 'When consumer purchases are tracked by barcodes, retailers can automatically re-order just enough products, just in time for restocking their shelves. . . With this just-in-time response comes the pressure on producers to deliver smaller orders, in less time, and according to tightly planned shipping schedules – or face fines for delays.'

Oxfam adds that, while brands are heeding demands that they eradicate labour exploitation, their own business methods limit the room for manoeuvre. In their quest for the cheapest and most efficient suppliers, and their desire for flexibility, they keep contracts short. Thus there is no sense of partnership or evidence of commitment. This encourages factory bosses to cut corners by insisting on unrealistic overtime, or by subcontracting work to other, less reputable suppliers.

The sportswear report quotes a Sri Lankan supplier to a major US sports-shoe company: 'I wish there was a system of compliance the other way around, that is to say a) buyers do not relocate orders to other suppliers based on a five to 10 cent difference in unit price; and b) that loyalty should be a two-way process – if we suppliers are compliant and open to meeting labour standards, than we should receive consistent orders.'

The charity admits that some leading brands are trying to address this apparent dichotomy. But, even with the best will in the world, codes of conduct are tough to enforce. Oxfam believes that suppliers, in their desperation to win and keep contracts, frequently conceal the true nature of their operations from visiting inspectors. Bosses bribe workers to lie about conditions, keep double payrolls, falsify timesheets and generally carry out a superficial clean-up of their factories before visits.

Finding and monitoring 'clean' factories in Asia for Western firms is becoming a métier in itself. Even before I'd approached Oxfam, a source at Zara told me, 'Suppliers are monitored very closely, with regular inspections to ensure that they conform to our standards. But there's always a nagging worry that you might not be seeing the full picture.'

Zara produces the bulk of its clothes at its own Spanish factories, but it sources basic items from external suppliers. According to its 2003 sustainability report, 30 per cent of its clothes are made in Asia, 5 per cent in North Africa and 3 per cent in South America. It hires social auditors to ensure that its factories comply with its code of conduct. They visit each factory and its facilities, closely question managers, and hold private interviews with employees. If breaches are detected, contracts are suspended.

H&M, the other 'fast-fashion' brand, employs 30 full-time 'code of conduct inspectors', who can drop in on its factories, unannounced, at any moment. The company believes that this is the most effective way of encouraging its suppliers to stick to the rules. Here's a quote from its social responsibility brochure (available at www.hm.cm/sr), which was handed to me on my visit to its headquarters: 'Before the Code of Conduct was produced, H&M's requirements were written on our order sheets. Unfortunately, a number of suppliers did not always bother with the finer points.'

H&M drew up its code in 1997, basing it on the UN Convention on the Rights of the Child, as well as on International Labour Organization (ILO) conventions. The brochure says, 'Child labour was an important issue to deal with – even though it was rare in the factories. . . H&M drew up its Code of Conduct. . . partially on the basis of consultation with Save The Children.' It adds, 'If the company discovers underage workers at the same factory or any of its subcontractors more than once, the cooperation is terminated immediately.' According to the document, an 'underage worker' is less than 15 years old.

Ingrid Schüllstrom, responsible for social responsibility at H&M, is also quoted within the brochure's pages: 'We needed more concrete efforts and active work on the part of H&M [at the time the code was created]. . . We have already made excellent progress. Now it is a matter of working on more specific and complex issues such as union rights.'

Unions are a sensitive area for Western brands, particularly in China. An organization called China Labour Watch is battling to make workers more aware of their collective rights, which it says are often provided for by government legislation but ignored by factory bosses (www.chinalabourwatch.org). Protests over pay occasionally lead to rioting.

But, with China set to become the world's dominant supplier of textiles, there are hopes that both wages and working conditions will improve. An article in *Le Figaro* ('*L'usine Chine tourne à pleine régime*', 14 December 2004) quoted Nicolas Giannoli, director of Quiksilver in China, as saying, 'We pay a great deal of attention and, in China, you won't find the problems that you do in India and Bangladesh.' The article adds that the increasing importance of China will prompt Western firms to delocalize large chunks of their head-office operations there, in order to get closer to suppliers and maintain greater control. 'Only the design and the marketing will stay with the Europeans,' opines Gianolli.

Already, most Western fashion and sportswear companies are not apparel manufacturers, but apparel marketers. Behind the familiar brand names are lesser-known supply-chain management companies such as Li & Fung (Hong Kong) and Makalot Industrial Co. Ltd (Taiwan), which co-ordinate the production of garments and footwear for their more famous clients. In order to arrive at the cheapest solution, these companies often dissect the manufacturing process, so that one item may pass through a number of different factories, and even several countries. To quote Oxfam, 'The company may, for example, source fibre from Korea, dye and weave it in Taiwan, buy zips from China, and send it all to Thailand for assembly.'

Today, if you're wearing a global brand, it may be just that.

SWEATSHOP-FREE CLOTHING

Bernard Arnault of LVMH has a low opinion of mass production; or, at least, of fashion brands that use mass production techniques but take on 'designer' airs. At the *International Herald Tribune*'s conference in Hong Kong, he said, 'We can see several companies trying to mix an image of luxury with a mass-market approach. In order to be able to sell a product at a relatively high price, you have to offer the craftsmanship and quality that goes along with it. There's an increase in products that have approximately the same look [as luxury brands] while providing a much lower standard. It's not counterfeiting, but it is misleading.'

Yet Louis Vuitton, also – albeit on a much lesser scale than H&M and Zara – has speeded up its production techniques to serve increased customer demand. Vuitton's marketing strategy, as we know, has been to introduce the short cycles of fashion into the previously static and timeless luxury sector. According to a report in *Le Monde*, the organization within its ateliers (the word 'factory' is frowned upon in the luxury sector) has been streamlined to improve productivity. Instead of using a long production line on which each task is compartmentalized, 'islands' of seven people are responsible for a single model. The idea, says the article, is that each member of the team eventually learns how to perform every assembly task. Whatever the strategy, the result is that the creation of a single bag, which took 25 days in 1995, now takes three and a half days. ('*Le renouveau du sac génère des emplois dans la maroquinerie*', 14 December 2004.)

Those in the know say that Louis Vuitton has one of the largest profit margins in the fashion business. But the article is keen to assert that, unlike other areas of the fashion industry, the luxury sector is creating employment in France. According to the Comité Colbert – the luxury-brand association – 12 factories opened in France in the period 2000–2005 to deal with the craving for upmarket wallets, purses and bags. Louis Vuitton, which employs 3,650 people in its ateliers – about a third of its workforce – has opened five new sites since 1999.

Hermès, also, is expanding in order to satisfy accessory addiction. At the end of 2004, again according to *Le Monde*, it opened new work-shops totalling 5,400 square metres on its existing site in the Ardennes. These ateliers are producing the famous 'Birkin' bag. (The cult object was named after Jane Birkin, wife of the late French pop singer Serge Gainsbourg. It was created for her when she complained to Hermès boss Jean-Louis Dumas that she had never been able to find the bag of her dreams.) Hermès has a number of sites like this dotted around France. It also has agreements with local schools to fund the training of students in leather-working skills, providing workshops and machinery.

All this is a refreshing change from the murky world of the sweatshops – but it is at the same time disheartening. If Vuitton and Hermès are to be believed, they are among the few globally renowned brands pro-viding desirable objects without exploiting underpaid workers. But they pass on this 'craftsmanship' to their customers in the form of high prices. Does this mean that political correctness is the preserve of the wealthy, and the rest of us have to swallow our pride in order to clothe ourselves?

Not necessarily. Enter American Apparel, the company that is, accord-ing to *The New York Times*, 'building a brand by not being a brand' (23 November 2004). Founded in 1997, American Apparel originally supplied plain and neat wholesale T-shirts to a range of US clients. Having relocated its factory from Mexico to Los Angeles, it began promoting its product as 'Made in downtown LA – sweatshop-free'. When it moved into retail in 2002, something about its bright, logo-free basics and anti-establishment stance struck a chord with consumers. Suddenly the company went into high gear, expanding across the United States and into Canada, Europe and Asia.

There have been other sweatshop-free brands – notably another US outfit called No Sweat – but American Apparel is the first that looks capable of becoming another Gap. There are a number of factors in its favour. One of them is its founder, Dov Charney, a fast-talking, extravagantly moustachioed entrepreneur who has deliberately made his droll 1970s persona part of the brand's appeal. Then there is the advertising: grainy, off-focus and provocative, featuring attractive young women in the brand's cute little knickers and tops. A man occasionally appears in the ads – more often than not, it's Charney himself. In fact, American Apparel has succeeded by being both politically correct and entirely politically incorrect at the same time. It makes doing the right thing feel pleasantly naughty.

The stores, too, hit the right spot. The minimalist white spaces, as well as being lined with T-shirts, underwear, abbreviated skirts and hooded sweatshirts, are photographic galleries featuring urban imagery from the 1970s, and snaps of beautiful rebels designed to inspire shoppers to get the look. The products have deadpan names like 'Baby Rib Sleeveless Crew', 'Classic Girl Flat Bottomed Panty' or 'Fine Jersey Leisure Shirt'.

The company produces a million units a week at its seven-floor garment factory in Los Angeles. It pays each of its 2,500-plus workers about US$13 an hour, well over the minimum wage. It claims that constant reinvention to create high customer demand, aligned with the sheer volume of output, make the profit margins practical. Charney explains to the press that his theory of 'vertical integration' – which brings designers, marketers, cutters, sewers and knitters together under one roof – reduces costs and improves quality control. He now shudders to recall the time when his factory was based in Mexico, where he was plagued by faulty phone lines and sub-standard equipment. 'It wasn't feel-good and it wasn't viable,' he told *The New York Times*. 'You think it makes you proud to pay someone forty dollars a week to make shirts all day? I spend forty dollars on a drink.' ('Sweatshop-free clothing industry growing in the US', 14 December 2004.)

In an earlier interview, with the trade magazine *Industry Week*, Charney argued that being closer to his customers enabled him to react more quickly, cutting down waste and saving money. 'People underestimate the cost of [going] off-shore. Instead of investing more money in R&D and investing money in innovation, a lot of companies find themselves putting an insurmountable amount of capital into financing the supply chain, because you need to constantly have stuff on the water and you need deeper inventories.'

He added that being based in Los Angeles made more sense because 'you've got to go to the top 5 per cent of kids that really set trends. You have to make products that they are going to want to buy two years from now or three years from now. And if you're going to focus on that, and then you're going to say, well I'm off-shore and I have this elongated supply chain and I want the cheap, cheap, cheap, you're going to lose that ability to be the trendsetter.' ('Home-run hitters', 1 December 2003.)

Perhaps due to his high media profile, Charney has occasionally attracted criticism – for instance, he's been accused of preventing his staff from joining a union. He denied the charges and pointedly slapped posters on the factory walls informing his staff that they were free to join the union whenever they liked. These stunts keep the company in the news, while at the same time expressing its flamboyant identity.

It's true that American Apparel's anti-corporate values have given it a handy marketing hook. But as the words 'sweatshop-free' continue to drive its worldwide expansion, other retailers have been forced to sit up and take notice.

ETHICAL FASHION

American Apparel, People Tree, Veja, Patagonia: brands that promise ethical working conditions, fair trade or the use of organic materials are becoming more prevalent, nibbling the market share of retail giants whose clothes are made by workers in developing markets. And the self-proclaimed capital of fashion has also become the location for the world's largest event devoted entirely to eco and fair trade clothing. The number of exhibitors at the four-day Ethical Fashion Show in Paris every October has grown from 24 designers in 2004 to well over 100 today.

The event was created by designer Isabelle Quéhé, who was inspired by a movie shot in Niger by her cameraman husband. '[It] featured a catwalk show by an African designer. I thought, well, Paris is supposed to be the capital de la mode, but we don't support anything like this, and we should.' ('Chic without the suffering: fashion displays its ethical face', *The Guardian*, 12 October 2007.)

Products on display at the show include fair trade jewellery from villages in China, hand-embroidered coats from Kabul and woven bags from Brazil. If all that sounds a bit neo-hippie, the event also attracts young designers who make clothes without using the chemical dyes and softeners that are so harmful to the environment. Another eco-friendly approach is to recycle clothing: the route taken by British designer Emmeline Child, who turns discarded and second-hand garments into unique new pieces.

At the 2007 Ethical Fashion Show, a group of consultants gathered to try and categorize the types of consumer who regularly bought 'ethical' clothing. They came to the conclusion that the market varied considerably in age and profile. The young – generally thought to be the most concerned about ethical issues – talked rather than spent. These 'ethno street' consumers were typified as the 'the "no" generation'. They seemed to be against everything, while offering no concrete solutions. Tribal in nature, they liked the idea of a 'global village'. They downloaded films and music illegally, while claiming to be part of the creative community they were short-changing. They poured scorn on big corporations, but many of them smoked and were not averse to the occasional Big Mac. And despite their penchant for piercings and tattoos, they were just as likely to shop at H&M as the next consumer.

In fact, older consumers were thought to be a more realistic target group for ethical brands. These ranged from women of a certain age who had discovered yoga and organic beauty products, to ecologically-aware middle class families. As well as being interested in 'fair trade' and organic products, this group had also become determined to support local goods and producers: hence their careful scanning of the 'Made in...' label. As they were concerned about climate change, they worried that importing clothing from cheap labour markets left a dirty great carbon footprint. Yet they also desired authenticity, looking for Shetland wool and Irish linen, for example.

Away from the speculation, it is certain that consumer interest in ethical fashion will continue to grow. Pop singer Bono was ahead of the curve when he started an ethical fashion label, Edun, with his wife Ali Hewson and the designer Rogan Gregory in 2005. The fair trade clothes are made in locally-run factories in Africa, South America and India.

A year later, Gap and Armani had signed up for Bono's Project Red collaboration – which encouraged brands to donate a percentage of their profits to helping women and children affected by HIV/AIDS in Africa.

Other mainstream fashion brands have added an ethical twist to their acts. Diesel pledged to cut down on the chemicals it uses to wash its jeans; and embarked on a company-wide drive to encourage its staff to save energy. Levi's added 100 per cent organic cotton jeans to its product line. The jeans had coconut shell buttons and their indigo finish was created by potato starch, mimosa flowers and Marseille soap. They were created in a separate section of the Levi's factory in Hungary, on machinery that complied with environmental regulations. The senior vice-president of Levi's product in Europe, You Nguyen, put the initiative down to the 'zeitgeist'. 'We found more and more consumers were making product choices based on the environmental and social impact. They were getting interested in apparel made using sustainable production methods, but they still wanted style and quality – it was no longer either/or.' ('Levi's launches green jeans', *The Guardian*, 24 November 2006.) The catch was that the jeans were pricey, retailing at around €120. Conscience comes with a price, which may explain why richer, middle-aged consumers are the ideal target for ethical fashion.

There are other problems, too. Those who work in ethical fashion say they are struggling with distribution issues. As *The Wall Street Journal* reported, 'Distribution of eco-fashion is broadening beyond catalogues and a few stores, now that big names from Barneys to Macy's are making a point of carrying eco-designs... Largely, though, eco-designers compete for floor space in stores with designers who aren't limited in their choice of materials or factories.' ('Green fashion: beyond T-shirts', 18 October 2007.)

The same article caught up with Rogan Gregory of Edun, who conceded the line hadn't sold as well as he'd expected. 'He faced a "laundry list" of problems: it was hard to find good organic cotton where the company needed it. It was impossible to create complex garments – or even cut a good fit – with the inadequately trained workers Edun focuses on. National infrastructure problems made transport and timely deliveries difficult.' Gregory said the company now had its 'head above water', but he confessed, 'It's hard enough to start a company, let alone do it with organic fabric and make it in Africa.' His comments may have persuaded consumers to support the brand, and others like it.

The other sticking point, as the *Journal* pointed out, is the foggy interpretation by brands of the terms 'ethical' or 'eco' fashion. 'Eco, green, sustainable… while you might expect the terms to mean the designers minimize harm to the environment or to workers, the terms are currently meaningless because there's no strictly guarded definition.'

Ironically, it may be that the best way to consume fashion ethically is simply to buy less of it.

22

Style goes back to the future

'None of us here are much interested in trends or brand names.'

This is a secret, so don't go around telling everyone. You know that little tweed jacket you picked up the other day from a leading chain store? You could have bought an even cheaper but much higher quality one in a cramped shop on a side street near the Pompidou Centre in Paris. The only disadvantage is that you may not have been the first to wear it.

'I've had them all in here,' says Aldo, manager of the vintage-clothing emporium Vertiges, on Rue Saint Martin. 'Designers from H&M, Gap, Zara. . . and bigger names still. Sometimes they tell me what they're after. Other times they come incognito, but I can tell what they're up to from the way they handle the clothes and take notes, and from what they buy.'

What they are looking for is the rare, ephemeral thing that Vertiges has in spades: inspiration. The narrow, musty, under-lit store, which makes no concessions to brand experiences or even rudimentary interior design (the general ambience is somewhere between cavern and attic) is a treasure-trove of second-hand finds. Aldo himself is a walking advertisement for the place. On the day I interview him, he is wearing an army-issue green parka with fur collar over an American university sweater and tartan trousers. Pointed shoes in patent leather complete the ensemble.

'The first piece of clothing I ever bought was second-hand,' says Aldo. 'In those days, mind you, I didn't have the choice. But it became a habit and after a while I didn't see the point of changing. This way, you get something that's original *and* cheap. Where's the problem?'

The search for originality – combined with a growing distrust of global brands – has driven a worldwide increase in demand for vintage clothes. Ironically, the brands have interpreted this as a desire to re-create the past, hence the race to emulate classic cuts and colours, and to develop high-performance modern versions of old-fashioned fabrics.

'Even new clothes are being sold as "vintage" now,' snorts Aldo. 'I can tell you one thing – clothes like that won't be hanging on these railings in 40 years' time. They'll have fallen apart long before.'

Students and nonconformists have been sifting through racks of old clothes for years. The terminology changes – in the hands of fashion editors, 'second-hand' became 'retro', which then became 'vintage' – but the pleasure of unearthing a treasure for a song remains the same. (Technically, I'm told, 'vintage' refers to pre-war clothing, although the term has come to mean garments made between the 1920s and the 1980s – anything before that is 'antique'.)

Long before they became acceptable fashion wear, second-hand clothes were simply the dress of the poor. In the 18th and 19th centuries, clothing markets like London's Petticoat Lane sold cast-off items to the needy. These were often bought for the fabric – considered far more precious than the garments themselves – which was reworked into 'new' clothes for husbands and children. 'Rag and bone men', those dealers in second-hand clothes and bric-a-brac who now seem like mythological figures, would travel from street to street scavenging for unwanted items. Jumble sales, car boot sales, charity shops and the vintage market did away with the need for such middle-men.

Today, used clothes that aren't resold in Europe and the United States often make it to developing countries in the form of donations. Others are sold in bulk to the 'flocking' industry and shredded to be turned into filler for insulation and furniture padding. Reclaimed wool can be mixed with new fibres to make low-cost fabrics. The UK's Textile Recycling Association, however, states that up to 40 per cent of 'post-consumer textiles' are worn again.

Aldo says, 'In Europe, the business first began to thrive between the wars. Rich Americans who'd been waiting out the Prohibition in Paris started going home, and a lot of them would sell half their clothes to reduce the weight of their luggage. Then, after the war, there was army surplus.'

In the 1950s, European teenagers wanted to get their hands on original American jeans. Over the years, this evolved into an obsession with retro Americana which, in Italy, would inspire a young man named Renzo Rosso to start a company called Diesel. Aldo says that the pop music and film industries, with their constant recycling of styles and frequent recourse to nostalgia, have always helped the second-hand market along. 'In the 1980s, everybody was after collectible American jeans, especially Levi's. Then the Japanese started making new jeans that looked second-hand, using advanced manufacturing techniques. It was really excellent work – sometimes even I couldn't tell the difference.'

But the innovation also killed off the second-hand jeans market. 'In any case, most of the American stuff gets sold straight to Japan now, either in bulk or on the web. We don't get a sniff at it. That isn't a problem, because the latest vintage trend is about old European designer clothing: while we used to go to the States to look for authentic American jeans, now they come here to look for original Chanel jackets.'

FROM THRIFT TO VINTAGE

Back in the days of Petticoat Lane, a wealthy person would never have dreamed of wearing second-hand clothing; and, of course, wearing a new garment that *looked* as if it was old would have been the ultimate in foolishness. Until the late 20th century, fashions were passed down from rich to poor. More recently, though, fashions have moved in the opposite direction, with disaffected urban youth sparking trends that are reinterpreted by designers and sold to wealthier, more privileged customers. This shift may partially explain the fascination with 'vintage', previously the domain of the imaginative underpaid.

Another factor may have been the creation of a magazine called *Cheap Date* in New York at the end of the 1990s. Its founders, Kira Joliffe and Bay Garnett, became the poster children for vintage; or 'thrifting', as they called it. Originally an anti-fashion magazine, thumbing its nose at the establishment, *Cheap Date* evolved into an alternative to mainstream glossies, attracting the attention of stylists, models and designers. Sophie Dahl, Karen Elson and Erin O'Connor have all appeared on its pages.

Co-founder Joliffe told *The Observer* that *Cheap Date* had begun 'as a magazine about thrifting for people who are into clothes and style but are really fed up. Fashion magazines have taken the fun out of fashion. It's now about commerce, not the love of clothes'. In the same piece, Garnett commented, 'If you succumb to the feeling of constant wanting and needing that comes from a Prada ad, there's never an end to it.' ('Why Prada is passé – and cheap is chic', 22 February 2004.)

Although it began in New York, *Cheap Date*, like its editors, had a very British aesthetic. The Brits have always had an edgy, eccentric, faintly grungy sense of style that makes them expert 'thrifters'. The concept is much newer in other parts of Europe, as Aldo confirms: 'Until recently, an Italian wouldn't have been seen dead in a piece of second-hand clothing. Even the French were snooty about it. But now they've all joined in the game.'

The economy inevitably played a part. The years of recession that followed 9/11 made even the wealthiest consumers a little more cost-conscious. Sarah Gray Miller, who launched a magazine called *Budget Living* in 2002, said, 'The logo mania of the late 90s is over now. There is something vaguely obscene – and not a little dumb – about spending hundreds of pounds on a designer handbag that everybody thinks is a fake from your local street market anyway. The word "luxury" has become so overused it has become completely meaningless. For the intelligent consumer it simply means overpriced and over-hyped. The new trend towards thrifty shopping is as much about being ahead of the curve as it is about saving money.' ('The drift to thrift', *The Observer*, 13 October 2002.)

That's one reason why vintage might hang around: what started out as an attempt to save pennies has become a statement of intelligence and personal taste. At the vanguard of that change is Cameron Silver, founder of the Decades store in Los Angeles. Silver specializes in what might be termed 'designer vintage', selling his clothes out of a cool and clean space that has nothing in common with flea markets or thrift stores. His customers include Nicole Kidman, Cameron Diaz and Renée Zellweger, as well as film companies in search of authentic items. 'I want all my clients to look like movie stars,' he says. (*'Une journée avec Cameron Silver'*, *Elle*, 6 September 2004.)

Silver started out as a cabaret singer, and it was during his tours that he began buying second-hand pieces. 'It wasn't always a glamorous life – quite often I'd find myself staying in pretty seedy places. So I'd go out walking. That's when I started visiting vintage fashion boutiques. I've always been interested in the history of fashion.'

Pretty soon, Silver had a wardrobe full of vintage items. With the touring life beginning to pall, he decided to open a store. 'I used the last few shows to round up some more forgotten treasures. I'd say to the audience, "If you've got any Pucci from the 1970s, come and see me after the show!"'

The store was discovered by Richard Buckley, editor of *Vogue Hommes International*, who spread the word. It was a fortuitous meeting, but it also shows that Silver has a keen eye. One of the most appealing aspects of vintage for fashion snobs is that not everyone has a talent for spotting decent pieces. This is clearly Silver's gift. He has since opened a branch of Decades in Barney's department store, New York. And he has helped to push vintage into the mainstream.

Increasingly, department stores are selling vintage pieces alongside contemporary designers. Bloomingdale's and Henri Bendel in New York both stock vintage. The Version Originale space in the basement of the Galeries Lafayette in Paris has a section devoted to the category, as does Topshop in London. And there is a new generation of independent outlets that sell second-hand in chic spaces. Lyell, in New York's Nolita, features original 1940s wallpaper and original pieces alongside 'vintage-inspired' designs.

The alert reader might have noted that the trend has started to cancel out its original purpose, with shoppers now being convinced by retailers to spend a great deal of money on items that are not even new. Why not go to charity shops and flea markets, where the same pieces can be found at a fraction of the price? For those with more money but little time, the benefit of upmarket thrift is that the collection has been pre-curated: they don't have to rummage through piles of crummy clothing in the hope of coming up with something fabulous.

British clothing brand Oasis took the theory to its logical conclusion with a line called New Vintage. This limited-edition range was based on one-off vintage finds, sourced in flea markets like Clignancourt on the outskirts of Paris and used as templates for mass-market products. Nadia Jones, the label's design director, explained the concept to *The Times*: 'We know our girl likes the idea of vintage because she sees Hollywood stars and Kate Moss wearing it. But she either doesn't know where to get it, or can't be bothered to search for it. So we do it in her dress size with no holes or stains.' ('Rags to Riches', 13 March 2004.) There can be no better example of the way fashion brands turn subcultural trends into marketing opportunities.

Not all vintage fans are such pushovers. Some neophyte thrifters have become as passionate about their hobby as the founders of *Cheap Date*. The names of brands such as Biba and designers such as Ossie Clark and Zandra Rhodes can be heard on the lips of those far too young to remember them the first time around. The web has become a fertile hunting ground – although there must be constant virtual battles between collectors and contemporary designers in search of an inspirational fix.

The brands' co-option of vintage has meant that collectors, archivists and 'thrifting' experts like Bay Garnett have seen their careers transformed. Mark and Cleo Butterfield, who run an operation called C20 Vintage Fashion, keep their huge collection of clothes in Devon. They list among their clients Topshop, Oasis, a clutch of Hollywood celebrity stylists, and Marc Jacobs. Their website boasts of 'an archive of thousands of pieces, individually chosen for their design features, available for hire as *inspirational vintage garments* [my italics] to design professionals' (www.c20vintagefashion.co.uk).

Butterfield told *The Times*, 'The market has totally changed… Old-style vintage collectors loved how things were made, and bought accordingly. Our celebrity clients now buy one-off vintage items in the same way as women used to buy couture – because they want to look fabulous and genuine.'

THE POLITICS OF NOSTALGIA

Although brands have done their best to get in on the act, the vintage phenomenon may have disturbing repercussions for them. For one thing, it shows that consumers are rebelling against high prices and mass production. For another, it was initially driven by word-of-mouth and alternative media, rather than conventional marketing. Indeed, one of the points of wearing an authentic vintage item is to prove you are not a 'victim' of marketing.

The trend is a global one. In Tokyo, a district called Nakameguro has become a 'vintage chic' oasis. Formerly edgy and working class, 'Nakame' can be compared to London's Shoreditch or New York's Meat Packing District – but it has a more underground ambience than either. The Meguro waterway, which divides the district in two and forms the backbone of this laid-back shopping area, was once vile and polluted. But since a government spruce-up, the river has become popular with strollers. This in turn has attracted entrepreneurs and small businesses. Shop fronts have been kept deliberately unobtrusive. In keeping with the emerging doctrine that status should be acquired rather than purchased, the best places are reserved for those who spend time looking for them.

Although brands such as Starbucks and APC have inevitably begun moving in, there is little sign as yet that they are forcing out the independent cafés and thrift shops that crowd the area. One resident sums up the situation: 'None of us here are much interested in trends or brand names. We dance to our own music.' ('Snobbishly vintage in a Tokyo hot spot', *International Herald Tribune*, 4 January 2005.)

The quote underlines the theory that 'vintage' is an attitude rather than a style of dress. It's a rejection of 'exclusive' yet global brands, an affirmation that cheap and unusual is better than expensive and everywhere – and a message to marketers that the fashion consumer of the future will be harder to snare.

Conclusion

*'The best marketing in the world comes down to a
person standing in front of a mirror.'*

The words 'fashion' and 'marketing' are virtually interchangeable. Yet
a fashion brand cannot expect to thrive on marketing alone. Consumers,
happily, just aren't that dumb. Jean-Jacques Picart, the Parisian fashion
consultant, told me, 'Over the years I've advised many brands, and
if there is one thing that I am absolutely sure of, it's that you can't
lie. You can bluff, you can rearrange the truth, but you can't cheat.
Marketing can persuade a customer to push open the door of a shop,
but if the clothes they find inside it are ugly, they will leave. Today, a
product at any level must achieve the correct balance between price,
quality, creativity, and wearability. If one of these factors is below par,
the customer will not be fooled. The best marketing in the world comes
down to a person standing in front of a mirror.'

Marketers often talk about the need to 'educate' consumers. The word
they are actually searching for is 'persuade' – or, perhaps, 'convince'
– but the process of education sounds less intrusive. None the less,
consumers are educated. In interview after interview, advertising executives have told me that consumers are highly sophisticated; that they
can decode marketing so swiftly and effectively that if the message is
not presented in a subtle and elegant manner, it actually damages the
brand.

Fashion consumers, I would argue, are the most sophisticated of the
lot. Fashion already relies on a complex array of barely perceptible signs

and symbols – the width of a lapel, the height of a boot – so the imagery behind it cannot afford to be primitive. Today's best fashion advertising barely resembles advertising at all. The most effective marketing campaigns are carried out under the radar, their targets unaware of the ruse until it is too late – or so appreciative of its shrewdness that they agree to accept the come-on.

Consumers have gotten wise, and they've become demanding. If fashion was ever a great swindle – with clothes sold for four times their value just because of a label – that is less and less the case. Every shopper has become a fashion professional. They are beginning to resemble those who work in the industry. Throughout my interviews with the people who package fashion, one thing struck me: none of them were particularly fashionable. They were often stylish, but there was never the slightest hint of the victim about them. They wore discreetly elegant clothes, or T-shirts and jeans. They understood the system so perfectly that they refused to get caught up in it. Increasingly, their target market thinks the same way. The designer Alber Elbaz says, 'I think the expression of a free and democratic beauty will progressively supplant the hegemony of trends.'

But this, too, is a trend. And there are others. I wouldn't have the temerity to claim they are definitive, but below are eight developments which, I believe, will have a dramatic impact on fashion brands.

THE CONSUMER AS STYLIST

The days when consumers were loyal to brands are long gone. Nobody wants to be decked from head to toe in clothes from the same source – especially if they are smothered in logos. Small 'curated' stores selling unusual but multiple brands – along with other lifestyle accoutrements – will become more common. Shoppers are increasingly drawn to environments that resemble markets rather than brand shrines. The emergence of 'fast-fashion' brands such as Zara, H&M and Mango has been driven by a demand for trendy, disposable items that can be mixed with expensive, classic pieces. Consumers don't just buy designer, or chain store, or vintage – they buy all three, and throw them together in a style that is uniquely personal.

REACTIVITY AND PERSONALIZATION

In their new guise as stylists, consumers are pushing for more choice and a faster turnover of products. Fabrics and designs are becoming more innovative, even at the lower end of the market. The quest for originality is also prompting the return of couture and personal tailoring – but in a more democratic form. This could also be termed 'the egg factor'. When packets of instant cake mix were first introduced, home cooks regarded them with suspicion. But when the formula was altered so that cooks were required to 'add one egg', they started to sell. People like being part of the creative process. If mainstream fashion retailers can establish a similar situation, it could be a powerful marketing tool.

CHOICE FATIGUE

New brands will have to work ever harder to win the loyalty of con-sumers. Younger shoppers zap from one brand to another, playing them off in terms of quality and price. Thanks to the web, they are better informed than ever before – and they certainly won't be fooled by advertising. Older, wealthier consumers may be loyal to a smaller clutch of brands. For that group, trustworthiness and authenticity will be key.

'SMART' CLOTHING

The appearance of 'faux vintage' clothes that paid homage to the past was driven, ironically, by cutting-edge fabric design that brought a new suppleness and practicality to tweed. Consumers will continue to demand better-behaved clothes: easily washable, iron-free, light enough to pack in a suitcase and arrive at their destination without a wrinkle. Budget airlines have seen to it that we're travelling more – and we want to look good when we arrive. The development of 'smart' materials will provide clothes that can react to their environment, changing colour or density, springing back into shape after being rolled into a ball. Fabric that can store data is not far off. Performance is likely to become a brand component.

BRANDING VIA BUILDINGS

In the rich west, shopping is no longer a functional task. It is a form of entertainment akin to going to a cinema, a show, or even an art gallery. Brands are responding by creating spaces that have more in common with museums or theme parks than traditional stores. These branded environments have become destinations – they are on the list of places to visit when you arrive in an unfamiliar city. If brands insist on a strategy of marketing via architecture, in order to hurdle advertising clutter and distance themselves from cut-price stores, they must provide rich and rewarding experiences.

HYBRID SHOPPING

One thing is certain: people still like shopping. In his 2006 book *The Long Tail*, author Chris Anderson suggested that 138 million Americans shop at Wal-Mart each week – almost half the population – making it the single most unifying force in the United States today. The internet has not supplanted the desire to pop out to the shops. In fact, after being first fearful of online shopping, and then embracing it, consumers are now becoming blasé about it. The time when consumers buy literally everything online is unlikely to come. While Nordic consumers are the keenest online shoppers, those in countries like Italy and Spain – with their sunny weather and focus on family and community – prefer to go out. This realization is reflected by the number of dotcom companies that are setting up bricks-and-mortar outlets for after-sales and service: the Apple stores being the perfect example. We will also see a rise in 'hybrid stores' like those offered by Ralph Lauren in New York and London, which give customers the chance to buy clothes electronically via touch-sensitive store windows.

NOMADIC DESIGNERS

Of course, not all designers can afford branded stores – or find the perfect distribution outlets. A third way is emerging, however. One brand to embrace the nomadic ideal is Clemens en August, a Munich-based fashion brand founded by Alexander Brenninkmeijer. (He is related to the Brenninkmeijer brothers, who founded the original C&A in the

19th century – by selling textiles to farmers.) As he could afford neither a shop nor a catwalk show, Brenninkmeijer decided to become the 21st century equivalent of an itinerant salesman. But rather than going door-to-door selling stockings or ties, he would take his entire collection on the road. Each season, the collection tours Europe, setting up shop in appropriate venues. You have to sign up to the Clemens en August website (www.clemens-en-august.com) to find out when the collection is coming to town, and where you can go and check it out. For those who prefer a more traditional look, how about an itinerant Savile Row-trained tailor? Originally employed by Anderson & Sheppard, top notch cutter Thomas Mahon still keeps an office on the Row, but these days he spends more time at his workshop in Cumbria, where he lives. Clients can make an appointment to get measured up in London, but he also regularly visits Paris, Brussels, New York, Chicago, Atlanta, San Francisco and even Sydney. He lets the faithful know when he'll be in town through his website, English Cut (www.englishcut.com)

THE END OF AGE

I find myself becoming increasingly irritated with forms that plonk me brusquely into an age bracket. It usually happens when I'm subscribing to a website. Am I aged between 25 and 35? No, I am bloody well not – thanks for reminding me. But, these days, what does that tell anyone? Age has ceased to function as a reference point for marketers. These days, a 36-year-old is just as likely to be a single DJ with a skateboard as a 25-year-old is likely to be married with two children. Mothers shop alongside daughters; fathers wear the same brand of jeans as sons. This is likely to affect the way the youth-obsessed fashion industry communicates with its customers. The trend-tracking organization Style-Vision already refers to 'mood marketing', suggesting that demographics are dead.

So there you go – as I said, it is not a definitive list. A few of the predictions may be wide of the mark, but as I shamelessly plundered them from some of the leading names in the fashion business, I'm expecting a reasonable degree of accuracy. The main problem, of course, is that this is a book about fashion.

Tomorrow, everything will have changed.

References

BOOKS

Agins, Teri (1999) *The End of Fashion*, HarperCollins, New York
Barthes, Roland (2001) *La Bleu Est à la Mode Cette Année*, Institut Français de la Mode, Paris
Baudot, François (1999) *Mode du Siècle*, Assouline, Paris
Erner, Guillaume (2004) *Victimes de la Mode?*, La Découverte, Paris
Frankel, Susannah (2001) *Visionaries*, V&A Publications, London
Lannelongue, Marie-Pierre (2004) *La Mode Racontée à Ceux Qui La Portent*, Hachette Littératures, Paris
Morand, Paul (1996) *L'Allure de Chanel*, Hermann, Paris
Vanderbilt, Tom (1998) *The Sneaker Book*, The New Press, New York
Various, *Repères Mode 2003*, Institut Français de la Mode, Paris
Various (2003), *Cool Brand Leaders*, Superbrands, London
Zola, Emile (1883) *Au Bonheur des Dames*, Folio Classique, Paris

ONLINE RESOURCES

Adbrands.net (www.adbrands.net)
Brand Keys (www.brandkeys.com)
Charles Frederick Worth Organization (www.charlesfrederickworth.org)
Dr. Martens (www.drmartens.com)
Ermenegildo Zegna (www.zegna.com)
Exposure (www.cxposure.net)

Fédération Française de la Couture, du Prêt-à-Porter des Couturiers et
    des Créateurs de Mode (www.modeaparis.com)
Gucci Group (www.guccigroup.com)
Harvey Nichols Ltd (www.harveynichols.com)
Hint Fashion Magazine (www.hintmag.com)
Nelly Rodi (www.nellyrodi.fr)
Nike (www.nikebiz.com)
The Photographers' Gallery (www.photonet.org)
SHOWstudio (www.showstudio.com)
Slate Magazine (www.slate.com)
Style-Vision (www.style-vision.com)
Victoria & Albert Museum (www.vam.ac.uk)
Vogue (www.vogue.co.uk)
Worth Global Style Network (WGSN.com)

Index